architectures of possibility:
after innovative writing

D1534482

Architectures of Possibility © 2012 by Lance Olsen

Published by Guide Dog Books
Bowie, MD

First Edition

Cover Image by Ivan Titor
Book Design by Jennifer Barnes

Printed in the United States of America

ISBN 978-1-935738-19-0

Library of Congress Control Number: 2011942820

www.GuideDogBooks.com

architectures of possibility:
after innovative writing

lance olsen
in collaboration with trevor dodge

Also by Lance Olsen

NOVELS
Live from Earth
Tonguing the Zeitgeist
Burnt
Time Famine
Freaknest
Girl Imagined by Chance
10:01
Nietzsche's Kisses
Anxious Pleasures
Head in Flames
Calendar of Regrets

SHORT STORIES
My Dates with Franz
Scherzi, I Believe
Sewing Shut My Eyes
Hideous Beauties

NONFICTION
Ellipse of Uncertainty
Circus of the Mind in Motion
William Gibson
Lolita: A Janus Text

Acknowledgements

Oceanic thanks to Trevor Dodge, who brainstormed with me, conducted most of the flash interviews interpolated through this book (save those with Kathy Acker, Joseph Cardinale, Robert Coover, Lydia Davis, Samuel R. Delany, Noy Holland, Shelley Jackson, Ted Pelton, Susan Steinberg, and Joe Wenderoth, which I conducted myself), and contributed to the writing of the opening of the chapter on publishing pragmatics. Without him and his friendship through the years, what follows would have been a different, lesser thing.

Each of the writers who agreed to be interviewed: thank you so much for your generosity, insight, and honesty. The idea behind those interviews was to create various counterpoints to (and occasional harmonies with) my own voice through the pages of *Architectures of Possibility*, and I couldn't have imagined in advance things would turn out as invigoratingly musical as they did.

I am grateful to Brian C. Clark for originally suggesting I write a version of this book, which I did, under his guidance, in 1997, for his press, Permeable; to Andy Watson and Cambrian Press for bringing that book to fruition as *Rebel Yell* a year later; to D. Harlan Wilson, John Lawson, and Jennifer Barnes at Raw Dog Screaming Press, and to Trevor Dodge, for convincing me to reimagine that version all this time later.

I am deeply thankful to my students from the beginning for teaching me what comes next, and to Melanie Rae Thon, for our extraordinary walks, talks, and joyful lessons in seeing; Lidia Yuknavitch, for our brain-sharing trust; and the Board of Directors at FC2 for challenging me with every manuscript we consider to rethink the innovative and embrace the collaborative paradigm.

And how, oh how, can I ever thank you, Andi, enough?

Table of Contents

For Andi,
Creative Righter Extraordinaire

"The aim of literature…is the creation of a strange object covered with fur which breaks your heart."

—Donald Barthelme

"I can't understand why people are frightened of new ideas. I'm frightened of the old ones."

—John Cage

"There's many a best-seller that could have been prevented by a good teacher."

—Flannery O'Connor

one

possibility spaces

Carefully follow what most textbooks on fiction tell you, and chances are you will end up producing a well-crafted piece that could have been produced just as easily in 1830.

You will end up producing, that is, a narrative where language is transparent and focus falls on your protagonist's psychology. That protagonist will be rounded, resonant, believable, and usually middle or lower-middle class. Your setting will be urban or suburban and rendered with the precision of a photograph, while the form your narrative takes will be so predictable, so patterned by convention, as to be virtually invisible: it will have a beginning, a muddle, and an ending through which your character will travel in order to learn something about himself, herself, or his or her relationship to society or nature.

You will end up producing some version of realism, in other words, and realism is a genre of averages—a genre about middle-of-the-road people living on Main Street in Middletown, Middle America.

In *For a New Novel*, Alain Robbe-Grillet calls this sort of writing the Balzacian Mode because in a sense its impulse stems from the early nineteenth-century work of Honoré de Balzac, although it could just as well be called the Defoean Mode—after Daniel Defoe and his 1719 puritanically detailed pseudo-reportage of Robinson Crusoe's daily accomplishments on his famous island. (Revealingly, Crusoe's first inclination after finding himself shipwrecked is to recreate as closely as possible a bourgeois European enclave…another kind of Main Street.)

Such fiction, according to Ian Watt, appeared in the eighteenth century with the rise of the new middle class in England and on the Continent. Rooted in the journalism, diaries, letters, and personal journals of the time, it is the stuff of Richardson and Fielding and their literary offspring: Flaubert and Chekhov, Ann Beattie and John Updike, Amy Tan and Jonathan Franzen. It represents a way of perceiving influenced by rationalist philosophers like Locke and Descartes that embrace a pragmatic, empirical understanding of the universe that emphasizes individual experience and consciousness.

Samuel R. Delany once pointed out those sorts of fictions aren't written for readers in, say, New York, where all the mega-publishing houses and slick magazines reside in the U.S., but for a certain imagined housewife living in a small-yet-comfortable house somewhere in Nebraska. If there's nothing in a given narrative she can relate to, nothing and no one she wants to know something about, then that narrative is out of luck so far as that publishing world goes.

"The housewife in Nebraska has, of course, a male counterpart," Delany continues. "In commercial terms, he's only about a third as important as she is. The basic model for the novel reader has traditionally been female since the time of Richardson. But the male counterpart's good opinion is considered far more prestigious. He's a high school English teacher in Montana who hikes for a hobby on weekends and has some military service behind him. He despises the housewife—though reputedly she wants to have an affair with him.... Between them, that Nebraska housewife and that Montana English teacher tyrannized mid-century American fiction."

One reason that virtual couple responds to the Balzacian Mode so positively, Fredric Jameson argues, is that it "persuades us in a concrete fashion that human actions, human life is somehow a complete, interlocking whole, a single formed, meaningful substance....Our satisfaction with the completeness of plot is therefore a kind of satisfaction with society as well."

What Jameson proposes, in essence, is that meaning carries meaning, but structuration carries meaning, too. The way you shape—or, perhaps more productively, misshape—a narrative *means*. Another way of saying this: every narrative strategy implies political and metaphysical ones—whether or not the author happens to be aware of the fact.

Creative writing is nothing if not a series of choices, and to write one way rather than another is to convey, not simply an aesthetics, but a course of thinking, a course of being in the world, that privileges one approach to "reality" over another.

Given the Heraclitean techno-global, multi-cultural, multi-gendered, multi-genred pluriverse our fluid selves navigate, the question thereby becomes: is the Balzacian Mode the most useful choice for capturing what it feels like to be alive here, now, in the midst of the twenty-first century?

Many of us no longer intuit existence is necessarily meaningful, if we ever did, and most of us certainly aren't satisfied with society, so why should we write as if we do and are?

Shouldn't our task as authors rather be to explore approaches to creativity that accurately reflect our own sense of lived experience?

If so, what might those approaches look like?

"If you don't use your own imagination," Ronald Sukenick once wrote, "somebody else is going to use it for you." This book intends to be a continual reminder of Sukenick's assertion, an invitation to conceive of writing as a possibility space where everything can and should be considered, attempted, and troubled. If success is defined as publication by a big publishing house or magazine, by joining the ranks of what Raymond Federman referred to as corporate authors, then this book is after the opposite. It believes that pushing as close to "failure" as you can in your work opens up myriad options you simply can't imagine while adopting conventional methods of narrativity.

Architectures of Possibility is all about taking chances, trying to compose in alternative, surprising, revelatory directions, about trying to move out of your comfort zone to discover what might lie on the other side.

Samuel Beckett: "Try again. Fail again. Fail better."

What follows is an extended proposal to think about where we are in space and time, to ask how each of us might most effectively capture that place and point in our own writing. Behind that proposal lies the assumption that writers work in a post-genre culture where there is no longer a significant difference between prose and poetry, between fiction and nonfiction. Theory, it takes for granted, is a form of spiritual autobiography, while all writing is always-already a kind of theorizing.

Architectures of Possibility doesn't intend to be a how-to text in the same way, for instance, Janet Burroway's *Writing Fiction: A Guide to Narrative Craft* intends to be one. Her guide and the profusion like it are designed to instruct writers how to construct in the Balzacian Mode. This one is designed to encourage writers to investigate various ways of re-imagining what creative writing is and can be, and how, and why.

Writing is a manner of reading. It is a mode of engaging with other texts in the world, which itself is a kind of text. And reading is a manner of writing, interpretation, meaning-making. Which is to say that writing and reading are variants of the same activity. Existence comes to us in bright, disconnected splinters of experience. We narrativize those splinters so our lives feel as if they make sense—as if they possess things like beginnings, muddles, ends, and reasons. The word *narrative* is ultimately derived, through the Latin *narrare*, from the Proto-Indo-European root *gno-*, which comes into our language as the verb *to know*. At some profoundly deep stratum, we conceptualize narrative as a means of understanding, of creating cosmos out of chaos.

Yet in many cultural loci these days we are asked to read and write easier, more naively, less rigorously. We are asked to understand by not taking the time and energy to understand. One difference between art and entertainment has to do with the speed of perception. Art deliberately slows and complicates reading, hearing, and/or viewing so that we are challenged to re-think and re-feel form and experience. Entertainment deliberately accelerates and simplifies them so we don't have to think about or feel very much of anything at all except, maybe, the adrenalin rush before spectacle.

Although, obviously, there can be a wide array of gradations between the former and latter, in their starkest articulation we are talking about the distance between David Foster Wallace's *Infinite Jest* and Dan Brown's *The Lost Symbol*; between David Lynch's *Lost Highway* and *Transformers: Revenge of the Fallen.*

In *The Middle Mind*, Curtis White contends that the stories generated and sustained by the American political system, entertainment industry, and academic trade have helped teach us over the last half century or so by their insidious simplicity, plainness, and ubiquity how *not* to think for ourselves. Little needs to be said about how the political narratives of the United States have led, as White says, to the "starkest and most deadly" poverty of imagination, nor about how, "on the whole, our entertainment…is a testament to our ability and willingness to endure boredom…and pay for it." A little should be said, however, about White's take on the consequences of this dissemination of corporate consciousness throughout academia.

For White, the contemporary university "shares with the entertainment industry its simple institutional inertia"; "so-called dominant 'critical paradigms' tend to stabilize in much the same way that assumptions about 'consumer demand' make television programming predictable." If, to put it somewhat differently, student-shoppers want to talk about *Spider-Man*, Stephen King, and hip-hop in the classroom, well, that's just what they're going to get to talk about, since that's how English departments fill seats, and filling seats is how they make money, and making money is what it's all about…isn't it?

The result, White continues—particularly in the wake of Cultural Studies—has been the tendency to eschew close, meticulous engagement with the page; to search texts "for symptoms supporting the sociopolitical or theoretical template of the critic"; to flatten out distinctions between, say, the value of studying James Joyce, Lydia Davis, and Ben Marcus, on the one hand, and Britney Spears, *The Bachelorette*, and that feisty gang from *South Park*, on the other—and therefore unknowingly to embrace and maintain the very globalized corporate culture that Cultural Studies claims to critique.

Architectures of Possibility advocates a practice of writing and reading against simplicity, renewing the Difficult Imagination—that dense space in which we are asked continuously to envision the text of the text, the text of our lives, and the text of the world other than they are, and thus contemplate the idea of fundamental change in all three.

In other words, The Difficult Imagination is an area of impeded accessibility essential for human freedom where we discover the perpetual manifestation of Nietzsche's notion of the unconditional, Derrida's of a privileged instability, Viktor Shklovsky's ambition for art and Martin Heidegger's for philosophy: the return, through complexity and challenge (not predictability and ease) to attention and contemplation.

"The technique of art," Shklovsky urged, "is to make objects 'unfamiliar,' to make forms difficult, to increase the difficulty and length of perception."

For Roland Barthes: "Literature is the question minus the answer."

In light of its natureless nature, writing of the Difficult Imagination will always make us feel a little foolish, a little tongue-tied, before an example of it. We will find ourselves standing there in a kind of baffled wonder that will insist upon a slightly new method of apprehending, a slightly new means of speaking, to capture what it is we have just witnessed.

Take, by way of illustration, J. M. Coetzee's *Elizabeth Costello*, which commences by telling the life and obsessions of a contemporary writer in her late sixties by means of a series of lectures she gives and attends. It begins, that is to say, in the realm of the Balzacian Mode, but a version faintly tweaked, askew, both by means of its structuring principle (those lectures, versions of which Coetzee actually delivered) and by a disquietingly flat prose style and series of odd narratorial insertions (the passage of weeks, months, or years, for example, is covered by the abrupt phrase: "We skip").

In the seventh of eight chapters, as the reader has come to feel settled into these conventions, the novel unexpectedly leaves the universe of logical mimesis and Freudian depth-psychology behind and veers first into a highly textured meditation, still from the protagonist's point of view (although her presence drops back decidedly from it, and symbol starts swamping personhood) about the relationship between gods and mortals in a variety of mythological iterations, and next, in the final chapter, into a retelling of Kafka's parable "Before the Law," in which Elizabeth rather than Kakfa's man from the country seeks entrance in vain, not from the quotidian world into the law, but from a purgatorial in-between place into some beyond-region—possibly heaven itself.

Coetzee's text ends with a brief, cryptic postscript that takes the form of an epistle from another (or is it somehow the same?) "Elizabeth C." (Elizabeth, Lady Chandos), this one quite possibly on the verge of madness, written on 9/11...not in 2001, as we might expect, but in 1603, the year the English Renaissance begins its concluding with the death of Elizabeth I.

With that, everything we have just read drifts into suspension. Is the narrative supposed to add up to the hallucinations of a seventeenth-century woman? A twentieth-first-century woman imagining from beyond the grave, or on her way to it? A serious postulation of cyclical rebirth or eternal recurrence? An ironic one? Or, more likely, a text not about character and mimesis at all, but rather about a series of philosophical problems, an investigation into a novel ripped open as unpredictably as our culture was on that glistery blue September day in 2001, a universe and a universe of discourse exploring the conditions of their own self-perplexing existence?

Writing of the Difficult Imagination asserts that language, ideas, and experience are profoundly, joyously complicated things, or, as Brian Evenson comments: "Good fiction, I would argue, always poses problems—ethical, linguistic, epistemological, ontological—and writers and readers, I believe, should be willing to draw on everything around them to pose tentative answers to these problems and, by way of them, pose problems of their own....It is our ability as [innovative] writers to stay curious, to borrow, to bricoler, to adapt and move on, that keeps us from becoming stale."

Staging the Difficult Imagination is, of course, an in-progress futile project—and an in-progress indispensable one. Its purpose is never a change, but a changing, an unending profiting from the possibility space of the impossible, from using our marginal status as innovationists to find an optic through which we can re-involve ourselves with the world, history, and technique, present ourselves as a constant prompt to ourselves and to others that things can always be different, more intriguing, than they seem.

Any such changing will occur—if it occurs at all—locally. That is, writing of the Difficult Imagination won't generate macro-revolutions. Rather it will generate a necklace of micro-ones daily: nearly imperceptible, nearly ahistorical clicks in consciousness that come when you make or meet an explosive, puzzling, challenging, enlightening writing thought experiment.

reading suggestions

Barth, John. "The Literature of Exhaustion" (1967) and "The Literature of Replenishment" (1979). Two cornerstone essays on the innovative by one of the most influential experimental authors of the second half of the twentieth century. The first focuses on the death of old forms of fiction, the second on fiction's postmodern reinvigoration.

Berry, R. M. and Jeffrey Di Leo, eds. *Fiction's Present: Situating Contemporary Narrative Innovation* (2007). Essays by such contemporary writers as Percival Everett, Michael Martone, Carole Maso, Joseph McElroy, Leslie Scalapino, and Lidia Yuknavitch on innovation's history and current problematics.

Federman, Raymond. "Surfiction: A Postmodern Position" (1973). "The only kind of fiction that still means something today," this key essay asserts, "is the kind of fiction that tries to explore the possibilities of fiction beyond its own limitations; the kind of fiction that challenges the tradition that governs it."

Marcus, Ben. "Why Experimental Fiction Threatens to Destroy Publishing, Jonathan Franzen, and Life as We Know It" (2005). Provocative explanation and defense of experimental writing in contemporary America that argues, in part, "the true elitists in the literary world are the ones who have become annoyed by literary ambition in any form."

McKeon, Michael, ed. *Theory of the Novel* (2000). An extraordinary compendium of narrative theories, including excerpts from Fredric Jameson's *The Political Unconscious*, Alain Robbe-Grillet's *For a New Novel*, and Ian Watt's *Rise of the Novel*.

exercise

Bring in to your writing community a short passage from one of your favorite writers of all time, and from one of your least favorite. Be prepared to explain why each affects you the way it does, paying close attention to style, voice, ear, form, character, and imaginative flair. What would you like to steal from the first? What can you learn by negative example from the second? What does each tell you about your aesthetic preferences? How do the aesthetics of each imply a politics, a metaphysics? How, if at all, do they, as Barthes suggests, provide the question minus the answer?

interviews

brian evenson

q: You have taught at a number of unique universities—Brigham Young, Oklahoma State, Syracuse, Denver—and currently direct the Literary Arts Program at Brown. What's the best thing about a university environment for creative writers?

> **a:** I think ideally that the university can provide a safe place for writers to experiment, expand their sense of the possibilities of writing, and take chances. If you have a good and fairly unbiased teacher leading the workshop in a way that puts the advancement of students at the fore, that can happen. But it's true that far too many teachers resort to universally-applied maxims and other easy ways out.

q: Your writing consistently and bravely tests the limits of popular genre fiction like horror and SF. Why are these particular genres compelling to you? What sort of challenges do they offer you as a writer?

> **a:** I grew up reading SF and I think my work's concern with mood and atmosphere and viscerality gives it a kind of natural connection to at least some of what's going on in horror. More than anything, I think that some of our genre divisions are outmoded and artificial, and that we're not taking advantages of possibilities that can make the writing more dynamic and challenging. I also think that cross-pollination between genres, and between literature and genre, is one of the things that can keep fiction alive and vibrant, that keeps it from becoming staid. There's a lot of good work being done within both genre and literature and a lot of bad work being done within both genre and literature, but the best work in both, I think, when taken together presents very interesting possibilities that I'd like to take advantage of as a writer.

q: The publication of your short story collection *Altmann's Tongue* quite literally became a crisis of faith for you at Brigham Young, and you ended up leaving your teaching position there over it. How did that incident impact your subsequent writing?

> **a:** I think it had a huge impact on my writing. The biggest thing was that it told me something at the beginning of my career that most writers may not experience throughout theirs: it told me that what I wrote mattered, and that if I was going to do it at all I had to be committed to it since I might well lose a job or even a religion over it. That also made me think carefully about what I was putting down on the page, made me feel like, if I was going to potentially suffer over it, I wanted it to be as good as I could make it. It made writing feel like anything but a frivolous activity.

Brian Evenson is the author of nine books of fiction, most recently Fugue State.

susan steinberg

q: One of the many things I adore about your writing is its gorgeous, obsessive rhythms. Would you talk a little about your sense of the innovative at the sentence level? What sort of attention do you pay there, and how, and why?

> **a:** The obsessive rhythms you mention grow out of a writing process which is also a little obsessive. I often tend to write a sentence and then quickly build the next one off of the one that precedes it, borrowing words or syntax or rhythm. I write fast, messy drafts, and don't focus on the fine-tuning and removal of individual sentences until much later in the process. For me, this is an effective way to build voice and story, as opposed to jumping in with a preconceived plot. It allows for unexpected turns in the narrative and interesting accidents in the language.

q: Does innovative narrativity engage with gender differently than other forms of narrativity? Or, to put it a little differently, what is the relationship, if any, between gender construction and innovative aesthetics?

a: I'm not sure if we're talking about the connection of innovative aesthetics to the gender of the writer or to writing gender. Either way, I write as female, and I generally write about what it is to be female. And, importantly, I view gender as a performance, and I view writing as a performance. For me, a more formulaic approach to the type of narratives I write wouldn't allow for a thorough enough exploration of the questions I raise about both gender and writing.

q: What is one of the most interesting/fun/successful/challenging writing exercises you offer your students?

a: The transcription project, in which students record themselves telling a story to a friend, then transcribe it word for word, including all "ums" and "likes." It sounds a little like cheating, but they then have the opportunity to revise, after discovering the rhythms of their own storytelling—in terms of how they construct both individual sentences and the narrative as a whole. When do they repeat words? How do they use delay? Where do they end the stories? How do their voices sound? It's very effective.

Susan Steinberg is author of three short-fiction collections. She teaches at the University of San Francisco.

joe wenderoth

q: If a poet were to read your *Letters to Wendy's*, I suspect s/he would encounter it as a chain of interconnected prose poems. If a fiction writer were to read it, I suspect s/he would encounter it as a collage of flash fictions adding up to a narrative whole. Is there still a productive distinction to be made between poetry and fiction, between any one genre and any other?

a: I guess it depends how you define "productive." I don't think the assignment of genre really accomplishes much in terms of increasing a reader's potential for being engaged with the text. In fact, it may be true that a serious reader (a reader of the literary) always wants to feel somewhat unsure of genre. Feeling unsure of genre may be a sign that something authentic (uncanny, fateful) is actually happening in the unfolding of the text. The counter argument—or peripheral simultaneous argument is more accurate— may be that there is in fact a difference between what poetry is and what fiction is (or at least what non-poetry is), and that the current lack of concern for the most poetic of speech is indication of some very serious problems in the realm of our species' habits. If this argument is constructed in a serious (careful) way, it leads us off in a different direction—more toward the issue of why people in our society read mostly unpoetic (and usually quite facetious) books—books that do not hold readers up in relation to reality…but which occupy them with fantasies that allow them to have no concern for reality. Anyway, I think the question of genre has this question sort of built in to it, at least when you include poetry in the mix. And like I said, I do not mean to suggest that I think of poetry as some always identifiable set of texts (let alone as some historically progressive set of texts). I certainly don't think that very much of what is now called poetry is possessed of much of the poetic, and I often come across the poetic in other genres. Most of the poetry written today, perhaps because it is unread by the people of the society and at the same time subsidized by an institution that intends to "educate" its consumers, falls off into what I would like to call the various intelligence-displays of lonely clowns. Harmless, one presumes, except with regard to the poetic, which the arising of such a clown (such an intelligence) sacrifices completely. The contemporary poet has accepted his or her position as intelligence-clown in exchange for a job in the educatory system, which brings with it some pseudo-prestige (title, a degree of notoriety in the intelligence-clown community), job security to the max, and decent pay. In exchange for this relatively luxurious life, the contemporary poet typically agrees to not be troubled by the fact that poetry is so rarely read—or read on purpose, anyway (unassigned). He or she agrees to go on producing texts that are not read by the society he or she lives in; he or she reasons that the nature of this work—its *essential difficulty,* i.e. the incredibly complex subtleties of its intelligence (which, coincidentally enough, cry out for help with interpretation from the institution in which it is housed)—is what causes so few people to be capable of rising up to consume it. Here, we can switch over to fiction and talk about what is probably much the same thing; while I am inclined to argue that the two genres most far apart are poetry and fiction, I do nevertheless believe that the best fiction may often be the most poetic fiction, and certainly the best fiction suffers from the same kind of neglect—though of course not nearly as profoundly. The question I'm most interested in is the question of how to define "literary," as that is the category to which most of the best writers are consigned, no matter their purported genre. I think that once "literary" is defined, it may be easier to ask about the divisions between the genres that make it up. My sense, as a teacher of young writers, is that the genre of a text should not be considered until it exists. Once a text exists, then it may be of use to talk about its structure, its manner of engaging the reader—all the genre questions. Young writers would be best served by the ability to be oblivious to genre— to have no set notions about what their voice is made of, or what it's for. Most students are hopelessly saturated with "knowledge" of genre, down to the fucking tone of each sentence. The best writers I see are the ones who are quite aware of genre, or of ideas about genre, but who use this knowledge to disallow its expected impacts. Disallowing the expected impacts is the first step in trying to find a voice of one's own.

q: The idea of the "innovative" is a fraught creative space. How would you go about defining it? Or, to put it somewhat differently, what's innovative about the innovative, and to what purpose?

a: Maybe I should say first that I do not think of writing as *intentionally* innovative. A writer who *intends* to be innovative—the self-described experimental and avant-garde and post-avant-garde writer—is a writer I beg you not to make me read. On the other hand, a *text* that is innovative is always welcome and much cherished. Perhaps I need to define the "innovation" I think a language-artist is capable of. Consider the preface to the first (1855) edition of *Leaves Of Grass*, where Whitman writes: "The direct trial of him who would be the greatest poet is today. If he does not flood himself with the immediate age as with vast oceanic tides…and if he does not attract his own land body and soul to himself and hang on its neck with incomparable love and plunge his semitic

muscle into its merits and demerits...and if he be not himself the age transfigured..."
It is terrible to interrupt the unfolding of this "if" in mid-stream, but I am satisfied
to speak to what he has thus far said. First, I like the way Whitman insinuates that
all innovation stems from simply being present, or from allowing one's presence to
become a desirous embrace with where one is. Land, body, and soul are "attracted" to
him—indeed, if he has work to do, it is to attract the land, body, and soul "to himself."
How is this attraction to be accomplished? Whitman does not say, but having read his
poems pretty thoroughly, I would say that, in his view, a profound sluttyness is required.
The "greatest poet" is profoundly slutty in that he has no past (or fixed) beloved—
his beloveds are too many to count, and they are all *current*, even *contradictory* (to
one another). He "floods himself" with "the immediate age," which is to say, with
everything that is in the present. He must allow himself to be *overwhelmed*—he must
give himself to what he later in the preface calls "lives regions previously unattained...
thenceforward is no rest." Of course, once the attraction is accomplished, the poet must
return the favor, hanging "on its neck" —he must even "plunge his semitic muscle in..."
He does not refer here to his Jewish muscle—the term "semitic" may also be used, as
it is here, to mean something like "pertaining to ancient knowledge, or the knowledge
of ancient cultures." What he is saying is that the greatest poet, engaged as he is in
this "incomparable love" embrace with land, body, and soul, instinctively transforms
his knowledge "muscle" so that it is "plunged" into the "merits and demerits" of the
immediate age. He figures old knowledge (which probably means all knowledge) as
a phallus—or a love-device, at any rate—which he must continually direct toward its
proper beloved: the immediate age. It is interesting that he qualifies the immediate age,
here, saying that the semitic muscle is plunged into the "merits and demerits" of the
immediate age. This again stresses the necessary sluttyness; one does not *know* (in the
biblical sense) the immediate age selectively, separating out the good from the bad, or
the pleasurable from the painful. One knows every part and every aspect of it—one
is randomly promiscuous, plunging that old muscle into *whatever offers itself up*. My
sense of innovation is squarely based upon this idea of sluttyness, of being open to
the immediate age with "incomparable love." Incomparable love is not intentional—it
simply happens. When someone is slutty enough in his soul, the immediate age is

attracted to him. It is the immediate age itself, then, that creates innovation in texts. It is always ready to do so. It just waits for those who are slutty enough to attract it, and then give themselves over to it.

q: What is one of the most interesting/fun/successful/challenging writing exercises you offer your students?

a: Exercise: THE MANY-MOUTHED CLOWN (the Dottie Lasky exercise)

Write a poem.

RULES:

1. Each line must be a sentence, with a period at the end.

2. Each line may be as many as 15 syllables, or as few as 8 syllables. You may have one line that is fewer than 8 syllables.

3. The poem must have between 12 and 20 lines.

4. Each line should be a description of something that is currently happening (i.e., something that is not yet "the past"). (This is a key rule for you to understand—it is important that you think of the something that is currently happening quite literally, which is to say, physically. Example: The wooden maze shrinks from the tired light's nerveless assault. It's okay, too, to bring in whatever abstractions occur to you—whatever seems emotionally resonant to you with regard to the present. Example: The poisoned cloak is given as a gift to each and every one. With the more abstract lines, the key is just to feel that, in the moment of its conception, it is descriptive of what is currently happening to the physical/spiritual space you sit at the center of.)

5. You may not use the words "you" or "he" or "she" or "they" or "us" or "we."

6. Each line should be beautiful—and by that I mean that you should enjoy the sound of it when you read it aloud.

7. Each line must make no reference—in terms of content—to the previous two lines. (This is the other key rule—it is the rule whereby you are encouraged to make leaps/transitions that you cannot explain—i.e., that do not manifest an intentional furthering of either of the two lines preceding. Of course, once you get to the fourth line of the poem, you may return to the subject matter of the first line—and the fifth line may return to the subject matter of the second line, etc.... You are not *required*, however, to return to the subject matter of *any* previous line.)

8. The challenge is to get to a sense of closure somehow. The challenge, that is, is to allow a complex scene to coalesce, and to find its fate.

Joe Wenderoth is Professor of English at UC-Davis.

two

eat your elders

Literary history can be viewed from one of two perspectives—either as series of ruptures (Romanticism rending Enlightenment norms, Modernism disorganizing Victorian aesthetics and moral assumptions), or as a complex network of continuities, complications, re-presentations, re-evaluations.

Choose the latter, and innovative writing becomes a conversation across space and time. Or, as one of Barry Hannah's characters says: "I live in so many centuries. Everybody is still alive."

American culture has at best a flawed sense of the past and at worst a nearly nonexistent one. Our attention spans are those of dexedrined flies in a cage strapped to the top of a Saturn rocket, nine million pounds of thrust behind us to get us away from yesterday. In good part this is because ours is a pioneer consciousness that doesn't like to look over its shoulder, check out the rear-view mirror, environmentally, politically, or otherwise, since objects back there are always larger than they appear.

Yet innovative writing demands historical awareness. In a sense, all innovative authors (as this book's subtitle suggests through its prepositional pun) are not only in pursuit of the innovative, but are also always-already writing subsequent to it—writing, that is, in its long wake. Without a strong sense of the past, an experimentalist is bound inadvertently to reinvent the same wheel of wrenched narrativity James Joyce did in the early twentieth century…or Laurence Sterne in the eighteenth…or Petronius in the first.

To innovate in any meaningful, purposive, resonant way, an author needs to make an attempt to know and understand as much as she or he can about the rules of conventional writing as well as the canonical and alternative traditions in order to challenge those rules and traditions, appreciate why and to what ends he or she is challenging them (even as she or he appreciates why they existed in the first place), and extend or modify or disrupt them. Otherwise, isn't it all simply an aesthetic whistling in the dark?

Take Pablo Picasso, who wrote: "I do not care who it is that has or does influence me, as long as it is not myself." For him, art history was a circus of minds in motion that demanded to be absorbed and fathomed to be both overcome and not overcome simultaneously. Look at him in 1891, barely 10 years old, producing exquisitely mimetic paintings, ingesting and digesting the academic tradition. Look at him fewer than five years later, mimicking a wealth of styles, including those of his fellow modernists from Toulouse-Lautrec to Gauguin. In 1900 he journeys from Barcelona, where he receives his early training, to Paris, where he spends years becoming conversant with the Old Masters in the Louvre, as well as with Classical and pre-Classical sculpture. In 1904, not yet 25, he moves into a tenement in Montmartre and surrounds himself with an ever-growing circle of friends and fellow artists, among whom are André Breton, Guillaume Apollinaire, Alfred Jarry, and Gertrude Stein.

Through a complex pattern of imaginative collaboration, Picasso erupts there into one of the most remarkable phenomena of the last century, reinventing himself and his art continuously, stunning for his versatility, prolificness, creative energy, range, and technical mastery. His work is marked by uninterrupted surprise and renewal, an exciting and impressive sense of the uncharted well into his eighties, even as it persistently both uses and abuses the canonical and innovative traditions.

Reaching that incandescent moment of what André Breton called convulsive beauty, which often feels rare and singular and intuitive and mysterious, consisted in Picasso's case (a case we can all learn from) in years of preparation, exposing himself as widely and deeply to as much art, music, philosophy, drama, poetry, and literature as he could, making reading and painting and connecting and traveling and exploring a daily addiction, teaching himself afresh every morning what Jorge Luis Borges knew as well with respect to writing: "the fact is that every writer creates his own precursors. His work modifies our conception of the past, as it will modify the future."

exercise

James Joyce recasts *The Odyssey* (ca. 800 B.C.) as *Ulysses* (1922), establishing an intricate series of parallels between characters and events in Homer's epic and his novel while shaping each of the 18 chapters into a new form and style that reflects its thematics. In *Snow White* (1975), Donald Barthelme resets the famous fairy tale in an absurd sixties commune in Manhattan peopled by seven dull men and one bored woman; coming to political awareness, the latter feels herself abused in her role as "horsewife" by the scripts that write her and which under scrutiny start seeming as outmoded as the fairy tale that she and her sidekicks find themselves forced to inhabit. Robert Coover looks to the Bible for his inspiration for "The Brother" (1969), retelling the myth of Noah and the Ark from the vantage point of the brother left behind to drown. Stephen Wright in *Going Native* (1994) re-narrates Conrad's *Heart of Darkness* (1902) by sending two affluent Americans from L.A. up a river in Borneo. Locate a fairy tale, folktale, myth, play, poem, short story, or novel you've always enjoyed, and retell it in a way that allows you and your reader to see it with fresh eyes. You might want to consider changing setting, time, point of view, and/or structure in order to employ the past to create something new, and not new, and not *not* new.

interviews

kate bernheimer

q: Your wide range of work not only includes writing fairy tales, but also building a small press to facilitate the publication of them. What's the most compelling aspect of fairy tales that draws your creative and editorial interests?

> **a:** Fairy tales are possibility spaces; they create new openings, fresh ways of considering the world. Fairy tales cross false boundaries of genre and time and belong to no one. They practice free love, lending themselves to all sorts of readers and writers from childhood to adulthood and back. Their rule is jam tomorrow, jam yesterday, but never jam today. I never will tire of reading them, the same way I never will tire of the delightfully weird childhood game of trying to catch up with your own shadow: you can't.

q: In your role of editor, what catches your eye in a submission?

> **a:** I love this quote from Gilles Deleuze: "I do not play the horse, any more than I imitate this or that horse, but I become a horse, by reaching a zone of proximity where I can no longer be distinguished from what I am becoming." I don't play the editor, but I reach a zone of proximity where I can no longer be distinguished from what I am reading. And I desire to read, so when my desire's ignited that work catches my fancy for sure. Whether I pick up an old Andrew Lang fairy-tale book, my own novel-in-progress, a student's manuscript, a solicited work, or a book off the shelf at the library, I want to read writing that makes me want to read more writing, that brings me in contact with a zone where I am indistinguishable from the work; I am becoming inside it. I seek this kind of sensation as a reader with new and old fairy tales, whatever

their form, and I hope that the work I publish (mine or anyone else's) inspires the same sensation in readers to read more fairy tales, too, experience their bliss.

q: Your book *Horse, Flower, Bird* is gorgeously illustrated by Rikki Ducornet. How important is the visual presentation of your work to you?

a: Rikki's a genius. She read the stories for *Horse, Flower, Bird* and said "Kate! I want to make you some pictures!" And the illuminations she made were beyond the beyond and completed the book. I was thrilled with the production by Coffee House Press, too, honoring the work's need for a lot of white space and these marvelous and frightening pictures. Yes. Visual elements are very important to me, but feel, somewhat wonderfully, out of my control. Even when I myself arguably gathered the illustrations for my trilogy of novels about the Gold sisters, over many years, I really felt I was discovering pieces of the characters' posthumous scrapbooks. To me words themselves are very visual, as numbers are. In a conversation along these lines, a fairy-tale scholar, Maria Tatar, recently reminded me of "Nabokov's colored numbers, the red five for example, which he evokes in his self-description as a syn-aesthete." Words are very sensory. If I don't like how one looks and feels, I won't use it. In similar fashion I did not like the number seven as a child and had a hard time multiplying it with anything.

Kate Bernheimer is the author of a trilogy of novels, including The Complete Tales of Lucy Gold, *and a story collection,* Horse, Flower, Bird. *She teaches at the University of Louisiana in Lafayette.*

robert coover

q: You use the tradition to subvert the tradition in your fiction, retelling everything from fairy tales to biblical myths through a postmodern lens. How important do you suppose it is for young writers to acquaint themselves with both the canonical and alternative lineage in fiction?

a: Many writers read nothing at all and get by very nicely. Writers who wish to ride along on the tradition will likely find "alternative" fiction of little use or interest, and the canon may only intimidate them. Innovative writers, however, are by the very nature of their ambition engaged in an ongoing dialogue with the form itself and therefore must read it all. Not in any particular order, though. It's all contemporary. The Gilgamesh Epic was written yesterday.

q: What sort of advice do you give your students approaching the zone of innovative fiction for the first time?

a: For the most part, I only teach mainstream fiction; of course the mainstream is being recut from generation to generation, so my definition of "mainstream" is probably different from most. When I was young, for example, the mainstream writers were Beckett, Burroughs, Borges, and the like; of course that's obvious now, though at the time they had few readers. When students (or friends) approach so-called experimental writing, I suggest that they apply the same severity of judgment they would apply to the typical bestseller, for novelty is not the same thing as quality (there's a lot of pretentious trivia published under the name of innovation, as we all know); but neither is imitation of conventional narrative, no matter how "pretty." Poor innovative writing is always more interesting than skillful conventional writing.

q: In what sense, if any, can fiction writing—especially innovative fiction writing—be taught? In what sense can't it?

a: The learning experience for writers is something of a mystery. Most writers learn only by writing. And reading, which is a kind of writing for them. Workshop dialogue can be useful to the writer with her ears open, but most student writers are deafened by their own egos and so frequently find workshop dialogue destructive. Expressing opinions sometimes helps, though. I often tell my workshops that on the day their stories are on the table they can absent themselves if they wish, for the comments will inevitably be aimed less at the story being discussed than at the failings of each of the speakers, who are working things out for themselves by way of critiquing the writing of another. I do try to break through conventional notions of form, and that can be done by example and challenge and exciting peer groups; I've found hyperfiction workshops especially useful in this regard, for conventional forms instantly vanish in hyperspace and, if wanted (why would they be?), must be reconstructed.

Robert Coover is author of many novels and short story collections, including Pricksongs & Descants *and* The Public Burning. *This interview was conducted in 1996.*

alan singer

q: How do you best achieve a sense of what is "real" in your writing? Is it setting, character, dialogue, point of view, style? All/none of the above?

a: What counts as real in my fiction is what happens: action. I don't mean what can be described as happening, but what happens within the sinews of syntax, both at the level of the sentence and in the juxtaposition of one sentence with another. Change matters most.

q: What is it that a well-crafted sentence does that no other form of expression can?

a: A well-crafted sentence overturns the notion that thought is distinct from thinking. A well-crafted sentence enacts the sense it makes rather than representing it. The result of writing well-crafted sentences is that your reader will have the most vivid sense that something is happening to him or her and with the irresistible urgency of their own dreams.

q: What advice would you give to a beginning writer about writing memorable sentences?

a: I would recommend to all beginning writers that they read first. Dedicate yourself to reading most energetically that which you don't immediately understand. Read with a special attention to the prospect that what doesn't appear to make sense matters most because of the possibilities of sense-making that are portended in it. This experience will fund your own capacity for writing memorable sentences precisely because they will not be mere echoes, mere memories of past writing.

Alan Singer's most recent novel is The Inquisitor's Tongue.

three

the mcdonaldization of the literary marketplace

Authors don't write solely from within disparate literary histories. They also write from within disparate economic ecologies. Despite the Romantic myths to the contrary, nobody ever sits down to compose in an ahistorical vacuum outside the marketplace.

A quick history lesson concerning that marketplace over the course of the last century or so. During the sixties, more than 100 publishing houses thrived in Manhattan. The seventies saw a major oil crisis and recession that resulted in a movement toward consolidation and commodification in the book industry—toward maximizing profits and minimizing risk. By the eighties, there were only 79 publishers left in Manhattan. By the nineties, 15.

Currently, there are only five that bring out fiction: HarperCollins, the Penguin Group, Random House, Simon & Schuster, and Time Warner. Only five, and yet they are responsible for 80 percent of the bestsellers out there. Combine them with the next five, and that figure rises to 98 percent. Most of the Big Five are subsidiaries of vast entertainment corporations (Random House, for instance, of Bertelsmann; HarperCollins of News Corporation), which in good part use those book outlets as tax write-offs.

Although it surely is not the case that the Big Five don't bring out some exciting innovative fiction (Mark Z. Danielewski, Lydia Davis, Mario Vargas Llosa, Thomas Pynchon, and J. M. Coetzee rush to mind), it is the case that the trend in commercial publishing over the last half century has been toward a narrower, safer, blander vision of writing driven by corporate authors like Anne Rice, Stieg Larsson, Stephen King, Dan Brown, and David Sedaris, not to mention the young ones publishers perceive and sell as The Next Hot Thing.

In other words, New York publishing some time ago joined the United States of Shopping. As if to underscore the point, Sonny Mehta, editor-in-chief at Knopf, wondered rhetorically recently: "Why should I publish books if they are not going to make money?" Why indeed, so long as one conceives of writing as commodity rather than art form.

Not long before, Philip Roth estimated the audience for "serious" fiction in the United States runs about 120,000. Nan Talese, Senior Vice president at Doubleday, puts it closer to 4,000. So while John Grisham's law-firm novels sell more than 4.5 million copies in hardcover alone and the romance genre more than $1 billion worth of books each year (50 percent of all mass-market paperbacks), most writers can't live from what their writing makes them. The average income of a "successful" author is usually well less than $5,000 a year.

Only about one percent of novels submitted to major publishers each year is published. New York editors won't look at a manuscript unless it comes through an agent (more on those and the pragmatics of publication in this book's penultimate chapter), and most agents won't look at a manuscript unless they believe it to be economically viable—rather than, say, aesthetically or thematically interesting. If the agent can place it, an $80,000 advance isn't out of the question (quite a low figure, even in the best of cases, considering most authors spend between two and five years of their lives working on a book and struggling to find an agent to represent it), but a $1,000 or $2,000 advance (if not less, if not none) is much more likely.

For argument's sake, let's imagine you do locate an agent who can place your book. And let's imagine that your editor doesn't jump ship or is fired from the publishing house bringing it out (an increasingly common occurrence these days). Your book then becomes one of the 50 an overworked in-house publicist must push that season, meaning he or she will send out 200 review copies, 400 press releases…and probably call it a day, moving on to the next product that needs peddling. Those advance review copies will join the other 300 or so advance review copies crowding book reviewers' shelves each month at a time when most print book review venues are scaling back on how many reviews they run in order to save space and cash. That means the chances of your book being nationally reviewed are slim to none.

Moreover, publishers send only about 10 percent of their authors on reading tours to promote their books, and then usually only the award winners and celebrities (not literary celebrities, mind you, but the pro-wrestler, political, self-help, or talk-show varieties).

Although your book may have a print run of 15,000, and although it may sell a respectable 6,000, it probably won't do well enough for your Manhattan publisher to want to buy your next one.

While we're at it, it might be illuminating to keep in mind that most books published in the U.S. each year are neither fiction nor poetry. Eighty-five percent are nonfiction. And no matter what the genre, the amount of the cover price that goes to the writer (called royalties) ranges anywhere from three to 25 percent. The average is six to 12. Most authors never receive even this because their books don't earn out their advances—moneys paid to an author before the book goes on sale, which must be made up before the author gets further royalties. Nor does one fare much better at the level of consumer magazines. Each receives a conservative average of 1,000 submissions a year. *Redbook* receives 25,000 short story submissions for five spots.

If you're out to make money through your writing, then, you would be better advised to play the lottery. Your chances of winning will be much greater, which is to say what Samuel Beckett once told Raymond Federman is truer now than ever before: "Whatever you write never compromise, never cheat, and if you plan to write for money or for fame, do something else."

That said, there has been a second trend in publishing since the seventies that has grown in response to the first, and in response to the rise of print-on-demand technologies, relatively inexpensive printing options, and the development of e-readers (ebooks outsell hardcover books): the proliferation of independent small and micro presses like Coffee House, Dalkey Archive, Chiasmus, Dzanc, Eraserhead, FC2, Jaded Ibis, Les Figues, Raw Dog Screaming, Small Beer, Spuyten Duyvil, Starcherone, and Wordcraft.

Small and micro presses are redefining the publishing/distribution paradigm to such an extent that people have begun to shop as much by press as by author. It is as if, next to the universe of commercial publishing, there has come to exist an alternate one, à la some Borges story, made up of innovative authors who live with a completely different set of aims and ethics than those found in Manhattan. These are the literary activists among us who are writers themselves, bring out each other's work, read and review it, teach it at colleges and universities and local writing groups across the country, study it in critical essays, urge others to start up journals and presses to help get the word out about the work they love.

If the early twenty-first century is the worst of times for American publishing because of the market pressures that favor writing that wants to be a film when it grows up, it is also the best of times because of these small and micro presses and the literary activists at their helms. Competition here has been replaced with collaboration. Corporate paradigms have been replaced with collective ones.

FC2 (short for Fiction Collective Two) is a case in point. Founded in 1973 as Fiction Collective by a small group of experimental writers (among them Jonathan Baumbach and Ronald Sukenick) increasingly frustrated by New York publishing's commodification and aesthetics of exclusion, FC2 developed a successful model based on alliance and partnership, a production model run by and for authors, and the idea that it is less important to make a profit than it is to disseminate significant innovative projects. The consequence has been to remind readers and writers with every book printed (now more than 200) that there are options that stand against the corporate milieu's structuring, functioning, and ambitions, not to mention a means of caring about innovative writing that Manhattan can't begin to begin to conceive of.

A manuscript can reach FC2 in one of three ways: 1) a non-FC2 author can enter his or her manuscript in either the Ronald Sukenick American Book Review Innovative Fiction Prize or Catherine Doctorow Innovative Fiction Prize; 2) her or his manuscript can be sponsored by an FC2 author; 3) as an FC2 author, one can submit one's own manuscript for consideration. If submitted to one of the contests, it is evaluated by screeners and the judge. If submitted directly into the editorial pipeline, it is evaluated by several FC2 authors and must receive two yes votes before two no ones in order to proceed to the Board for a final vote. Each manuscript that reaches the Board is read in full by at least two Board members, each of whom writes a reader's report. All Board members read at least 50 pages of any manuscript that has been approved for continued consideration by the first two readers. The Board as a whole makes the decision whether or not to publish each manuscript. Out of the hundreds of manuscripts received annually, FC2 accepts approximately six for publication. About half are by previous FC2 authors, about half by authors never before published by FC2.

The one constant for FC2 is that there are no constants—except, of course, a commitment to its original mission statement: "to publish books of high quality and exceptional ambition whose style, subject matter, or form push the limits of American publishing and reshape our literary culture." The Collective has always stood against, as one of its founders, Peter Spielberg, pointed out in 1974, "books designed by cereal packagers, marketed by used-car salesmen… and ruled or overruled by accountants."

Dispersed among several universities and structured as a not-for-profit publisher, FC2 fashioned itself as an adaptable, flexible entity. Nearly 40 years on, it has brought out some of the most important and diverse innovative writers of the second half of the twentieth century and first decades of the twenty-first, including Kate Bernheimer, Lucy Corin, Samuel R. Delany, Jeffrey DeShell, Brian Evenson, Raymond Federman, Noy Holland, Harold Jaffe, Stephen Graham Jones, Clarence Major, Vanessa Place, Leslie Scalapino, Ronald Sukenick, Melanie Rae Thon, Steve Tomasula, Curtis White, Diane Williams, and Lidia Yuknavitch.

The paradigm constructed around the idea of the literary activist has gone a good distance toward erasing distinctions between editor and writer, critic and poet, reviewer and novelist, academic and publisher, or blogger, or tweeter, or reading series coordinator, or volunteer at a small press or journal. A new mandate for innovative writers pulses behind it: *Ask not what publishing can do for you; ask what you can do for publishing.*

This landscape has concomitantly foregrounded the materiality of the book, the beauty of and possibilities inherent in the thing itself, and the beauty of and possibilities inherent in emerging delivery systems that run the gamut from various social networking tools to new-media writing (more on this later)—all of which aid in making the book's present future, as Michael Martone has pointed out, increasingly viral, collaborative, and ephemeral.

Publishing over the course of the last half-century, then, has come down to a new iteration of the David and Goliath myth. The individual's reaction time is fast, the corporation's reaction time slow, and innovative fiction has accordingly discovered over and over again abundant opportunities in which to flourish.

And that's why, despite the McDonaldization of the corporate marketplace—or, rather, to a great extent because of it—this is an immensely exciting moment to be an author.

exercises

1. Go to your campus or local library and follow *Publishers Weekly*, the primary gloss on the New York publishing industry, for a month. Compare what you discover there with several issues of *American Book Review* or *Rain Taxi*, two of the leading print venues for reviews and discussions of innovative writing and publishers. What sort of trends, concerns, themes do you find? Do these jibe with the salient points made in this chapter, or do you perceive different ones? What does what you see tell you about the current state of innovative writing in the United States?

2. Visit the websites for three of the following innovative presses: Burning Deck, Chax, Coffee House, Cuneiform, Dalkey Archive, Dzanc, Fairy Tale Review Press, Featherproof, FC2, Granary Books, Jaded Ibis, Raw Dog Screaming, Small Beer, Starcherone, Tinfish. What similarities and differences do you find among their histories, mission statements, publishing paradigms? What can you take away with you about the current state of innovative writing in the United States?

interviews

davis schneiderman

q: A good amount of your work is in collaboration with other writers and artists. What does writing/creating with others afford you that working solo does not?

> **a:** Collaboration lets me stop being an Author with a capital "A" and start being a writer with a small "w": a conduit for the language of our particular time, wherein my words lose their bulky ego-trips about genius and creativity and get churned up in the cement mixer of other people. When I collaborate, I break my own bad habits, shrug off the quirks of my prose, all because I surrender even the illusion of control cultivated by the Romantic myth of the Author. Put another way, I break myself in pieces.

q: Your novel *Blank* takes big risks with its concept and execution, wherein entire pages of the printed book are intentionally left as pure white space. Can you briefly describe your method?

> **a:** *Blank* uses a morphological strategy in the style of Vladimir Propp's work on Russian folktales. Propp identifies the structure that all the folktales he studied have in common, and he so develops a list of these structures. The chapter titles for *Blank*, which is thus not a fully blank book, do the same with a set of over-exaggerated narrative structures. Chapter titles such as "A Character" or "They Fall in Love" provide ballast to the emptiness of the interior chapters. The book doesn't so much ask the reader to contribute in filling the spaces as it asks the reader to dismantle other books that are already overfilled. In a world of information overload, *Blank* is antidote *and* disease.

q: Where a lot of creative writers teach in M.F.A. programs at universities, you've chosen to teach at a liberal arts college. What do you think a liberal arts education might afford a creative writer that the more tried path through a university might not?

a: The liberal arts environment prides itself on the creative synthesis of its broad subject areas through the close collaboration of its individuated parts. For the student, we hope that at a certain moment the language of economics bleeds into the language of mathematics and so into the language of philosophy. As a faculty member, I teach as a writer and a literature professor, offering courses in everything from fiction writing to postmodernism to Chicago and science fiction. Thus, the borders between everything remain wonderfully slippery, which is perfect for the writer, a figure who must press through different zones as the same syllables press through a billion different mouths.

Davis Schneiderman's novels include Drain *and* Blank, *with audio from DJ Spooky. He is Chair of the English Department at Lake Forest College.*

david shields

q: Your book *Reality Hunger* makes a compelling argument for a deliberate composing methodology of appropriation and assemblage. What was the most difficult part about your executing that particular project?

a: Taking 618 prose fragments—about half written by me and about half originally written by others—and repurposing them into a sustained argument, a unified voice.

q: What advice would you give a beginning writer about today's publishing realities?

a: Ignore them. There is no "today." No "publishing." And no "reality." In 10 years, if not sooner, there will no longer be a "publishing" "industry."

q: You describe your own writing as "mainly collage nonfiction." Can you describe what you mean by this?

> **a:** I'm interested in work that takes the banality of nonfiction (the literalness of "facts," "truth," "reality"), turns that banality inside out, and thereby makes nonfiction a staging area for the investigation of any claim of facts and truth, an extremely rich theater for investigating the most serious epistemological and existential questions: What's "true"? What's knowledge? What's "fact"? What's memory? What's self? What's other? I want a nonfiction that explores our shifting, unstable, multiform, evanescent experience in and of the world.

David Shields is the author of a dozen books, including Reality Hunger, *which was named one of the best books of the year by more than 30 publications, and* The Thing About Life Is That One Day You'll Be Dead, *a* New York Times *bestseller; his work has been translated into 15 languages.*

four

workshop model(s)

Founded in 1936, the Iowa Writers' Workshop was the first program in the country to offer a Master of Fine Arts degree in creative writing. It is also one of the most esteemed in the world, and one of the most paradigmatic. Each year about three percent of applicants are admitted, while almost every other program in the U.S. and Canada—more than 300 of them—designs itself with Iowa's model in mind. Graduates include T. Coraghessan Boyle, Sandra Cisneros, Michael Cunningham, Steven Erikson, Allan Gurganus, John Irving, Bharati Mukherjee, Jane Smiley, and Joy Williams.

Flannery O'Connor attended, too. She was never especially fond of her alma mater or its workshop model. "I don't believe in classes where students criticize each other's manuscripts," O'Connor wrote in "The Nature and Aim of Fiction." "Such criticism is generally composed in equal parts of ignorance, flattery, and spite. It's the blind leading the blind, and it can be dangerous."

Vladimir Nabokov was even less generous about showing work before it was done: "Only ambitious nonentities and hearty mediocrities exhibit their rough drafts. It is like passing around samples of one's sputum."

Although many writers, innovative and otherwise, have graduated from M.F.A. programs (John Barth, Louise Erdrich, Thalia Field, Lily Hoang, Rick Moody, David Shields, and David Foster Wallace, for instance), it is also true that at its worst the pedagogical approach that forms the core of these programs is the aesthetic equivalent of a Ford assembly line. As the pseudonymous Chris Altacruise argues in his vitriolic attack on them, work generated within their hermetically sealed walls almost always "displays the hallmarks of committee effort: emotional restraint and a lack of linguistic idiosyncrasy; no vision, just voice; no fictional world of substance and variety, just a smooth surface of diaristic, autobiographical, and confessional speech." Poems, of course, fare no better.

"The average workshop is a profoundly conservative force in fiction writers' lives," Brian Kiteley warns in his collection of innovative writing exercises, *The 3 A.M. Epiphany*, "encouraging the simplifying and routinizing of stories." He goes on: "the most damning criticism I've heard of workshops is that they promote mere competence."

Anyone who has ever attended one probably senses a nip of truth in such statements. Workshops can and frequently do devolve from energizing, theorized, revelatory and liberating discussions of the formalistics, thematics, and problematics of writing into therapy sessions and/or Ebertization exercises in judgment where participants voice uninformed opinions about what they like and/or don't about the piece before them. Many workshops end up producing what Altacruise calls Groupthink, "an unspoken consensus on politics and aesthetics that completely controls student work—from the story genre, down deep into the psychic creation of character, and out into the writer's very ability to imagine and create a world." They can become less a case of the blind leading the blind than the bland leading the bland.

Still, it is too easy to dismiss writing programs and other intimate writing communities out of hand. If nothing else, M.F.A. programs provide writers with between two and three subsidized years to do very little except write, think about writing, read, and in many cases teach writing and literature. Creative writing Ph.D. programs, generally recognized as a writer's best preparation for a tenure-track teaching career at the college or university level, provide the same while emphasizing, in addition to creative-writing workshops, courses on advanced theory, film, literature, and so on. There are many less productive ways to spend one's formative writing years.

Another way to conceptualize this: since, roughly, World War II, universities have come to fulfill the role rich patrons used to in the Renaissance, affording support to talented writers— both students and teachers alike.

Moreover, workshops (whether inside or outside academia) surround you with relatively attentive, well-read, committed readers. Even if you find yourself agreeing with them only intermittently, they can nonetheless serve as useful sounding boards off of which to bounce your own ideas about what writing is and should be. And it is always enlightening to view one's own work through the eyes of others. In some instances, fellow participants will turn out to be among your most influential and challenging teachers long after you have moved on.

Both undergraduate and graduate programs in creative writing also provide the opportunity to take a wide array of courses in intellectual movements, literary history, aesthetics, the short story, the novel, poetics, and film, not to mention ones in far-afield areas that can feed your writing in rich and unexpected ways, from art history and new-media studies to tennis and forensics. In addition, graduate programs usually provide students an opportunity to teach and/or edit, which may help students determine if those might be careers they would enjoy. Equally important, graduate programs provide students with a support network that will see budding authors through the rest of their lives, while on occasion serving as portals to publication and jobs in academia, publishing, editing, journalism, advertising and public relations, business and technical writing, educational writing, and book selling, among others.

Needless to say, education is not something your professors make for you. It is something you make for yourself. If you do your homework in advance, research where authors with whom you'd like to study teach, check out their reputations in the classroom, get a sense of various programs and options around the country and abroad, compare and contrast the visions and resources of those programs, perhaps even email their directors with follow-up questions after carefully studying their websites, contemplate the environment you'd like to inhabit and ask yourself why you'd like to inhabit it. Give yourself permission to follow your own interests and instincts, and most likely you won't be disappointed. That said, some people prosper in graduate writing programs while others don't. Only you know, if anyone does, which you're likely to do.

For those interested in innovative writing at the M.F.A. level, among the programs to look into are those at Brown, Columbia, Notre Dame, University of Alabama, University of

Massachusetts-Amherst, University of Colorado-Boulder, Brooklyn College, CalArts, The New School, University of Washington, University of Illinois-Chicago, SUNY-Buffalo, University of Albany, Temple University, Naropa, University of California-San Diego, and Johns Hopkins. Consider faculty, curriculum, journals and/or presses associated with the program, other programs at the university in question from which you might benefit, duration, cost, support, what graduates have done upon leaving.

For those interested in innovative writing at the Ph.D. level, the three major programs to look into are those at the University of Utah, the University of Denver, and the University of Southern California. Once upon a time, the M.F.A. was considered the so-called "terminal" degree when pursuing creative writing. That is no longer the case. While many M.F.A. programs are "studio" ones—i.e., programs focusing on "applied" or "practiced" writing—the Ph.D. offers that in addition to a more rigorous course of study in which you participate in all the work students in literature/theory Ph.D. programs do and, while also taking workshops, complete a creative rather than academic dissertation.

Another possibility to consider at the graduate level is the low-residency M.F.A., especially for those with already established careers and/or families that don't allow them to move easily to another city for several years of study. Low-residency programs usually last four semesters, yet participants are only required to spend a week or two on campus each year participating in a series of intensive workshops, craft lectures, discussions, and readings. Participants stay at home the rest of the year, developing a reading list and workshopping online with a faculty advisor and sometimes his or her fellow participants. Low-residency programs open to innovative writing include Warren Wilson College.

If you don't find the idea of entering an academic program particularly appealing, but do find appealing the idea of a writing community, you may want to investigate local college or university extension programs, online workshops, or private tutorials and workshops. In larger cities, the latter are fairly prevalent. Online workshops exist throughout the world. To find them, just Google. You may also want to think about starting one around your own aesthetic interests.

All of which begs a more fundamental question: Can creative writing—let alone innovative writing—be taught? "There are three rules for writing the novel," W. Somerset Maugham once observed. "Unfortunately, no one knows what they are." This might be closer to the truth than most teachers of creative writing would like to acknowledge, no matter what the genre. No one would disagree, naturally, that grammar can be taught. Certain guiding principles that tend to work in certain modes of writing surely can be pointed out and discussed. That laundry list of clichés called craft can be unfurled.

Yet every writer writes differently from every other. Each has a unique compositional process, a unique set of gestures, a unique way of manifesting those gestures, a unique worldview, a unique voice. Furthermore, each piece of writing—conventional writing is no exception—succeeds exactly to the extent that it doesn't quite follow the rules established for it. Each is both always-already in conversation with every piece that has ever been written in the genre, and strives to steer that conversation in a slightly unusual, individual direction.

Nevertheless, the fundamentals of creative writing can be taught in the same way, say, that the fundamentals of piano can. You learn, metaphorically speaking, how to hold your hands and not arch your wrists, the difference between grace notes and glissandos, the difference between a sonata or a sinfonia. What can't be taught is innate talent. While no music teacher can make Bob or Barb into Beethoven, most good ones can certainly give the Ludwigs out there a hand in order to reach their full potential. Most writing teachers can help authors compose a little better by the time they exit a workshop than when they entered—assuming, of course, another key principle, this one from Thomas Edison: "Genius is one percent inspiration and ninety-nine percent perspiration."

It took Beethoven years of practice to become a natural. Being a writer (to change metaphors midstream) is a lot like practicing to become an Olympic swimmer. No one would imagine the latter could attain his or her goal without years of hard work, a rigorous daily regimen, an obsessive personality. Why would anybody think it would be any different for an author? The more you write, the more you read and think and talk about writing, the more accomplished you will become.

Hemingway promised himself he wouldn't leave his writing studio until he had written at least 500 words every morning. William Makepeace Thackeray, who wrote precisely three hours each day, rain or shine, once discovered he had just completed the novel he had been working on for the last nine months and yet still had 15 minutes left. He began a new one. Which is to say: whether or not you enter a writing program, or a community workshop, or decide to create on your own, develop a writing schedule and stick to it, and your writing will improve.

Writing every day is best, even if it is only for 45 minutes or an hour, but if that isn't possible, then write three evenings a week, or every Saturday and Sunday morning. Melanie Rae Thon suggests wisely that, even if your life is too hectic to write on a regular basis, you should somehow touch your writing every day—edit a few lines of what you're working on, take a few notes, brainstorm for a few minutes, read something that nourishes your words. To put it another way, writing is more than touching fingers to keyboard. The less you write, the easier it will be not to write. The more you write, the more you will want to write. The more you write, the more your writing will continue to become itself.

All of which begs yet another fundamental question: Does a workshop, whether it takes place inside academia or not, by necessity have to follow the Iowa model? Sometime before each meeting, according to that model, two or three participants turn in material for critique. At the workshop proper a discussion ensues, guided by the teacher, during which the other participants offer impressions about and suggestions for each piece in front of them. The teacher usually sums up—usually authoritatively—at the end of each workshop. Sometimes the workshop is broken up with the discussion of a story or two by professional writers, a poem or two, from a limited range of aesthetic possibilities. The goal is for authors whose work is up to leave with insights into the strengths and weaknesses of their own writing, and everyone to leave with insights into the craft of writing—with a distinct emphasis on the word *craft*.

But why not instead consider turning the workshop into a possibility space analogous to that which defines innovative writing where everything can and should be considered, attempted, and troubled? Why not, in other words, conceive of the workshop along the same lines as David Markson conceives of experimental work generally—as a "kind of research and development arm of the culture industry"? A zone, that is to say, where writers can and should take multiple risks in order to imagine in new ways, explore fresh strategies for finding and cultivating story ideas, re-view what it is they are doing and why, what "writing" is and why, and, at the end of the day, understand better from the inside out, at the cellular level, what Samuel Beckett's dictum about failure really means.

Why not as well build innovative workshops around specific problematics to investigate—the question of hybridization, say, or pla(y)giarism, or paraliterary genres' impact on innovative writing, or, maybe, the relationship of print to digital forms, the rise of the book arts movement(s), or architecture and music to prose, or the thematics and formalistics of metamorphoses or collage? Rather than granting the assumptions behind such craft elements as scene, plot, and fully-rounded character, why not stage a workshop that investigates those assumptions, asking what they imply aesthetically, philosophically, socially; or asking what the limits of those gestures might look like; or asking what would happen if we tried to create our way beyond them? What would the results look like? What could they teach us about narrativity or how we construct ourselves and the world?

Rather than spending the full workshop on the pieces under discussion, why not also invent as a collaborative group a number of generative prompts for each other, while reimagining the "teacher," not as expert or judge, but as facilitator? Read a book or several short pieces each week—sometimes theory, sometimes poetry, sometimes fiction, sometimes hybrid projects, sometimes new-media ones—that challenge us to re-see how our writing might work, what it might do if we envision it other than we have up to this point? Read and discuss along the course of the workshop two fiction-writing textbooks that approach the topic from diametrically opposed directions in order to ponder the cultural assumptions behind the act(s) of writing? Discuss current marketplace pragmatics and how to navigate as well as subvert them? Talk about how we might self-consciously ruminate about the very ideas of "workshop" and "workshop critique," what their boundaries are, their assumptions, and how we might as a community push our ways beyond them—all in order to bring into greater relief why and how we do what we do?

reading suggestions

Altacruise, Chris. "Stepford Writers: Undercover Inside the M.F.A. Creativity Boot Camp" (1990). Scathing—and unsettlingly accurate—indictment of the conventional creative writing workshop model.

AWP Official Guide to Writing Programs (updated regularly). Online. Indispensable listing of all undergraduate and graduate programs in creative writing in the U.S. and Canada. Outlines various courses of study, enumerates current faculty and contact addresses.

Poets & Writers (Updated regularly). "M.F.A. Programs Database." Online. Also includes Ph.D. programs. Again, excellent resource for those searching for the right academic place to study.

exercises

1. If you decide not to go into an academic writing program, then join a local community-based writing group or, better yet, start your own and people it with an animated assortment of imaginations on your wavelength. Build a Do-It-Yourself workshop online or locally. Hang up fliers around town, making sure to target independent bookstores, cafés, and reading venues; advertise in local alternative papers or zines; develop a website; put together an email list of writers you think might be interested; pass the news via word of mouth among your friends, at work, in your classes.

2. If you decide you might be interested in entering an academic creative writing program, begin your homework. Talk to faculty at your present college or university to get their sense of good matches for you. Study websites for the innovative writing programs listed above. Look through the *AWP Official Guide to Writing Programs* and *Poets & Writers* "M.F.A. Programs Database" to discover additional possibilities. Make a list of programs that appeal to you in terms of faculty, course of study, resources, location, cost, support. Don't be shy: if you have questions, approach the directors of those programs by email in order to find out the answers. Since acceptance rates are low, plan to apply to about 10-12 programs at the M.F.A. level, six-seven at the Ph.D. Always apply to three or four safety schools in addition to your top choices.

interviews

r. m. berry

q: You describe your novel *Frank* as an "unwriting" of Mary Shelley's *Frankenstein*. What was your process like?

a: My goal with *Frank* was to acknowledge what Shelley's novel couldn't acknowledge, while doing justice to her discoveries about masculinity and creative autonomy. My premise was that the book itself was the monster, which was something I believe Shelley had to repress. I then rewrote her book almost paragraph by paragraph consistent with that premise. Of course, I set *Frank* in the present and in Florida (the American Southeast) because the goal of unwriting her creation was to write mine.

My process was to figure out what the equivalent would be in my present circumstances for the elements of Shelley's story, section by section. Her writing needed to show through mine, as though my words were struggling to free themselves from hers (which, of course, they were), and I didn't want to repeat the violence of her male characters, killing off the women who gave them life. I wanted Shelley to be my literary mother without any hovering threat of emasculation. I found a parallel for that task or goal in the theme of fate in her novel. Victor Frankenstein repeatedly feels that his doom has been foretold, that he isn't free. That becomes literally the case in *Frank*, where Frank Stein's life is dictated by Shelley's book.

A last remark: Shelley's book was originally published in a heavy German or gothic type font, and as I became interested in how to demonstrate the real basis of my book, I hit on the idea of including certain of her phrases, or sometimes just a Shelley-sounding word, in gothic type. I came to feel that the whole originality of my work was comprised in that gesture.

q: You are an accomplished critic as well as a creative writer. Why is it important to you to wear both hats?

a: I have always felt that they were a single hat, that wearing one already meant I was wearing the other, but that viewpoint, which today seems stranger than when I began writing 40 years ago, may be because of the way I have always thought of fiction. I only care about fiction that raises the question of what fiction is, and that question is a critical or theoretical one. Writing criticism isn't the only way to answer it, of course, but it is one way, and when it's good, criticism can help fiction writers think about what they're doing. I try to write criticism of that kind, both to help other writers and to help me understand myself, both as a writer and a person.

I should add that I'm a philosophical rather than historical critic, and philosophy, as I have learned from Wittgenstein's writing, always poses the question of itself. Although metafiction in the sixties and seventies came to be identified (reductively) with fiction that wanted to expose its own fictionality, I have for some time felt that writing that reflects critically on itself joins a philosophical aim to a literary one. That conjunction has always been something to which, as a writer and critic, I've aspired.

q: You not only teach in a university setting, but serve as chair of your department. What is the best thing a university can offer a creative writer?

a: A job. I don't see how any serious fiction writer today can hinge her financial security on the sales of her fiction, so finding other employment is crucial. Universities are particularly attractive because the work performed in them can be collaborative and meaningful, does not have to be competitive and worthless, as is often the case in business. However, I hasten to add that universities cannot and should not be expected to function as patrons. Being part of a faculty means contributing in all the ways other academics do. I'm chair of my department because I'm a member of my department, and sharing in the administrative burdens is something all faculty members do.

R. M. Berry is author of the novel Frank *and editor of the anthology* Forms at War: FC2 1999-2009.

monica drake

q: Where a lot of creative writers teach in M.F.A. programs at universities, you've chosen to teach at a fine arts college. What do you think an art school education might afford a creative writer that the more tried path through a university might not?

a: Art school often draws students who value self expression, are into making things, are in love with ideas, and are less concerned about conventional systems of judgment and reward like grades. That mix lends itself to a fantastic, active arena. There's a constant blending and cross-pollination between disciplines.

I studied painting and art history before I started writing. Standing in front of a canvas, working alone, was an active meditation. I'd mess around with paint and idly follow random, tangential thoughts, which would deepen, in a way that doesn't happen in daily life. I found meanings, moments, or sentences that I brought to my written work. The creative processes are cognitively linked. There's crossover in the language of the disciplines, too: line, shape, form, composition, armature, tone, value, texture. These all apply to written work. When you have experience physically building visual art, externalizing ideas, while considering these terms, you develop an internalized sense of what the words really mean, which then can apply to writing in a more specific yet still abstract way.

Beyond all that, for me making art is always a good time. Writing is hard and solitary and offers never-ending homework. I grow obsessive about words on the page. Trading thoughts with visual and performative artists keeps it fun, builds a creative community, and keeps ideas alive.

q: What's the greatest thing about using a peer group of other writers to workshop your in-progress work? What might be the not-so-greatest thing?

a: Workshop is a form of marriage between a pack of people—it's intimate, vulnerable, fabulous, sexy, drunken, mind-blowing, and sometimes rocky. It's a great way to develop a sense of audience. When I drift away from workshop my writing can grow ruminative. When I vow to pull my pages out and read them out loud to my crew, I immediately cut away whatever I think won't charm them. I try to make the work be "about" something, so I'm in conversation with the other writers I'm fortunate enough to be in workshop alongside.

The downside might be a sense of self-consciousness about work in its infancy. I'm not sure. You can always let those pages develop for a while, working on them at home. Most of all, though, I've found that taking even very new work in can be incredibly helpful, as feedback from good readers expedites the necessary revelations.

q: Your first novel, *Clown Girl*, was published by Hawthorne Books and is being optioned for a possible feature film. What did you and/or your publisher go through in order to get your book a level of visibility to warrant such attention?

a: I flew to Los Angeles twice, on my own dime, when one man in Hollywood expressed an interest in the book. I scheduled a meeting with him and with anyone else who would talk to me. I spent days driving to meetings. L.A. is a place where everyone seems to be interested in who has what deal going on, so once you have one person's interest, you can parlay that into additional meetings. The phrase, "It's not what you know; it's who you know," rings true. I met a lot of people. After a second trip, Kristen Wiig invited me to send a copy of the book to her. To my great happiness, she fell in love with it. Slowly, it's all moving forward.

Monica Drake is the author of Clown Girl *and* The Stud Book, *as well as many essays and short stories.*

matthew kirkpatrick

q: A lot of creative writers go into M.F.A. programs, but you chose the Ph.D. route. When you were deciding on a post-graduate path, what ultimately tipped the scale for you towards the doctorate program instead of the M.F.A.?

a: It was a tough decision. I was fortunate to be accepted to several great M.F.A. and Ph.D. programs. Ultimately, the Ph.D. seemed like a better fit for me because one of the things I wanted out of graduate school was a deeper exploration of literature than I was able to do on my own, in addition to the mentorship of creative writing workshops. My workshops during my Ph.D. have been enormously enlightening, but the work I did for my comprehensive exams was, to me, the most valuable part of the experience. I don't think there's any one path for every writer, whether it's an M.F.A., a Ph.D., or neither, but for what I'm interested in accomplishing, the Ph.D. was the best fit.

q: What's the one short story that best exemplifies not what a story should be but what one *could* be?

a: "In the Heart of the Heart of the Country" by William Gass was a story that really opened my eyes, as a new writer, to what a story could be. It has been a tremendous influence on the way I think about short stories. It's a formally innovative story that wouldn't work in any other way; each unit of the narrative builds to create an emotional impact that comes from a collage of setting and character details.

q: What do web-based art forms afford a writer that traditional print can't?

a: I'm interested in pushing myself in new directions. I like to try things and see what happens. I've always been interested in computers (I was a web developer before returning to grad school), so for me, new-media writing and audio are ways in which to experiment with form that don't necessarily translate or aren't possible on the printed page. I think new-media narrative is, in many ways, still very young, so using these technologies is exciting because they're quickly and constantly evolving.

Matthew Kirkpatrick is the author of Light Without Heat.

curtis white

q: A good amount of your work—especially books like *The Middle Mind* and *The Spirit of Disobedience*—is dedicated to exploring the philosophical and political landscape artists have to navigate in a culture that largely doesn't care about art. What do you think is the hardest thing about being a creative in this culture?

> **a:** The hardest thing is figuring out a way to thrive in the massive indifference, the massive self-satisfaction, the massive delusion of American culture. In the end what matters is whether or not the artist finds a way to freedom, to the kind of play that at the same time distances itself from culture and invents itself in some sort of "outside." Art has been utterly de-socialized, which means that it mostly doesn't exist any more. The "art" we're left with—Harry Potter, etc.—is just sedation for the slaves.

q: You recently retired from a distinguished university teaching career at Illinois State University. In your experience, what do you think the university setting affords creative writers that makes it worthwhile?

> **a:** Nothing, really. M.F.A.s lead to mostly mistaken assumptions about what makes art worthy. It's just another petty biz for the slaves: M.F.A., more fucking adjuncts. (I steal that from the poet Linda McCarriston.)

q: What's the best advice you might offer a beginning writer?

a: Nietzsche said the only heroes, the only fit warriors, were artists, and that artists ought to be Free Spirits. He meant something very subtle by that, so I won't be able to explain it here. So my best advice is to read Nietzsche until you understand him and go from there. Artists are Romantics, if you know what that term really means, and Nietzsche was the triumph of Romanticism. Artists will always live under his massive shadow, until there are no artists. We're getting close. I just hope to live long enough to see the Romantic explode again as it did in the sixties. How beautiful that will be.

Curtis White is writing a novelish thing in Normal, Illinois.

five

the garbage disposal imagination

Why do you write? In a sense, there are probably as many answers as authors. Some do so to pick scabs, some to help heal wounds. Some to learn why and how other human beings feel and think the way they do, some to shake things up, some to dramatize an ideal, some the real, some to warn, some to entertain, some to discover where our hearts are, some to effect change, some to delight in technical constraints, some to educate, some to explore the boundaries of language, some simply to make what they consider beautiful, euphonious things.

Some write to begin to imagine the impossible, some to make money, some to make readers or fans, some to procure jobs, some to feel a little more like themselves, some to touch others, some to be touched, some to be remembered, some to forget who they are for just a little while, some to make sense of lived experience, some to enter an alternate state, some to taste what it feels like to be free a couple hours every day.

Some agree with Gertrude Stein: "In the midst of writing in the midst of writing there is merriment." And some with Walter Wellesley Smith: "There's nothing to writing. All you do is sit down at a typewriter and open a vein." Some with Gaston Bachelard: "Art is an increase of life, a sort of competition of surprises that stimulates our consciousness and keeps it from becoming somnolent." And some with Kathy Acker: "I write it to get it out of me. I don't write to remember it." Some with William Gass: "Getting even is one reason for writing." And some with Marcel Proust: "The real voyage of discovery consists not in seeking new landscapes but in having new eyes, in seeing the universe with the eyes of another, of hundreds of others, in seeing the hundreds of universes that each of them sees."

Annie Dillard: "Assume you write for an audience consisting solely of terminal patients. That is, after all, the case. What could you say to a dying person that would not enrage by its triviality?"

Most of us write for a crisscross of contradictory reasons, all at once, all the time. With such a multitude of motivations, how do you even begin to begin to start a piece? Perhaps the best advice is simply this: envision your imagination as a huge garbage disposal, and throw everything into it you can: weird utensils, odd facts and impressions, a phrase you overheard at the grocery store, the fragrance you smelled while strolling down the street yesterday, a gesture somebody made an hour ago in the park, snatches of interstellar void. At some mysterious instant, someone or something will flick the ON switch, and surprise will happen, and you will find yourself in the midst of a starting.

Incorporate travel (in all senses of the word) into your life both in order to experience new sensations and to re-view where you usually live with fresh eyes. Go places you've never been. Do things you've never done. Try cutting down a tree with a chainsaw. Visit an emergency room. Get in your car and start driving. Go to the nearest city, throw away all your maps, and lose yourself for a day.

If you live in an urban area, visit the smallest town you can find. If you live in a small town, go to the country. If you live in the woods, go to the desert. If you live in the desert, go to the mountains. Along the way, notice details. How are things different from what you're used to? Listen to how people speak. Look at how they dress, wear their hair, shave, shrug. How is the air texture unlike what you're used to breathing? How about the way the night comes on? What are the dominant colors in this new landscape?

Writing comes down to learning a little each day how to sharpen determined noticing.

Listen, look, smell, taste, and touch with focus.

Enjoy inhabiting your body.

"Pay attention," Susan Sontag advised. "It's all about paying attention. Attention is vitality. It connects you with others. It makes you eager. Stay eager."

"For godsake, keep your eyes open," William Burroughs said. "Notice what's going on around you."

William Gass: "He knew why one normally didn't look. There were too many things to see. Every feature was a forest where you'd get lost in leaves, in their serrated edges, their dim red veins, to fall through the small holes eaten by insects."

Determined noticing applies not only to the text that is the world. It likewise applies to print and electronic ones. A writer is somebody who reads as if her or his life depended on it, which, in a very real sense, it does. Take in as many books as you can (see the list in the last chapter of this one for some ideas). Study the history of the "experimental," "avant-garde," "modern," "postmodern," "a-modern," "alternative," or whatever other troubled and troubling term we might choose to deploy and interrogate in this situation. Study books regarded as the opposite of those.

"Read, read, read," William Faulkner chanted. "Read everything—trash, classics, good and bad, and see how they do it. Just like a carpenter who works as an apprentice and studies the master."

Samuel R. Delany: "It is almost impossible to write a novel any better than the best novel you've read in the three-to-six months before you began your own. Thus, you must read excellent novels regularly."

Read close to home and far afield—in different genres and forms, different periods and cultures. Pick up *People* magazine. *Scientific American.* That strange monograph on Roswell conspiracy theories you saw in the bookstore yesterday. Notice billboards, status updates, shampoo bottle ingredients, what websites your friends are frequenting, recipes, biographies, government reports. Subjects and techniques are everywhere. They appear serendipitously. All you have to do is open yourself up to the world to stumble across them.

Despite what lots of textbooks about creative writing will tell you, don't write about what you know. Write about what you want to know. Write the piece you've always wanted to read but haven't been able to locate anywhere except in your own imagination.

Welcome research. Embrace the invitation to notice even more, and more acutely. A not atypical case: in preparation for my novel *Nietzsche's Kisses*, about the philosopher's last mad night on earth, I reread his complete oeuvre, steeped myself in biographies and critical studies about him, examined photographs of him and of those who played important roles in his life, and traveled extensively, making notes and videos I could later draw on along the way, through places he lived and visited in Germany, Switzerland, and Italy.

Always carry a pen and small notebook with you that you can tuck in your shirt pocket or backpack. An idea might be waiting for you at the end of the next block, in the middle of a movie or a dream, and you don't want to miss it. Don't attempt to convince yourself you'll remember it when you get home or wake up. You almost surely won't. Somehow that's how memory works.

Write down overheard lines at the local bar, in the aisles of Walmart, the art museum restroom. Write down descriptions of places, people, their accessories, nifty devices your friend mentioned in passing the day before yesterday that didn't seem important to you at the time but now do. Your dreams. Your best and worst memories. The fight you had with your partner last week in a way that puts yourself in his or her shoes. Sentences from novels or poems or plays you wish you'd written. A list of books you want to read. The sound your bicycle chain makes.

Ron Carlson keeps a bag filled with little scraps of paper by his computer. Each scrap has written on it some snippet he appropriated from a supermarket tabloid, a conversation he overheard, something strange he saw. When he can't think of anything to write, he reaches into that bag of tricks, pulls out one of those scraps, and begins riffing on it to see what will happen next.

To a person with a restless imagination, one who makes a practice out of staying awake, the world is the next writing project waiting to be told.

reading suggestions

Pick up an anthology of writing composed in genres with which you're not especially familiar and read it cover to cover. A few good places to start: a) *Extreme Fiction* (2003), edited by Robin Hemley and Michael Martone; b) *The Anchor Book of New American Short Stories* (2004), edited by Ben Marcus; c) *PP/FF* (2006), edited by Peter H. Connors; d) *Forms at War: FC2 1999-2009* (2009), edited by R. M. Berry; e) *30 Under 30: An Anthology of Innovative Fiction by Younger Writers* (2011), edited by Blake Butler and Lily Hoang.

exercises

1. A difficult one from Truman Capote. He advised (and he listened to his own advice) that to learn about the process of writing from the inside out you should take your favorite novel and type it word for word. A condensed version of the exercise will suffice: dig up your favorite flash fiction or poem and copy it, noting how the author introduces and composes character and/or voice, creates style, moves from scene to summary and back again, effects transitions, constructs dialogue, employs punctuation and white space to his or her advantage. While that might sound like a huge endeavor, it will take you a single afternoon and teach you more than most semester-long creative-writing courses.

2. Begin a journal or notebook and get into the habit of writing in it regularly. While there are no rules for keeping either, you may want to bear in mind that a journal or notebook isn't a diary. That is, it's not there to record what you did on a particular day. Rather, it exists as a catalyst for starting to think and feel about what you're thinking and feeling. It exists as a chronicle of your experience and the geography of your imagination, a space to discover your voice and writing rhythms, experiment, draft stories, contemplate books you're currently reading, jot down great quotes, compose letters you'll never send, record memories and expectations and snippets of overheard dialogue, probe sense impressions. To put it simply, it's a place to hone determined noticing. If you're having trouble getting started or keeping going, try one of these: a) record a dream you had last

night; b) write the letters of the alphabet down the left-hand margin of the page, then use each to create a poem or story in 25 words or fewer; c) in a short paragraph, answer the question: how does the weather taste today?; d) remember the best or worst moment from your childhood; e) pen a letter to an earlier version of yourself offering advice for the shellshock called the future.

interview

doug rice

q: In 1997, your novel *Blood of Mugwump* was part of a congressional brouhaha on obscenity involving your book, your publisher (FC2), and the National Endowment for the Arts. How has that experience impacted your subsequent writing?

> **a:** Not at all. I continue to simply write writing. I continue to tell stories about the people I care about even if the lifestyles of these people risk offending some. For me, the pleasure of writing is in the writing, the absolute joy of being in the present moment of writing the sentence. What happens afterward—senators bemoaning words they do not understand, critics praising work—has nothing to do with writing, so I ignore it.

q: Your writing walks a very interesting tightrope between the highly theoretical and the deeply personal, and is something you explore in your latest book, *Dream Memoirs of a Fabulist.* Where's the line between fiction and memory for you?

> **a:** That line is only a shadow cast by one (memory or fiction) over the other (fiction or memory). Once I place memory into language, memory becomes a rumor that makes room for uncertainty. Memory slips into fiction but then fiction becomes memory once again in an/other way. In the long journey of revising my writing, these fictional stories are then transformed into my memory. Photographs also help me to see into memory (especially photographs of dreams) in ways that language fails to see or sees in different ways. It is difficult to separate fiction from memory, which is different from separating truth from lying.

q: What's the most important thing a beginning writer needs to know?

a: He or she needs to cultivate solitude and sensuality for reflection. He or she needs to become curious about seeing by being patient and by learning to see into mysterious moments. Then he or she needs to contemplate these moments with playful language that experiments with what she or he thinks s/he already knows. And read. They need to read as slowly as possible, devoting time to seeing how writers write.

Doug Rice is the author of Between Appear and Disappear, Dream Memoirs of a Fabulist, *and three other works of memory-fiction. He teaches film theory and creative writing at Sacramento State University.*

six

beginnings

When an idea visits, let it haunt you as it wants to haunt you—while you're trying to sleep, shower, take notes in class, drive down to the corner store for a gallon of milk. Let yourself forget it for days at a time, because it won't really be forgotten at all, but working on your unconscious behind your back. Jot it down in your notebook, return to it regularly, sit at your processor and start playing with it to see what develops. Don't think too hard. Give your imagination permission to wander as it will around and through it. Type whatever comes to mind in whatever order and form it appears.

One of the wonderful things about word processors is they transform all composition into continuous process. You can rearrange, rewrite, tinker, copy, cut, paste, open separate files for separate chapters or story sections or poem fragments, a window for notes, another for your outline, and still another for your list of characters and their attributes, and have them all on your screen simultaneously so you can flip among them as necessary while your web browser provides you with a dictionary, a thesaurus, a Wikipedia page, a website to aid you checking this fact or that.

(The less than wonderful thing about word processors is they make every draft look like a final draft, sloppy writing look as polished as just-published. Careful about being duped by the sheen, and don't disregard the notion of trying to compose on a lined tablet unless you've already tried it and found it lacking; it is a method that both slows perception and increases conscientiousness.)

Some writers don't feel comfortable talking to others about their intentions until those intentions have been fully realized. That's completely understandable. It is possible, after all, to burn out an idea before it has left the confines of your head. But if you do feel comfortable doing so, sit down with a friend and/or fellow author and tell him or her about your plans. You might be surprised by how much can come from such an informal give-and-take session.

Sometimes such conversations can help you break through writer's block, as well—that feeling many authors succumb to at some point in their lives that they can no longer produce new work. Sometimes that impression can descend on you as a passing difficulty. Sometimes it can last for months on end, even years. Try to use those give-and-takes with friends to move your writing in a new direction, steer your way into creative light. But whatever you do, don't sweat it. Don't obsess about not producing. The more you do, the worse it will get.

Remember, too, that you're in good company. "Every writer I know has trouble writing," Joseph Heller said, and Joan Didion affirmed: "There is always a point in the writing of a piece when I sit in a room literally papered with false starts and cannot put one word after another and imagine that I have suffered a small stroke, leaving me apparently undamaged but actually aphasic."

Writer's block, in a phrase, is just part and parcel of the art form. If you hit a wall, give your imagination a rest. Distract it. Go for a walk. See a movie. Travel somewhere new. Maybe take your journal or notebook along and simply practice observing for a while. Busy yourself with your day job. Read a few pages from your favorite writer. Lie on the floor, put on some music, daydream. Chances are you just need to step away from your work for a couple hours or couple days. And when you return, you'll be ready to pick up where you left off.

Set aside what you were working on and go elsewhere creatively. If you can't get started on a new piece, visit the Surrealists. Their first manifesto, which appeared in France in 1924, advocated the expression of the imagination as realized in dreams and presented without conscious control. They have a lot of productive exercises for hotwiring inventiveness. Two of my favorites:

> **Leapfrog.** Assemble three or more players around a table. Give the first a sheet
> of paper. Tell her or him to write for a specified amount of time—one to three

minutes is usually enough. Stop him or her (in mid-sentence, if necessary) when time's up, and pass what he or she has done to the next player, who must take up where the first player left off. Repeat until a story-like-object is complete or an hour has transpired. Now (this is an addition to the original) use the results as a springboard into a new piece of your own writing.

Automatic Writing. Put on some music that fits your mood (the fewer lyrics, the better), or find a quiet corner in a café or park, and get out your journal or notebook. Before you dive in, read these lines from André Breton's 1934 manifesto, "What is Surrealism?": "Let your state of mind be as passive and receptive as possible. Forget your genius, talents, as well as the genius and talents of others. Repeat to yourself that literature is pretty well the sorriest road that leads to everywhere. Write quickly without any previously chosen subjects, quickly enough not to dwell on, and not to be tempted to read over, what you have written... Punctuation of course necessarily hinders the stream of absolute continuity which preoccupies us. But you should particularly distrust the prompting whisper. If through a fault ever so trifling there is a forewarning of silence to come...break off unhesitatingly the line that has become too lucid. After the word whose origin seems suspect you should place a letter, any letter, *l* for example, always the letter *l*, and restore the arbitrary flux by making that letter the initial of the word to come." Then see what happens. Is there something in the outcome—a few lines, a phrase, an image, a character revelation, a detail, a plot point, a voice—that can lead you into a new piece of writing?

Another productive group of writers to visit for a creative jumpstart are the Oulipoeans. *Oulipo* is short for *Ouvroir de littérature potentielle*, or "workshop of potential literature." Founded by Raymond Queneau and François Le Lionnais in France in 1960, Oulipo seeks to create work by exerting various technical constraints on one's writing in order to (paradoxically) open that writing up to unexpected possibilities. It may be thought of as a subset of Conceptual Writing— that mode in which the idea or concept is the most important aspect of the work, and therefore in which decisions concerning the work's framing mechanisms are made well in advance of the work's execution. Two of the best-known Oulipoean exercises:

> **Lipogram.** Compose a text that deliberately excludes one or more letters. Georges Perec, by way of illustration, wrote a 300-page novel called *A Void* (a pun on *avoid*) that sidestepped the use of the letter *e*. Such a move might strike one as gimmicky—until one realizes the novel is all about absences, about, ultimately, the loss of his father (*père*) on the battlefield in World War II and mother (*mère*) in a Nazi deathcamp.

> **N+7.** Choose a short text (your own or someone else's) and replace every noun in it with the noun seven entries after it in a dictionary. Results will vary depending upon the dictionary used. This technique can also be performed on other lexical classes, such as verbs.

Whatever you do, however, the takeaway message here is this: motivated or not, write regularly. As I mentioned earlier, writing every day is best, even if it is only for 45 minutes or an hour. Consistency is key. Gail Godwin once admitted she went into her writing studio and simply sat there each morning, whether she thought she had something to say or not. That way, she reasoned, she would always be home if the muse happened to drop by.

A writer isn't a person whose work sells, or is well known, or has published, or possesses a single reader besides him or herself.

A writer is a person who writes.

It's as straightforward as that. Write and you're a writer. Don't write and you're not.

"The way to write a book," Anne Enright reminds us, "is to actually *write* a book." And so establish that work schedule. Recall that most authors seldom write for more than three or four hours a day. Many—maybe most—do so in the morning, but, again, you'll soon discover what works best for you. Many prefer late nights. One side of dreamtime or the other seems most productive. Give yourself word counts. Deadlines. Don't answer your phone when you're in the thick of it. Don't check your email. Don't do your laundry or think about that appointment you have later in the day. Let your writing sphere exist as a special territory outside geography and the clock.

Sometimes you will commence with one idea in mind and before long realize your writing has taken you across the border into another country altogether. Go where your writing leads you. The act of composing is perpetual discovery. E. L. Doctorow explained he rarely knew what he believed until he had written about it. Dostoevsky would start authoring a given scene, assuming he understood precisely what he believed about the issue discussed in it, only to have one of his characters convince him otherwise. Frequently it is only through the actual act of creation that we locate what we really feel and think about a subject.

It isn't unusual to lack a clear idea of where your piece is going until you are already swimming deep inside it. What you have in the beginning is frequently little more than a vague sense of some character you want to probe, a voice you hear, a phrase that you can't get out of your head, an issue, a picture, the dimmest sketch of a scene, the mistiest outlines of a place, an action, a sound, a smell. Don't wait for more. That's plenty. Dive in. Keep your heart and mind open as you move forward.

In essence, all conventional narratives are about the frustration of desire. So ask yourself what your protagonist wants. Create a character who craves something more than anything else in the world—to be loved, to get away with murder, to remove that annoying sirloin gristle stuck between her or his front teeth (it doesn't matter how much or how little)—and refuse to let him or her have it. In that checked longing is the plot's birth. Now ask yourself why she or he wants it, who is blocking that want, how and why they are doing so, and you've already begun to understand your protagonist.

Speaking of plot, do you have a general sense of your story's arc—i.e., how its action will be shaped, where it is heading? It isn't necessarily a problem if you don't. Many authors barely know what's going on at the start of their narratives. Some possess only an unformed sense of what's going to happen in the middle. Others can scarcely make out the end but not how to get there. Half the pleasure in the process comes from the surprises you will encounter along the journey from alpha to omega. A scaffolding of outline (which you give yourself permission to veer from at any moment) may encourage you to imagine in advance, get you to think about what you want to accomplish and by what means. You may want to give one a try to see if such a thing suits you.

Do you have a sense of how (and here we begin to turn away from conventional narrativity) your approach to your subject matter will be unique—or at least unique to you? Early in the twentieth century, Ezra Pound advised Imagist poets to make it new. That's still an invigorating call to arms. Is it possible to tell your narrative from a point of view other than the one usually employed to tell it? To use an innovative structure or presentation to match your theme? Distort chronology in order to lend your narrative a new perspective? Recast your sentences' lengths or rhythms or complexities to suggest, say, your protagonist's worldview? Disturb narrative expectations by upsetting genre conventions? If you're playing with the murder mystery, perhaps the bad guy won't get caught after all, or the murderer is really the good guy, or maybe there hasn't really been a murder at all, or maybe it's impossible to tell. (Alain Robbe-Grillet's novella *Jealousy* is a rich model to consult in this context.)

More on those elements later. Before concluding this chapter, one last point about the notion of beginnings, and this has to do with the actual opening sentences of your piece. Always be aware: they do a *tremendous* amount of work. In fact, they do nothing less than build a world that has never existed before for your reader to inhabit. First there is white space. Then there is an undiscovered planet on the page.

Think about it. Those first few lines establish tone (comic, satiric, somber, wistful, etc.), voice (word choice, sentence length, diction level, rhythms), point of view (first, second, third), setting (where the story takes place), character (most narratives start with the protagonist's point of view, then within a few quick brushstrokes commence giving a sense of who she or he is), the socioeconomics of your universe (subtle clues indicate your protagonist's social rank, how he or she makes her or his living, etc.), conflict (that frustration of desire just mentioned), tense (present, past, even future), authorial distance (are we dealing with an unreliable first-person narrator, a god-like omniscient one, something in-between?), theme (what the piece is about in its largest terms), and genre (the contract established between author and reader raising expectations about what the latter can and can't anticipate in her or his reading experience).

Put that together with what labor you can do with your title, which should act as an arrow into your writing's concerns (recall, for instance, Pynchon's gorgeously named *Gravity's Rainbow*, a two-word poem that describes the arc of a V-2's trajectory, and hence the maximalist novel's guiding metaphor), and your reader comes to know volumes more than he or she probably thinks she or he does by the time he or she has moved a fourth of the way down the first page of what you've written.

This is why the first few lines are often the most difficult part of a piece to get right. Composing them is not unlike juggling 40 knives, some of which are on fire. No wonder authors work so long and hard on them, and no wonder few editors read beyond them in manuscripts that come across the transom. Usually what follows will simply confirm the impression established by them. Hence the importance of spending a lot of time and energy on them—if not initially, then surely during revision, when you have a better sense of the whole.

Look briefly at two examples of beginnings in fiction. What catches your eye? What would you like to steal from them? Why? What different sorts of work are they doing—or undoing? How do they go about their business of world-building?

1. Boys are playing basketball around a telephone pole with a backboard bolted to it. Legs, shouts. The scrape and snap of Keds on loose alley pebbles seems to catapult their voices high into the moist March air blue above the wires. Rabbit Angstrom, coming up the alley in a business suit, stops and watches, though he's twenty-six and six three. So tall, he seems an unlikely rabbit, but the breadth of white face, the pallor of his blue irises, and a nervous flutter under his brief nose as he stabs a cigarette into his mouth partially explain the nickname, which

was given to him when he too was a boy. He stands there thinking, the kids keep coming, they keep crowding you up.

2. Where now? Who now? When now? Unquestioning. I, say I. Unbelieving. Questions, hypotheses, call them that. Keep going, going on, call that on. Can it be that one day I simply stayed in, in where, instead of going out, in the old way, out to spend day and night as far away as possible, it wasn't far. Perhaps that is how it began. You think you are simply resting, the better to act when the time comes, or for no reason, and you soon find yourself powerless ever to do anything again. No matter how it happened. It, say it, not knowing what. Perhaps I simply assented at last to an old thing. But I did nothing. I seem to speak, it is not I, about me, it is not about me. These few general remarks to begin with. What am I to do, what shall I do, what should I do, in my situation, how to proceed? By aporia pure and simple? Or by affirmations and negations invalidated as uttered, or sooner or later? Generally speaking. There must be other shifts. Otherwise it would be quite hopeless. But it is quite hopeless. I should mention before going any further, any further on, that I say aporia without knowing what it means.

The first passage is the opening paragraph of John Updike's *Rabbit, Run*. Notice how Updike foregrounds vibrant, painterly language (his second love was in fact painting) to the point where it very nearly becomes a second protagonist. That is, language leaps to consciousness like those kids playing basketball in the two-word sensory-charged second sentence ("Legs, shouts."); in the repeated choice of active verbs (Rabbit doesn't "stick" a cigarette into his mouth; he "stabs" it in); in the alliterative use of significant detail ("the *m*oist *M*arch air *b*lue a*b*ove"), and in the striking metaphors ("he seems an unlikely rabbit, but the breadth of white face, the pallor of his blue [there's that color again] irises, and a nervous flutter under his brief nose…").

The distance between 26-year-old Rabbit Angstrom (his last name riddled with a rabbit's angst, and hence already beginning to make character resonate for the reader) and the young kids in

Keds (another flawless use of significant detail, along with that "scrape and snap" on the alley pebbles) playing basketball announces just how isolated Rabbit feels from his own past—the novel's central theme and conflict, the place he wants to get back to but cannot, the desire he cannot realize. Notice, as well, how Updike establishes setting, socioeconomic reality (that telephone pole with the backboard bolted to it, that alley, that business suit), tense (a glossy present), authorial distance and point of view (limited omniscient), and genre (psychological realism). That's extraordinary, extraordinary work for 123 words.

The second passage is the first half of the first paragraph of Samuel Beckett's *The Unnamable*. Notice how instead of establishing conventional setting and building traditional character, it immediately unsettles both: "Where now? Who now? When now?" That first trio of question marks broadcasts the thematics of the writing ("novel" may be too strong a word) that will follow: it is all about a voice (or, perhaps, voices), a consciousness (maybe, again, too strong a word), often genderless, removed from place and chronology and socioeconomic reality, hovering in a state of perpetual doubt. All it knows is what it doesn't know, and its not-knowing is blackly, sardonically comic. The Unnamable is the embodiment of an unreliable narrator—a subject position that can't trust itself, let alone be trusted by a reader. It contradicts, takes back, digresses, undoes what it just did, forgets, lies, hallucinates.

Notice as well that Beckett's use of language couldn't be more different from Updike's. Yet language is also foregrounded in the second passage to the point where it very nearly becomes a second protagonist, too—or, arguably, the primary one, the only one. Here though, it is abstract, disembodied, devoid of sensory data, grayish rather than painterly in texture. Without knowing this passage is from a novel, a reader might well conclude s/he were reading a patch of Cartesian philosophy. It might be helpful to conceive of what Beckett is doing as an example of post-genre writing, then, or perhaps what Raymond Federman referred to as critifiction—a mode that blurs conventional distinctions between theory and narrative.

It might be helpful, too, to conceive of *The Unnamable* as a Limit Text—a variety of writing disturbance that carries various elements of narrativity to their brink so the reader can never quite think of them in the same terms again. To the brink, and then (for most readers, at least) over. Karl Jaspers coined the word *Grenzsituationen* (border/limit situations) to describe existential moments accompanied by anxiety in which the human mind is forced to confront the restrictions of its existing forms—moments, in other words, that make us abandon, fleetingly, the securities of our limitedness and enter new realms of self-consciousness. Death, for example.

If we carry this notion of *Grenzsituationen* into the literary domain, we find ourselves thinking about the sorts of books that, once you've taken them down from the shelf, you'll never be able to put back up again. They won't leave you alone. They will continue to work on your imagination long after you've read them. Merely by being in the world, Limit Texts ask us to embrace possibility spaces, difficulty, freedom, radical skepticism. Which writings make up the category will, naturally, vary from reader to reader, depending on what that reader has already encountered by way of innovative projects, his or her background, assumptions, and so on, but it is likely *The Unnamable* will show up on most lists, along with, say, everything after chapter three in Joyce's *Ulysses*, William S. Burroughs' *Naked Lunch*, Young-Hae Chang's text films, Anne Carson's *Nox*, and Patrik Ourednik's *Europeana*. (N.B. See the last chapter in this book for a list of 101 of them.)

The more Limit Texts one reads, the less one tends to feel the impulse to return to more conventional narrativity.

reading suggestions

Kiteley, Brian. *The 3 A.M. Epiphany: Uncommon Writing Exercises that Transform Your Fiction* (2005). Exactly what it says.

Nelson, Victoria. *On Writer's Block* (1993). What it is and how to survive it.

Smith, Hazel. *The Writing Experiment: Strategies for Innovative Creative Writing* (2005). Offers an exploratory approach to creative writing, with exercises.

exercises

1. If you haven't already, take time to sit down and work out the most productive weekly writing schedule for yourself. What days? What time of day? How long? Remember: it usually takes about three weeks to change an old behavior or start a new one.

2. Visit a bar, a diner, a shopping mall, a park, and practice short, medium, and long descriptions. Describe one person you see in language that will single her/him out from all the others. Practice seeing, hearing, smelling, feeling. Try to capture setting, dialogue, everything.

3. Take a published flash fiction or poem by one of your favorite or least favorite authors and edit it to half its original length without losing its essential meaning. What did you cut, and why?

4. Write a three-page story or one-page poem about nothing.

5. Find a photograph or painting to which you're drawn. Write a monologue based on one of the characters in it that emphasizes the sense of place, the thereness of the scene, being present in all senses of the word, which makes place a central character.

6. Write a flash fiction or poem that tells the story of a scar on your body, or perhaps inside your or a character's body (exploring, perhaps, a disease, the personal history of an organ, etc.) Think, in other words, about how the world has written on and in us.

7. Another Surrealist exercise, this one called Tzara's Hat: Everyone in a group writes down a word (alternative: phrase, line) and puts it in a hat. Construct a narrative according to the order in which words (phrases, lines) are randomly pulled from the hat. (Solo: pick a series of words or lines from books, newspapers, magazines to put in the hat, etc.)

8. Misheard: Write a flash fiction or poem composed entirely of misheard song lyrics, overheard conversations, news headlines, menu items, etc.

9. If everything else fails, write a story or poem about somebody who can't write a story or poem.

interviews

lucy corin

q: Like many writers, you teach in a university. What about the university environment is most beneficial to creative writers?

a: Well, I can't honestly answer this question without mentioning the changes that are happening in our current university system. When I was making choices about how to make my way as a writer, I saw the university as the closest thing in our culture to a place free from market concerns, where artists and thinkers were valued for the way they contributed to the history of making and thinking, rather than their ability to feed a proven desire for some product (i.e., making things that we already know people want to consume/buy).

I was right in some ways and in some ways not. Personally I have benefited hugely from universities: I get money from them to live, I get artistic and intellectual friends, I get my mind challenged, and I get access to people with more power than I have who are apt to be interested in what I care about and do. I still don't know of another way to support myself that also allows time and mental space to write.

As research and education are privatized, this is less and less the case, and I think university jobs are increasingly filled by people who are supposed to draw attention/ funding to the institution because they are successful in the marketplace or re-enforce existing trends. Certainly a lot of good art happens in and because of university support and community, but a lot happens regardless of it, and despite it. More and more I find myself interested in what is possible outside of the university, and I think the next generation of interesting artists is going to have to create structures to support what it does, as existing structures become less and less relevant to what they're doing.

q: What's the one novel not nearly enough writers have read, and why should they read it?

> **a:** Too many people read Beckett as a playwright and they should look at him as a novelist—or better, as a *writer*. No one can show you the implications of uniting form and content like he does. It doesn't matter which book you read, which is most "successful"—the point is the completeness of his approach, the way of doing narrative, work by work, and within that, line by line and word by word, taking nothing for granted. For a fiction writer, that radical option for conceiving of the point of telling a story, even a long story, on the page, is crucial. It says that you can write a novel by taking a sensibility that is true to you—your mind, your experience—and following it through to a built (fictional, dramatized) space made of language, and that this is what creates meaning about the world.

Lucy Corin is the author of the novel Everyday Psychokillers:A History for Girls *and the short story collection* The Entire Predicament.

michael mejia

q: What do you most look forward to when beginning a new writing project?

> **a:** Journeying to and exploring a place I've never been before. By "place" I mean a conceptual creative space that's new to me both as a writer and as a reader. Its attributes may be articulated through specific details, sure—i.e., verbal representations of a work's world, such as it is—but also through uncommon logic, the rhythms and sounds of various languages, a peculiar manner of speech, a baroqueness or sparseness of style, the mixing of media, the incorporation of research, etc.: through the work's form, that is. This sense of experiencing something new is not so much about being

in, or coming into, tune with any particular zeitgeist, but rather is based in me: what is new to me now? What kind of novel experience am I looking for as a reader? What do I need as a writer/reader living in my particular place and time and how can I begin to produce that and with what materials? Of course, I feel really fortunate to connect with other readers after a work's published, but thinking about them too much at the outset might steer me away from risk, which I think is essential, and which is another way of naming what I look forward to.

q: What, if anything, do you dread?

a: Dread is an interesting word here. I associate it less with loathing or aversion, I suppose, than with a kind of productive fear. Do I dread a project's failure? Sure, who doesn't? Who wants to waste time on something that comes to nothing, or is un-readable? But then, what do these terms mean, and who or what defines a work as a "failure," as "waste," as "unreadable"? Should a work actually try to interrogate and exceed these conceptual limitations? My tendency is to write into dread in order to reveal to myself, as much as to any reader that may come after, the varied complacencies that make other, mostly more conventional writings, readable. It's at the frontier between readability (security) and unreadability (terror) that I want to live creatively. That frontier is dread, a dread with moral, ethical, political, social, cultural, psychological, historical, and aesthetic ramifications, any or all of which become visible in a dreadful work. As a writer/reader, not to mention as a human, I live best in dread. Now, if there's something I actually fear when starting a project, it's probably not being able to complete the work, but then there's something dreadfully interesting about fragments and incompleteness, too.

q: What advice might you give to someone suffering from writer's block?

a: Practical advice: Keep your eyes off the screen or page and keep your fingers typing or your pen or pencil moving. To me, "writer's block" means an excess of editorial pressure imposed pre-writing, pre-empting the creative process. The writer does not recognize him- or herself as a reader and is imagining a reader outside him- or herself who makes prescriptive and proscriptive demands based on what that imagined reader (i.e. culture) thinks he or she deserves or needs from writing. But the writer is a reader, too, and the writer/reader needs to retain, to actually forge, control over his or her process. What does the writer/reader need from writing? What is the writer/reader thinking about now? This is no time to adhere to any rules of genre, any theory, any grammar, or to know (i.e., to be fixed by) any history, literary, personal, or otherwise. Those things may acquire value as tools in the editing process, but this here is the time to write, and any seeming stumblings along the way should be viewed by the writer/reader not as faults, but as opportunities. Stay nimble, then, and fleetly pursue and blindly love right now your writing.

Michael Mejia is the author of Forgetfulness.

seven

narrativity

Samuel R. Delany once proposed science fiction is a tool to help us think. The same could be said for innovative narrativity. A tool, perhaps, to help us re-think, re-feel, re-perceive, as well.

All narrativity, innovative or not, is also about change, about creating in yourself and your readers the sense we have been somewhere, transitioned from one condition to another. In conventional narrative—whether story, film, video game, poem, or other mode—that may mean moving through a fast-paced plot toward a conclusion that neatly ties together loose ends. In innovative narrative, that may mean instead moving through a complex language display or investigation of structural opportunities. Through a problematics concerning the material nature of the page itself. The phenomenology of the reading experience. An exploration of what writing is, or what a transgressive politics or sexuality or spirituality might look like. Through a compelling consciousness (think again of Beckett's *The Unnamable*), an unimaginable world …or maybe something else altogether.

It is often useful when working on your own narrative to ask: How are its key components undergoing significant transformation? How, for example, is your protagonist growing, gaining control (or at least a comprehension) of her environment, losing his grip on reality, reaching her goal, losing his path, finding what she wants, doubting his universe in interesting ways, succeeding or failing? How will she or he in some way be different at the end of the action than at the beginning, and why? If you can answer those questions, you are probably operating within viable narrativity. If you can't, you need to ask yourself why not. It may be that you have some provocative and liberating reasons, or it may be that you need to reinvest yourself in the process.

The idea that change is an integral part of narrative structure tracks back at least to 1863 and the German playwright and novelist Gustav Freytag. He drew the now-famous (some would say infamous) diagram of the basic mechanics of a five-act tragedy in his book on the subject, *The Technique of Drama*. That diagram describes the movement of the conventional short story and novel, too. It has come to be known as Freytag's Pyramid, and is still valuable for providing a sense of how most narratives develop in five fairly distinct (though many times overlapping) stages.

First comes exposition, or the introduction to the protagonists, the conflict, the setting, and so forth. (Note how well that opening passage from Updike's *Rabbit, Run* quoted in the last chapter models Freytag's notion of exposition.) Second comes rising action, wherein the basic conflict is complicated by the insertion of related secondary conflicts, including various obstacles that frustrate the protagonist's desires. Those complications generate a sense of forward momentum that carries the narrative toward the climax, crisis, or turning point—that decisive action which marks a change in the protagonist's state of affairs.

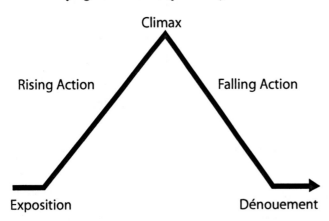

Traditionally, this is the big showdown: the shootout, the major argument and split, the maximum disorder in the narrative system. If the plot at hand is a comedy, things will begin to go well for the protagonist after that. If a tragedy, the opposite will be the case. Things will move from bad to worse. Fourth is falling action (also known as resolution or reversal), wherein the protagonist either wins or loses against the antagonist. Finally there is dénouement (literally "unknotting," also known as the catastrophe or resolution), wherein solutions, explanations, or other outcomes take place. In comedy, the protagonist is in a better place than at the narrative's outset. In tragedy, a poorer.

Even when applied to nineteenth-century drama, Freytag's Pyramid is of course an oversimplification. Think of Ibsen or Strindberg, whose play structures are nothing if not complex.

Yet Freytag's Pyramid remains a constructive way to discuss the architectonics of what many think of when they think of narrative.

Notice in passing how it follows that, in addition to change, conflict is always an essential feature of narrativity. Trouble is more engrossing than harmony to read about, Hell more intriguing than Heaven. In Milton's *Paradise Lost*, as William Blake and others have pointed out, Satan strikes most readers as the far more engaging character than, say, Christ or the good angels. Or as Nietzsche put it: "In heaven all the interesting people are missing." Place your protagonist in danger (thereby creating conflict), and everyone will want to know what happens next. That doesn't mean dynamite and car crashes in every paragraph. Subtle psychological conflict is usually much more tempting for readers—at least grownup ones—than the overt, hyperbolic, physical kind.

Story and *plot*, by the way, are two different concepts, although most of us use the terms interchangeably. In his groundbreaking book on fiction writing, *Aspects of the Novel*, E. M. Forster defines the former as "a narrative of events in their time-sequence" and the latter as "a narrative of events, the emphasis falling on causality." More plainly, story is a series of events in chronological order. Plot is a series of events deliberately arranged for maximum dramatic, thematic, and emotional intensity. Story, that is, is the stuff of the world. Plot is the stuff of fiction. Story is event. Plot is event shaped.

There are two ways to shape event in your writing process: outlining and improvisation. Both carry risks and benefits. You should experiment to see which feels like the best fit for you. Outlining works in different ways for different writers. Some keep only the most nebulous sense of their project's narrative arc in mind, while others sketch out in advance every scene with a few sentences on index cards or processors or paper. However one conceives of it, outlining gives you a leg up about what you want to accomplish before you find yourself adrift in the midst of the thing itself. What are your motives? What are your characters' motives? How will your plot move both in the direction you want? Outlining will get you to ponder such things before you commence typing, while also helping you separate major from minor plots, discover plot inconsistencies before you've enacted them, and keep you and your story well-paced and on track.

If you'd like to try an outline, first block out your narrative in a very general way—a single-paragraph synopsis is plenty. Next, break that paragraph up, making each sentence into its own scene or chapter (depending on whether you're writing a short story or novel), then tease each of those sentences out into its own single-paragraph mini-synopsis. Once you've actually begun writing, give yourself permission to veer from your outline at will. Revisit and re-orchestrate regularly.

The danger of outlining, obviously, is that it can make the writing process feel mechanical and rigid. That's where improvisation comes in. Improvising means following your own narrative rhythms and intuitions, seeing where the composition takes you, letting every sentence, every move of your characters, be a surprise. Many times the result is liberating, leading you into territories you couldn't have ended up in otherwise. Moreover, improvisation tends to allow you to produce more quickly, get more prose down, build up pages, move through your narrative relatively unhindered. Unfortunately, of course, it will also lead you down dead ends and unnecessary detours and into runnels of narrative adipose. That's okay…so long as you conceive of those diversions as part of your piece's evolution, and so long as you understand that when you're finished drafting you'll need to go back and shape.

In other words, you'll essentially need to outline either before or after the fact, and usually both. Outlining versus improvisation may at the end of the day come down to a question of emphasis. There always remains a trace of the former in the latter, a trace of the latter in the former.

How can you deploy either in the service of reimagining the aesthetic, political, and existential assumptions behind Freytag's Pyramid? The question leads us back to our earlier discussion of the Balzacian Mode, and to Fredric Jameson's proposition that our satisfaction with conventional plot's harmonies and completions is indicative of our satisfaction with society as well—our satisfaction with, that is, the dominant culture's narrativization of reality. Once again, then: meaning carries meaning, but structuration carries meaning, too. Deciding to put together a narrative one way rather than another *means.*

If that is the case, are there meanings—political, metaphysical, and otherwise—to be articulated on the far side of Freytag's vision? About a century before Freytag published his book, Laurence

Sterne published *Tristram Shandy*, a ribald anti-novel masquerading as an autobiography composed of digressions within digressions authored by a de-narrator who finds it impossible to tell a story in a straight line. It takes him until volume three, for instance, to reach his own birth—no small feat when narrating one's life. "I should beg Mr. Horace's pardon," Tristram comments about his undertaking at one point, "for in my writing what I have set about, I shall confine myself neither to his rules, nor to any man's rules that ever lived." Influenced by Locke's philosophy, which argues consciousness moves by association rather than along logic's line (thereby looking forward to Joyce's, Woolf's, and Faulkner's experiments with stream-of-consciousness), Sterne continually unsettles notions of the well-made plot and any sense of an orderly, easily interpretable reality behind it. In an attempt to schematize his narrative's progress, Tristram offers the reader the following diagram:

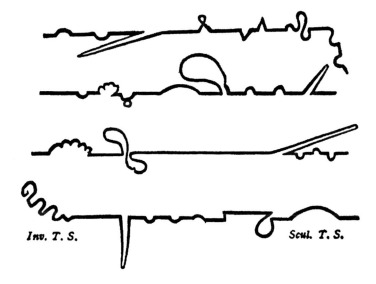

Behind that narratological blueprint resides the question: What structures capture your sense of lived experience? For Sterne, the answer isn't a neat pyramidal one. The answer is one that points to writing as thinking, and thinking as prolix meander.

There are a plethora of other options, some already discovered, and some waiting for you to discover them. Christopher Miller, for instance, constructs a novel as a string of CD liner notes in *Sudden Noises from Inanimate Objects*. In *The Last Novel*, David Markson constructs one as a collection of note cards (on which are written anecdotes about and quotes by authors, musicians, artists, and philosophers) arranged by an elderly writer. In *Dictionary of the Khazars*, Milorad Pavic constructs one as a lexicon. Robert Coover writes a short story called "Heart Suit" on a deck of real playing cards that you can shuffle. Carole Maso in *Ava* evinces "plot" as a series of disconnected thoughts and literary-theoretical quotations broken by white space by a woman on her deathbed. In *Changing*, Lily Hoang builds a book made up of 64 hexagrams based on *I-Ching*.

One could argue each represents a variation on the collage form. From the French word *coller* ("to glue"), collage originally referred to artwork made by appropriating and manipulating parts of other artworks. In compositions by Georges Braque, Hannah Höch, and Richard Hamilton, by way of example, you can make out newspaper clippings, ribbons, bits of colored paper, railway tickets, stamps, and photographs attached to canvas. While antecedents reach back at least to tenth-century Japan, where calligraphers glued bits of paper and fabric together to create backgrounds for the brushstrokes of their poetry, the method became a signature part of modern and postmodern art.

Robert Motherwell went so far as to advance "collage is the twentieth century's greatest innovation," and Donald Barthelme, who employed the technique in many of his short stories and his novel *Snow White*, contended "the principle of collage is the central principle of all art in the twentieth century." With social networking tools, music sampling, and similar hybrid forms of the appropriation and repurposing of small discrete units, Motherwell's and Barthelme's statements may seem even more true of the twenty-first.

In writing, collage can work at multiple strata, from phrase to sentence, voice, page design, overall structure of the text, even genre itself, while combining drawings, photographs, *trompe l'oeil* effects, found objects, you name it. In 1929 Max Ernst published his first series of collage novels. They took fragments from nineteenth-century wood engravings and forged surreal combinations out of them. He went on to define collage as "the noble conquest of the irrational, the coupling of two realities, irreconcilable in appearance, upon a plane which apparently does not suit them." Collage is the quintessential art of the non-sequitur. Shelley Jackson, an early practitioner of hypertext writing, itself an electronic form of collage, comments that "in collage, writing is stripped of the pretense of originality, and appears as a practice of mediation, of selection and contextualization, a practice, almost, of reading. In which one can be surprised by what one has to say, in the forced intercourse between texts or the recombinant potential in one text." She concludes: "We are all collage artists."

Jackson is echoing a notion of intertextuality articulated by such poststructuralists as Roland Barthes, who embraced the supposition that every text is "a multi-dimensional space in which a variety of writings, none of them original, blend and clash." Every act of writing, put plainly, is either a conscious or unconscious act of what Raymond Federman used to call pla(y)giarism and Kenneth Goldsmith calls uncreative writing, a method of self-conscious thieving and transcribing. Collage thus becomes a limit case of citation, quotation. Every sign, linguistic or non-linguistic, can be cited, put between quotation marks. In so doing, it breaks with every given context, engendering a network of new ones. Through its very process of cutting up and cutting off, collage opens up and out. By snatching and quoting out of context, collage releases new and often unexpected meanings, networks, recontextualizations that can surprise author and reader alike.

Collage thereby foregrounds continuous expeditions into what Mikhail Bakhtin championed as *heteroglossia*, or *multilanguedness*: a variety of social dialects, professional jargons, genres, languages of generations and age groups, cultural sign systems, and so forth, occurring within a single space. By its very nature, there is always an *aleatoric* or chance component to collage aesthetics, as well as an ongoing understanding of what Ronald Sukenick called the Mosaic Law—the question of "how to deal with parts in the absence of wholes."

Yet collage is only one structure among many for capturing what it feels like to be awake here, now. The next time you begin to write, ask yourself where else you might go to search for triggers that you can repurpose into rich, vibrant formal possibilities. Medical textbooks? Car manuals? Subtitles? Indexes? Footnotes? The look of the CNN screen on TV? The safety card in your airplane seatback? Menus? Comics? Tables of content? Appendixes? Your favorite or least favorite video games? And is the only sort of conflict that can appear in a text centered around characterization? What about style entering into conflict with style? Language with language itself? Material with theme?

If, as Louis Sullivan, proponent of the International Style in architecture, claimed, form follows function, then what form will best serve your writing's function? The more you keep tuned in to your environment, the more possibilities you will identify.

reading suggestions

Aristotle. *Poetics.* The Ur-Text on the question of narrativity in the Western tradition.

Bal, Mieke. *Narratology: Introduction to the Theory of Narrative.* A classic introduction to the major elements comprising a comprehensive theory of narrative texts.

Chatman, Seymour. *Narrative Structure in Fiction and Film.* Still one of the best overviews of narratology.

Genette, Gérard. *Discourse: An Essay in Method.* Another Ur-Text about how to analyze fiction (especially the novel) from a writer's point-of-view.

Prince, Gerald. *A Dictionary of Narratology.* History, literature, religion, myth, film, psychology, theory, and daily conversation all rely heavily on narrative. Cutting across many disciplines, narratology describes and analyzes the language of narrative with its regularly recurring patterns, deeply established conventions for transmission, and interpretive codes, whether in novels, cartoons, or case studies.

Richardson, Brian. *Unnatural Voices: Extreme Narration in Modern and Contemporary Fiction.* Offers a model of narrative voice that is both supple enough to attend to the dizzying variety of innovations in fiction and precise enough not to add to the confusion such works often produce.

Rimmon-Kenan, Shlomith. *Narrative Fiction: Contemporary Poetics.* Addresses key approaches to narrative fiction, from New Criticism to Phenomenology, but also offers views on and modifications to these theories.

exercises

1. The next time you sit down to write, try an outline if you've never done so before, or, if that's the way you normally work, try a round of improvisation. Don't be too fast to judge: give both some real time and effort to see which yields better results for you.

2. Use Freytag's Pyramid to compose a number of extremely short stories—each no more than a paragraph long, fewer than 100 words, the size that can fit on the back of a postcard—to familiarize yourself with the components that make up most fiction and to practice concision. Now make each narraticule part of a longer narrative mosaic, or actually write them on the back of postcards in a way that creates resonant tension between text and image.

3. Write a collage fiction or poem about a car crash using at least three different voices and points of view. What elements other than written text might you employ? Think about the very paper you're writing on as part of your narrative—engage, in other words, with the materiality of the page.

4. Appropriate words, phrases, and/or sentences from the first page of J. K. Rowling's *Harry Potter and the Prisoner of Azkaban* and collage them with those from "Différance," the famous essay by Jacques Derrida, and an excerpt from Kathy Acker's *Blood and Guts in High School* in order to create a new, surprising, and disruptive multilanguaged text that uses none of your own words and yet is completely yours. If those "primary" texts don't suit you, find three other ones (each radically different from the rest) you would prefer and work with those. Perhaps use images from a medical textbook, comic, or newspaper as one of your choices.

5. Identify a model for formal possibility that you haven't employed before. Car manuals, film subtitles, indexes, footnotes, the look of the CNN screen on TV, the safety card in your airplane seatback, menus, tables of content, appendixes, and video games were mentioned above. Use one of those, or come up with your own. Repurpose them into a flash fiction or poem.

interviews

kathy acker

q: Would you talk a little bit about your writing process? My sense from reading your work is that it grows organically...as Robert Coover once said of Donald Barthelme's, like barnacles on a hull. Is that right?

> **a:** That's right. It grows organically. That is, I have to listen to it in the same way that I have to listen to whatever I'm reading. And seeing, experiencing, the whole bit. My sense is that I write by listening, by reading, etc. Which is to say—with a leap—that I write by being written.

q: Have you ever tried outlining? Would you ever recommend it to others?

> **a:** I only outline writing that's done for money. (I used to say: writing that's not much fun.) Only when the article is too complicated to write directly. When I have outlined, I have always, in subsequent drafts, neglected the outline. So the outline is just a device to get from point a to point b (in forgetting point a). I'm more interested in the forgotten than in facts.

q: What sort of advice would you give a young writer about the actual writing process?

> **a:** Well, when I taught, I tried to listen to each student. Where he or she was at. Tried to say: you have to listen to yourself. Not to that screaming ego self, but all the rest. If it's human, it's not formulaic. And then there's (the problem of) writing in the world. Money, publishing, etc. I've never been great about those babies, but it still seems to me that patience or endurance and some extremely thick duck feathers are necessities.

Before her death in 1997, Kathy Acker stood at the forefront of literary inventiveness in the U.S. with works like Blood & Guts in High School *and* Pussy, King of the Pirates. *This interview was conducted in 1996.*

deb olin unferth

q: What's the one novel for you that best exemplifies what a novel *could* be instead of what it *should* be?

> **a:** *The End of the Story* by Lydia Davis. That book showed me that a novel can daringly disregard expectations about story structure and still feel full of passion and urgency. And a novel can talk about itself and not feel cute. And a novel can be about only one thing, one thought. It doesn't have to show the universe. One thought is a world.

q: Can you talk a little bit about how you selected the stories that became your collection *Minor Robberies*? What do you think is the most important thing in preparing a short story collection for publication?

> **a:** It's most important that there is a conversation going on between the stories. Listen to your inner voice about which stories are part of that conversation and which aren't. My original title for *Minor Robberies* was *A Serious Explanation*, and I chose stories that I felt explained, seriously.

q: What one piece of advice would you give to a beginning writer about "becoming" a writer?

> **a:** Don't be afraid to repeat yourself. Think of visual artists, the way they draw the same piece of fruit over and over for years. They're trying to figure something out. If you find yourself returning to the same sounds, structures, subjects, objects, follow that. It's likely leading you somewhere.

Deb Olin Unferth is the author of the novel Vacation, *the memoir* Revolution, *and the story collection* Minor Robberies.

eight

settings

Setting provides the sense of place in narrative, the environment through which characters travel, against which they struggle, the time of the action, the physical details of their world, the atmosphere of their story.

Sometimes settings are simple, sometimes even sketchy. Think of those found in fairy tales and the Bible. Sometimes they are elaborate, especially when in the service of creating the illusion of realism, a fully imagined universe in which shared knowledge is recognizable. Look at this passage from Don DeLillo's *Falling Man* and notice how setting is quickly actualized and how it functions:

> He was walking north through rubble and mud and there were people running past holding towels to their faces or jackets over their heads. They had handkerchiefs pressed to their mouths. They had shoes in their hands, a woman with a shoe in each hand, running past him. They ran and fell, some of them, confused and ungainly, with debris coming down around them, and there were people taking shelter under cars.
>
> The roar was still in the air, the buckling rumble of the fall. This was the world now. Smoke and ash came rolling down streets and turning corners, busting around corners, seismic tides of smoke, with office paper flashing past, standard sheets with cutting edge, skimming, whipping past, otherworldly things in the morning pall.

Look at how much data these 126 words supply about where and when and how we are. Some information is given directly. Some of it is implied. Although never spelled out, for instance, it doesn't take long for the reader to realize the scene takes place during the minutes immediately following the collapse of the Twin Towers after the 9/11 attacks in lower Manhattan. In order to assemble environment, DeLillo appeals to several senses at once—sight, surely, but also sound (e.g., "the roar was still in the air, the buckling rumble of the fall") and smell, taste, and touch (suggested by the ubiquitous ash, the people pressing handkerchiefs over their mouths, holding towels to their faces, those "seismic tides of smoke").

Another way of saying this: DeLillo privileges specific, definite, concrete details over vague abstract ones. Each detail answers the question: How is this space and time different from every other? Janet Burroway recalls that in *The Art of Fiction* John Gardner "speaks of details as 'proofs,' rather like those in a geometric theorem or a statistical argument." Carefully chosen sensory details are the essence of world-building in normative narrative.

Interestingly, though, DeLillo withholds a key one here—the protagonist's name. By doing so, he emphasizes the facelessness of all the victims before us, how the shock here is general, not specific to an individual. If we translate the scene into filmic terms, we see DeLillo providing us with an establishing pan in which the protagonist is merely one of many in a mass of confusion and wreckage. Knowing when to withhold a detail, then, is as significant as knowing when to employ it.

The smoky, panicky, claustrophobic atmosphere charged with a sense of disorientation is underscored by several of the sentences' wrenched, disjointed rhythms and repetitions and syntax: "They had shoes in their hands, a woman with a shoe in each hand, running past him. They ran and fell, some of them, confused and ungainly, with debris coming down around them, and there were people taking shelter under cars." Such stumbling lines do something else as well. They tell us not only about the world the protagonist is navigating, but also about the protagonist's perception of that world. While the narration never moves inside him, it is always as if he were telling it, and the telling is fraught with a numbness, an inability to integrate this tear in reality's fabric with the protagonist's own existence—an inability that will dog him through the rest of DeLillo's novel.

While many readers think of setting as relatively expendable background noise in narrative, then, the opposite is the case. As author, you need to know your setting inside and out—or, as we shall see in a moment, know and be able to explain to yourself why it isn't important to you and your narrative. Do your research to get those specific bits of data right. Take notes. Close your eyes and imagine every item in a scene before you begin composing it. What does the world you're constructing smell like? Taste like? Look like? Feel like? Sound like? The world in conventional narrativity is a fully embodied one—so much so that it is a good idea to consider setting as one of central characters in it.

"The question," Thoreau wrote in his 1851 journal, "is not what you look at, but what you see." A productive exercise to run daily: walk through a room in the apartment or house where you live, or drop into your favorite café, or visit a park, or sit in the back of your creative writing workshop, and look around, take in, record without taking notes, shut your eyes and let the sounds and scents and textures sink in, then go back to your writing space and try to recall all the specific, definite, concrete details you can in a list.

What makes the place you just visited only itself, and other?

Because it is virtually impossible (not to mention tedious and unrevealing) to catalogue *every* detail of the world your character inhabits, you should ask yourself which are the most significant ones to understanding him or her. DeLillo doesn't slow down to cite the make of the cars under which the people in his scene are taking shelter or the brand of shoes the woman is carrying. He doesn't mention the weather conditions that day because his readers already know them. He doesn't take time to describe the buildings on the street down which his protagonist is moving, or what color hair he possesses, or whether he is black or white, Asian or Swedish.

You should always be able to answer more questions about your characters' environment than you share with your readers. Always know what season it is, what the temperature is, what time of day it is, what the precise slant of the light is, the feel of the air, the geography, the architecture, the socio-economics, and so on. But only mention those that help us quickly situate your readers and fathom the characters.

The important questions that have been silenced in our discussion of setting so far are these: Is setting invariably, fundamentally necessary to all narrative? Are there ways to reconceptualize setting that can point to other ways narrativity may exist in our world? What happens when we try to do without it? Redefine what setting is and how it works? Once again we are back to Beckett's Limit Text, *The Unnamable*, which deliberately withholds and/or unsettles information about time and space. In a sense, the only "setting" in that text is what goes on between the narrator's ears. The reader exists in a gray Cartesian field sans body.

In some of his short stories, to cite another example, Donald Barthelme, whose fiction owes a great deal to Beckett, does away with setting by composing completely in the form of disembodied, unsituated dialogue that now and then indicates a when and where, but more often than not doesn't. When asked why he made such a move, Barthelme answered: "The opportunities are those of poetry without the stern responsibilities....The sentence rhythms are rather starkly exposed, have to be weirdly musical or you send the reader off to Slumberland posthaste....I'm talking about a pointillist technique, where what you get is not adjacent dots of yellow and blue, which optically merge to give you green, but merged meanings, whether from words placed side by side in a seemingly arbitrary way or phrases similarly arrayed, bushels of them."

Shelley Jackson explores the opposite impulse in her early hypertext, *My Body.* The opening screen takes the form of a sketch of a naked female torso accompanied by the sound of breathing. As the reader scrolls over the image of a shoulder, an eye, a breast, she or he is linked to a narraticule associated with that body part. It is as though the only setting here is the flesh itself, which when touched opens into memory and imagination. Yet Jackson complicates the equation by setting those stories in the non-space of the Web, making her narrative one of embodiment composed in a digitized mode that refuses any sort of embodiment.

In addition to imagining mind and body as ways of challenging conventional notions of setting, it is possible, as writers as different as Jorge Luis Borges and Ben Marcus do, to imagine impossible environments. In Borges' "The Library of Babel," a postmodern parable about the inability to attain knowledge, the narrator describes an endless library composed of an infinite number of hexagonal galleries (a sort of beehive library also known as "The Universe") that houses all possible books—those that have been written as well as all those that will be written (including ones that group meaningless sequences of letters compiled into random arrangements with no purpose). To make matters more difficult still, the light in the library is insufficient to read by.

Ben Marcus' *The Age of Wire and String* is made up of a series of "explanations" and "definitions" concerning a world that can only exist in abstruse, short-circuiting language games. The definition for "Age of Wire and String, The," for instance, reads: "Period in which English science devised abstract parlance system based on the flutter pattern of string and wire structures placed over the mouth during speech. Patriarchal systems and figures, including Michael Marcuses, were also constructed in this period—they are the only fathers to outlast their era." The kind of sense a reader can make of this is the kind (as Barthelme said about his dialogue stories) one can make of poetry. In Marcus' definition, we discover an extended metaphor about the nature of logical, phallogocentric systems of representation and control, but nowhere anything remotely resembling traditional setting.

Beckett's, Barthelme's, Jackson's, Borges' and Marcus' innovative approaches to re-envisioning the idea of setting obviously aren't by any means the only ones. They are simply offered here as challenges to you to contemplate both why conventional notions of setting obtain in the first place and to ask how and why one might profitably move through or around them into new ways of knowing and apprehending.

exercises

1. Your protagonist is an alien who has just landed on earth. He/she/it enters a setting we earthlings feel wholly at home in—a Walmart, for example, or a Pizza Hut, or the student union—but for him/her/it it spells nothing but nightmare. Why? Write a flash fiction or poem to find out.

2. Write a flash fiction or poem made up of (à la Donald Barthelme) dialogue sans setting, or dialogue that naturally and subtly suggests setting while focusing on something else. For inspiration, take a look at Barthelme's narrative "Margins."

3. Think of a character you would like to write about or perhaps are already in the process of writing about. Now compose a narrative about him/her that is a list (and only a list) of items in that character's special room (bedroom, attic, bathroom, etc.); allow the list to reveal who that person is.

4. Is it possible to write a sudden fiction or poem in which setting is exclusively important, and where character doesn't exist? Or where setting is radically redefined, maybe always in transition, or something other than we as readers might anticipate? Take a look at Borges' "The Library of Babel" or Ben Marcus' *The Age of Wire and String* and think in terms of impossible settings.

5. Write a flash fiction or poem in which the only setting is (à la Beckett) the mind creating it. There is no "out there," only "in here."

6. Write a flash fiction or poem in which the only setting is (à la Jackson) the body. Perhaps you want to focus on a particular body part (eyes, fingers, arm hair) or organ (liver, pancreas, lungs). Perhaps you want to explore the body from the point of view of a disease taking it over. Perhaps you want to create a narrator who can't think beyond his or her own flesh and blood.

interviews

laird hunt

q: Your novel *Ray of the Star* uses a lush, European setting in inventive and striking ways. At what point do you decide on a setting for a narrative you are writing, and how important is this particular element to your composing process?

> **a:** Setting has been there from the start in all of my books whether it has been Paris, lower Manhattan, Barcelona, rural Indiana, or a barren stage set. If I don't know where my characters are standing, sitting or lying, I don't know what they are doing or saying. There is no why in my books without the where. Setting saturates it all.

q: What's the best executed setting you've seen in another novel?

> **a:** Georges Perec's *Life: A User's Manual* (trans. David Bellos). Perec's great novel imagines an apartment building that has had its front façade taken off so that the rooms and corridors and staircases (there are 100 individual areas) are exposed. Chapter by chapter, using a method borrowed from the game of chess, he leaps around the building—never once returning to somewhere he has been before—describing the various species of the spaces encountered. The result is highly active (setting is where action takes place) and highly static (setting is also where nothing takes place), and it is always interesting.

q: What should a beginning writer try to keep in mind about setting?

> **a:** Fictional worlds are built out of words. Words take time to unveil their meanings. So do worlds. Don't rush.

Laird Hunt's novels include The Impossibly, Indiana, *and* The Exquisite.

michael martone

q: A good amount of so-called "experimental" fiction attempts to downplay the truth of place, oftentimes in deference to a larger philosophical or theoretical truth. Your writing has always struck me as finding a wonderful balance between the two when it comes to using setting in smart and resonant ways. Can you talk a little bit about the importance of setting that you see within your own work?

a: In the nineteenth century, "regionalism," "local color" was the thing. It continues through the modernists—Joyce's Dublin, say, Lewis' Main Street—even as place as a subject was being erased by those writers and the great abstract placelessness of a writer like Stein. The interesting drama for me is the one between locality and mobility, and for two centuries mobility has been winning. Rebecca Solnit's great book *River of Shadows* speaks of the industrialized amplification of the human body as the annihilation of space and time. So what is an author supposed to do when setting is rapidly steam-rolled and abstracted? In what way can "place" be made interesting again, a postmodern regionalism? I am not a narrative writer. I don't tell stories. Instead, I think, in this vacuum of real "places," the fictions I like to create are constructed as environments themselves. Installations of words that simulate place. A map more real than the thing it represents, as Borges suggests. Is setting an important part of my work? For me, it is the work, the whole work. I have little interest in characters doing something that a reader observes. I am much more interested in creating a space in which the reader is immersed and then interacts. So I am very interested in places out there such as Hannibal, Missouri, and Dublin, Ireland, that have become "real" through fiction, fabrication. People actually travel to Hannibal to see Tom Sawyer paint a fence. Place culturally has been obliterated long ago. It is maintained through fiction. Thousands of people travel from all over to run with the bulls, an effect of a fiction. The story in the Hemingway text is long forgotten, the place, the setting survives, expands.

q: Your book *Michael Martone*: what is it, exactly? And where do you distinguish within it what's real and what's fiction?

a: Well, the book of the collected contributor's notes is like an afterthought. The real project survives within the 30 some magazines in which the notes first appeared. Part of the fun was negotiating with the editors to have the pieces placed in the contributors' notes section even though I had nothing else in the front of the magazine. I think of that—that scattered, disparate publication—as the book. The collection into a book book is a kind of afterthought. The notes, I think, are better when framed differently and separately.

As for distinguishing between what is real and what is fiction—think of physics. The book ends with a piece where life is compared to the tracings on cloud chamber windows. The scientists, great fiction writers by the way, are asking us now to believe in many dimensions, many parallel realities. In the subatomic world we know things exist by their not existing. Anti-matter, dark matter. These notes play out those strings. A fact, you know, is a thing done. Once it is finished it has no existence. A fiction, on the other hand, is a thing made. Once made it is real; it has an existence. These words, "true" or not, are made; they have existence; they are real. The fact of my typing them, once I am finished typing, is over, gone, insubstantial. All that is left is the residual debris of the typing. And all the residue of all the facts ever can be faked, manipulated, deformed, repeated, recreated, fabricated further. All fictions in that sense.

q: What advice would you give a beginning writer about the importance of place in their stories?

a: I don't know if I would give that advice. I know I am supposed to be in the advice business as a teacher of beginning writers, but I find most of the advice I give is to simply write. Much of the teaching of writing comes out of the "how to" tradition with manuals and guides and models. Writers teaching in universities get lulled into the institution's essence—that is the desire to curate, to norm, and create hierarchies of all sorts. As a teacher of creative writing, I try to resist the institutional bias about institutionalizing bias. The place of Place in any given writer's story is up to the writer. As with my own stories, I like to think that in the classroom I create interesting and complex environments of possibilities. It is up to the student to actually employ or disregard or expand on any and all the different techniques and props and styles and genres he or she finds there. I think of my role as someone who facilitates, a medium, in which to grow. I am not an expert but a medium. I like that. My students' stories are their stories, and I shy away from advising them on manners and matters that they know far better than I ever will.

Michael Martone's newest book is Four for a Quarter.

nine

characters: flat & round

In *Aspects of the Novel*, E. M. Forster distinguishes between two kinds of character, flat and round. Flat ones function as background in a narrative. They exist to help out the round ones. If your protagonist needs to get from Long Beach to West Hollywood to have dinner with the woman with whom she is falling in love, and she takes a taxi, a flat character will most likely be the driver. Flat characters don't change, won't surprise you, are constructed around a single idea or quality…the sponge-nosed street person in the water-logged refrigerator box on the corner between Avenues C and D in Manhattan the protagonist passes while taking a call from his doctor, who breaks the news to him he has pancreatic cancer.

If flat characters lack depth, round characters are bursting with it. They are your leads, the ones on which to keep your narrative camera trained. They're sufficiently complex to change over time, rich with conflicting emotions. Their actions can ambush the reader without losing credibility. They intrigue us, shock us, bore holes in our hearts. Think of Hamlet in Shakespeare's play, Raskolnikov in Fyodor Dostoevsky's *Crime and Punishment*, Humbert Humbert in Vladimir Nabokov's *Lolita*, the narrators in T. S. Eliot's poetry.

To flesh out a flat character into a round one, give him or her a past, at least one strength, and at least one weakness. The sponge-nosed street person in the water-logged refrigerator box begins to resonate when we discover his name is Byron Penumbra, and he used to be a successful stockbroker on Wall Street…until, that is, three weeks ago, when he got sick of his nice pat suburban life and decided simply to step out of it, which he did one night without warning or fanfare, right through the front door and down the green-lawned avenue in northern Jersey, sprinklers ticking, rat dogs yapping, leaving behind his pudgy real-estate-agent wife, Joan, who has been attending church with more regularity than makes Byron strictly comfortable recently, and their two Republican teenagers, June and Jedd. Byron has never felt more liberated and shameful than at this very minute.

What makes a round character interesting? Surely that sense of complex motives and conflicting emotions. Surely her ability to change during the course of the narrative—to grow, wither, learn, forget, escape, fall, go insane, attain a brief epiphany (the term James Joyce employed to refer to that sudden manifestation of meaning that scuds into some characters at climactic moments in life), and, in the final analysis, startle us in ways that never veer from who we feel she is and can be. A rule in conventional narrative: no psychological change, no plot.

As already mentioned, character becomes interesting at the distance she or he exists from goodness. Nabokov's Humbert Humbert is a child molester and aesthete who almost never sees himself as anything but a sweet, gentle, cultivated, intelligent lover of nymphets, yet comes to despise himself, yet relishes his memories of Lolita as the one true love of his life, while being brilliantly funny, and a gorgeous stylist, and impressively educated, and a terrific gamester, and ready to provide an excuse for his actions in the wink of an eye, profoundly in lust, a murderer who didn't believe the murder he committed was so terribly bad after all, not really, not at all.

Nor does a character need to be honest with him or herself—or with the reader—to be engaging. In fact, dishonesty is where things start heating up and turning fun. Recall Humbert Humbert once more, as well as some of the most compelling paper people in literature: Twain's Huck Finn, Faulkner's Benjy, Salinger's Holden Caulfield. They are all unreliable narrators— narrators, that is, who err in their understanding of themselves and/or their worlds, and who sometimes attempt to mislead the reader. They may simply be innocent (Holden) or mentally challenged (Benjy), or they may be purposefully devious (Huck and Humbert). In order to develop them, authors rely on the use of verbal irony (the distance between what a character says and what he/she means) and dramatic irony (the distance between what a character knows and the author/reader does).

Repetition for emphasis: characters must want something they can't have. Pair frustrated desire with making your protagonist the central point-of-view in your narrative, and your reader will usually want to learn more. Normative characters must also be believable (consistent in her or his actions) and possess some sympathetic qualities with which the reader can identify (Humbert's intelligence, artistry, and pain; Raskolnikov's remorse; Hamlet's very human ongoing doubt). Steven Pinker once said "fiction is empathy technology." Reading and writing, that is to say, are usually acts of telepathy, the ultimate mode of virtual travel, journeys into the minds and feelings of creatures who are just like us, only more so. That's one of the reasons writing exists in the first place.

To feel fully rounded, a character must be an individual rather than a stereotype, more than a mere oversimplification of an idea or undercooked trait or two, more than the dumb blond, the absent-minded professor, the red-neck trailer trash. The same question applied to setting, then, should be applied to character: What makes him or her only him or herself, and no one else?

A good place to start individuating character is by gifting him or her with several defining physical characteristics—a unique speech pattern, a trademark gesture, a particularly revealing cut of hair or turn of lip or hunch of shoulder. Close your eyes and picture him or her. What events from his past help account for who he is? What are her key memories? These will allow you to witness how his awareness processes the universe, put us inside her psyche. Humbert returns over and over to his beatific relationship with another nymphet, Anabel Lee, when he was an adolescent, arguing (quite likely fallaciously) that that relationship informs all the others he has with young girls.

Now imagine your protagonist experiencing various facets of life. How would he or she react to each? Imagine him moving through what comprises a normal day for him. What would it look like? How and when and why does she wake up, go to sleep? Each time you confront him with new stimuli, force him to interact with them, you're going to discover a different part of his character. Imagine character as prism. Try to explore all the ways s/he refracts existence's light.

Just like you should know more about setting than you make plain in your narrative, so you should know more about your character than you openly share with your reader. You want him or her to sense more than the text says. A few constructive questions to ask yourself: How old is my character, how tall, how much does he weigh, what does she wear when dressing up, dressing down? Where was he born? Raised? Who are her parents and what do they do? What was his childhood like? What events define it? Does she have siblings? If so, what are their names and what are they like and how does he get along with them? Is she sociable or reclusive, optimistic or pessimistic, trusting or skeptical, serious or fun-loving, organized or disorganized? What is his favorite and least favorite food, book, film, album, website, color, animal, holiday, possession, hobby? Name three of her interests, three of her fears. How would those differ from what he would post on Facebook? What makes him happy, angry, sad, frustrated, nervous, embarrassed? What are her best qualities? His worst? What sort of education does she have? Where has he traveled? Where does she want to travel? What does he do for a living and how does he feel about that? What would she rather be doing? What are his goals in life? Does she have pets? What is his best friend's name and where did they meet and what is he or she like?

In *Writing Fiction*, Janet Burroway outlines two methods for presenting character: indirect and direct. Indirect presentation means the author does all the telling. He or she intrudes into the narrative at hand to give us the character's history, motives, and beliefs in abstract summary: "No one who had ever seen Catherine Morland in her infancy would have supposed her to be born to be a heroine," Jane Austen begins *Northanger Abbey*. "Her situation in life, the character of her father and mother, her own person and disposition, were all equally against her. Her father was a clergyman…and a very respectable man.…Her mother was a woman of plain sense, with a good temper, and, what is more remarkable, with a good constitution."

Indirect presentation relies on telling, on summary, rather than on showing. It also relies on a godlike omniscient perspective. These days it tends to sound faintly faded and dated. From the early twentieth century forward, first film and then television heavily influenced our perceptions of what narration ought to look like, feel like, read like. Showing and scene building—direct methods of presentation—have become more and more the privileged vehicles for relaying information.

There are four major modes of direct presentation: appearance, speech, action, thought. Conventional narrative is a continuous mixing and matching of these. A few words about each:

Appearance. Another way of phrasing this: exterior presentation. What does your character look like, dress like? How does she or he carry him or herself? Aim for those details that create a singular personality—that worried vein squiggling like a blue worm across the librarian's left temple; that blurred purple-green tattoo of the naked girl on the lawyer's inner right forearm that he keeps hidden under his suit. We live in a highly visual culture. People love to see and are usually quite adept at semiotics. So appearance can and should convey lots of news: socio-economic status, degree of emphasis your character puts on tidiness and cleanliness, whether she reads or works at a computer a lot (does she wear glasses?), how fashion-conscious she is, her age, race, gender, et cetera. Too, consider what aspects of another person's appearance your character dwells on—namely, what does he notice when initially meeting someone, where do her eyes first fall?

Speech. A character's appearance can be in harmony or in conflict with her or his speech. Does your character lisp, stutter, use pet words, employ malapropisms, speak in incomplete sentences, possess an accent? Does she dress down but talk up? What sort of diction does he manifest? What sort of grasp on metaphor does he have? Does she speak in self-absorbed monologues, balanced sentences, shy single words? What's his syntax like—clear as an unmuddied stream or cat's-cradled with convolution? Does she respond to questions asked or mishear incoming data and respond to the questions she wished she were being asked? Does he say what he means? Or is what she says always at odds with what she is thinking?

Action. A third direct exterior mode of presentation. How does your character move when she enters a crowded room? Is that different from how he moves down a busy street? An empty street? In front of her mother or lover? What gestures define who he is? Does she scratch at her wattles, tug at his earlobe, surreptitiously pinch at the right knee of her torn prewashed jeans when talking with her teacher, his boss, her buddy, his older sister?

Thought & Feeling. Thought, like feeling, is an interior mode of experience, and no art form does interior better than writing. Film is concerned with surfaces, from which the viewer must infer internal states. Writing is capable of creating those states for thousands of pages on end, teasing out nuances, exploring the formation, shape, and progression of thoughts and emotions. Narrative can turn the world inside out, allowing the reader to perceive external reality solely through the interior perambulations of a consciousness in process. Written narrative can and does often transform photograph into x-ray. And so: does your character think a lot, or prefer feats to philosophizing? If she does live an examined life, then what sorts of things does she contemplate, and what do his cognitive movements look like? Does she obsess on minutiae, the sign of the slightly unhinged mind, or over and over again relive a crucial event from childhood that helped make him who he is today? Does she think logically or associatively? Is he the kind of extrovert who is forever talking, or the kind of introvert who is forever paralyzed by self-conscious reflection, or something in between, or something else altogether?

Many authors base characters on people they know. Such an autobiographical approach to writing can be profitable, especially in the early stages of creating character, but it may be even more so to let your characters develop organically. To rephrase: use the people you know as a starting point, then blend them, alter them, let them become who they need to be for your narrative to happen into itself. If someone you're borrowing from the world is tall, make her short and dumpy. If popular, make him unpopular. If a male, make him female. If 30 and thin and geekish, make her 13 and muscular and a self-assured swimmer. Always search out a corner of his psyche that matches a corner of yours, because if you can't find something within him with which to sympathize, chances are your readers won't be able to, either.

Finally, avoid falling into the myth that states your characters have free will, they do things the author (that would be you) isn't expecting. While on rare occasion that might be the case, it is not for nothing that Nabokov used to refer to his characters as galley slaves, and John Cheever griped: "The legend that characters run away from their authors—taking up drugs, having sex operations, and becoming president—implies that the writer is a fool with no knowledge or mastery of his craft. The idea of authors running around helplessly behind their cretinous inventions is contemptible."

That may be too strongly asserted by half, and yet the gist of Cheever's admonition remains important. More times than not, writing is an exercise in premeditation, a continuous education into who is really sitting behind the curtain in the narratological city of Oz.

exercises

1. Choose a character you want to write about, or perhaps are in the midst of writing about, and, as a way to get to know him or her better, author his or her obituary, answering all the questions above—how old is s/he, how tall, how heavy, what does s/he wear when dressing up, dressing down, etc.?

2. Choose a character you want to write about, or perhaps are in the midst of writing about, and compose one page about him or her solely through indirect presentation. Next write a two-page scene enacting what you've written through one scene of direct presentation.

3. Choose a character you want to write about, or perhaps are in the midst of writing about, and build a Facebook page or blog for him or her. Keep it up and running for two weeks, adding to it every day. Use photographs from his/her life, favorite music videos, clips from favorite films, etc., as well as her/his words.

4. Choose a character you want to write about, or perhaps are in the midst of writing about, and compose a letter by him or her describing his or her most recent and revealing recurring dream.

5. Find a photograph or painting to which you're drawn, and write the interior monologue of that photograph's or painting's protagonist, making sure to develop a multi-dimensional character capable of surprising the reader in the process.

6. Imagine a dreadfully stereotypical character—the dumb blonde cheerleader, the absent-minded professor, the redneck trailer-park dweller mentioned above, for instance—and write a flash fiction or poem from his or her point of view that turns him or her into a sympathetic, fully-rounded character, possibly by giving him or her a crucial memory that no one else knows about, and/or a surprising strength or weakness.

7. Choose a character you want to write about, or perhaps are in the midst of writing about, and write an interior monologue about him or her from the point of view of the person he or she has hurt most.

8. From Brian Kiteley's *The 3 A.M. Epiphany*: "Write 100 short sentences about a character you are working on in a piece of fiction. The sentences should not connect and should not follow one another in any logical way. The idea of this exercise is to force you to outrun your own thoughts and intelligence and critical mind."

interviews

katherine dunn

q: Your novel *Geek Love* has some of the most interesting and compelling characters I've ever encountered. What were the first steps you took in creating them?

> **a:** Asking questions. For me the first question is often about desire because that's an engine that drives action. Who would want this situation or result? Or, what would this particular person want? All the rest grows out of that question—what their background is, what they look like, wear or eat for breakfast, how they try to achieve their desire, how they react to the results. The fun is in avoiding the off-the-rack item, going for the meticulously layered and tailored specimen who grows and is revealed in the material of the story. The trick is to imagine what it's like to be him, to see through his eyes.

q: In a *New York Times* interview, you quipped that "there should be unemployment insurance for fictional people." How do you know when it's time to cut a character from something you're working on?

> **a:** Occam's Razor, which I define roughly as, "Simplest Is Best." If I discover that a character's function in the story is unnecessary or can happen more directly without him, I fire him. Sometimes it takes me a long time to realize this, so the severance can be painful and messy.

q: What advice would you give a beginning writer about the importance of building strong characters?

a: You don't have to like them but you have to be interested in and by them. If you aren't interested, the reader won't be, either. If a character isn't interesting, you haven't had enough fun creating him.

Katherine Dunn's third novel, Geek Love, *was a finalist for the National Book Award.*

dave gibbons

q: What's the one thing comics can do for a storyteller that no other media can?

a: I suppose with comics the same person has control over the pictures and the words. I mean, movies are visual storytelling, radio can be audio storytelling, prose books are just the voice of the author having to describe pictures, but I think comics are that unique yet instinctive hybrid of words and pictures that allow the same person very economically to run the visual track and the audio track at the same time. The actual art of telling stories isn't exactly the same as the art of draftsmanship in the traditional sense. You can tell a very effective story with really quite simple pictures; as long as they carry some sort of emotional or informational content, the pictures are doing their job. Unlike movies or stage plays or radio, comics are essentially a reading experience. The readers can experience the story at their own pace. He or she can go backwards and forwards, return and study some particular passage, have time to think before the next event is upon them.

q: Your illustration and writing styles do much to capture the essences and motivations of your characters. When you are creating your characters—especially when you are writing them—what do you focus on to get started?

a: Characters have to have a sense of reality in your head. You have to feel that they're like people you know or people you would like to know: maybe like the persona of media personalities, maybe grade-school teachers, maybe childhood friends, maybe current coworkers, maybe current friends, maybe wives, maybe children. You actually kind of *gather* characters, or kind of make mental notes of character aspects that you feel are interesting or appealing (or maybe even unappealing). You have to be quite clear in your head before you start writing or drawing what the characters are about, possess some idea of how they behave or how they talk. It is a truism, but I've found certainly with writing well-established characters, like Superman for instance, that as you write his dialogue you have to have a very clear idea of what he would and would not say. You know, writers speaking about characters writing themselves is perhaps not quite as clear-cut as that, but certainly if you've realized the character fully before you've come to write it, it makes it actually much easier to write because you have a sense of motivation and attitude. So I think, like a lot of creative things, it kind of comes about from having a vague feeling about something that you then examine and refine.

q: What advice would you give a beginning writer about the importance of creating strong and memorable characters?

a: If the characters aren't real or don't have a coherence to them, then it will undermine the story you are trying to tell. People have to act in character—although, as we all well know, sometimes people will act completely out of character. When a story is said and done, it's not so much the plot that stays in people's heads; it's actually the characters and how they are virtually our avatars. How they reacted, how they behaved, and whether we like them, love them, or loathe them is actually where the emotional impact of a story lies.

Dave Gibbons is the co-creator of Watchmen, Give Me Liberty, The Originals, Rogue Trooper *and* Beneath a Steel Sky.

thomas e. kennedy

q: Your work is often described as "literary." What does that term mean to you as a writer?

a: I suppose literary fiction, much as I dislike such labels, is a kind of escape that delivers you back to a more lucid reality (even if that lucidity is a comprehension of darkness). What is important to me in writing fiction is the same as in reading it—not only do I seek to be entertained (make me laugh, make me weep, make me fear, surprise me, dazzle me with language, with complexity, with simplicity) but also to find existential discovery and wonderment (make me think, make me *see*). In short, I like fiction whose author has gone down into the existential pit and found something, forged it in words and brought it back up to the surface to share with us.

q: How do you go about creating your characters?

a: By trying to catch myself thinking. Especially when the mind police are asleep. Because if you can catch yourself thinking, you can reach a more profound understanding of yourself and of others. Take Oedipus for example: he thinks he knows so much; he has avoided the blind seer's prophesy that he will kill his father and marry his mother; he flees from them, but he doesn't think, is blind to the fact that they are not his real parents, and, in fleeing, he runs straight into the fulfillment of the prophesy. The play is about our blindness to our own understanding of ourselves and about our lack of control over ourselves, and Oedipus' blindness and his arrogance that he is *not* blind leads us to see that.

Another essential part of it is observing others, listening to what they say and how they say it, and seeing how they move and how they respond to others. Alec Guinness once said he didn't understand a character he was portraying until he understood how that character walked. I once saw Guinness portray Jonathan Swift on the stage in London, and at one point Guinness has Swift walking, moving his feet precisely like a horse's hooves—it was an astounding performance. He used to go to the zoo to watch how the animals move to understand how the character he was going to play walked, to understand that character.

q: What advice would you give to beginning writers who are creating their own characters for the first time?

a: Observe the world around you, observe the people. Their tics, the balance or imbalance of their faces. How they speak, how they phrase things. Where their eyes focus. Where their eyes do *not* focus. What they say about themselves. The lies they tell. And of course, once again, turn that observation on yourself as well.

But don't confine yourself to observing and thinking. Let your intuition take over. Let your language. The process of language is our connection with the divine. Follow your language as it leads you toward the thoughts and actions of your characters. Trust your language in all its shamelessness and all its beauty. Follow your imaginary characters through real landscapes to see how they respond in your imagination to what you see. Go to the zoo. Observe the animals.

*Thomas E. Kennedy's more than 25 books include the first two novels of his Copenhagen Quartet—*In the Company of Angels *and* Falling Sideways, *both from Bloomsbury. He lives in Copenhagen and teaches at Fairleigh Dickinson University's M.F.A. program.*

ten

characters: the metaphysics of the pronominal hoax

The last chapter focused on conventional character formations that are always-already profoundly Freudian—and hence deeply conservative—in nature. They assume a depth psychology, a roundedness, a complexity to composed consciousness. But is it conceivable to invent beyond them, beyond those we encounter in fictions by, say, Dickens or Fitzgerald, Chekhov or Morrison, that accept selves as dense products of past traumas, current conflictions and neuroses, unconscious fires and conscious tumblings? Character formations which are, in a phrase, emblematic of identities that are relatively solid through time and space, which assume there are great swathes of us-ness that remain constant and complete, autonomous and stable, that aren't invented minute by minute, second by second, from outside as well as inside, aren't continuously changing constructions flickery as those vibrating strings we are told make up the metalogical essence of what we used to think of as "reality"?

"The creators of characters, in the traditional sense, no longer manage to offer us anything more than puppets in which they themselves have ceased to believe," Alain Robbe-Grillet wrote… in 1957.

"The novel of characters," he went on, "belongs entirely to the past, it describes a period: that which marked the apogee of the individual."

Is it conceivable, and, if so, how, to put it differently, to become self-conscious about the assumptions behind conventional characterization, to invent paths into character formations (and deformations) that make us feel more like (and thus help us think more about how) we feel on this side of the age of uncertainty: i.e., mediated, remediated, illegible, dispersed? Something closer, by way of illustration, not to Freudian interpretation, but Baudrillardian: schizoid selves as pure screens, switching stations for all the data networks flowing within us and without? What would such a "character" look like on the page? What would the page on which "he" or "she" existed look like?

Yet again we are back to Beckett's astonishing Unnamable, that indeterminate, disembodied subject position ("character" is far too strong a word for he/she/it), uncertainly human, pulsing in and out of existence between gender and genderlessness, thereness and nowhere/nowhenness. Its modes of expression are hesitation, skepticism, and comma-spliced syntactic entropy. "But enough of this cursed first person," it announces at one point in its self-canceling word cascades, "it is really too red a herring....Bah, any old pronoun will do, provided one sees through it. Matter of habit." And, later, almost an aside: "I. Who might that be?"

Beckett's Limit Text serves as a penetrating reminder, in a Nietzschean/Derridean vein, that the pronoun (the heart of the heart of character) is, at the end of the day, a sort of hoax foisted upon us by the culture's language. That character, self, and identity are quantum fields rather than Newtonian nuggets. The rules of grammar, Beckett's "novel" undertakes to perform, have been repeatedly misunderstood by philosophy and fiction as a metaphysics.

In Patrick Ouredick's *Europeana: A Brief History of the Twentieth Century*, like the brutal period about which he writes, characters remain nameless and pastless, reduced to measurements and formulae, while being subsumed by monstrously absurd historical events in a paratactic style that privileges coordinating rather than subordinating conjunctions, and thereby juxtaposition without clear causal connection:

> The Americans who fell in Normandy in 1944 were tall men measuring 173 centimeters on average, and if they were laid head to foot they would measure 38 kilometers. The Germans were tall too, while the tallest of all were the Senegalese fusiliers in the First World War who measured 176 centimeters, and so were sent into battle on the front lines in order to scare the Germans....And the English invented tanks and the Germans invented

gas, which was known as yperite because the Germans first used it near the town of Ypres, although apparently that was not true, and it was also called mustard because it stung the nose like Dijon mustard, and that was apparently true, and some soldiers who returned home after the war did not want to eat Dijon mustard again.

Kathy Acker populates her Limit Texts with impossible protagonists. Janey Smith in *Blood and Guts in High School* is simultaneously a ten-year-old girl sexually abused by her father, and, depending on page and paragraph, a literary critic dismantling Hawthorne's *Scarlet Letter* or Marxist theorist critiquing late-stage capitalism. "Character" becomes metaphor for socio-economic construction. Social and gender theory, poetic suggestive indirectness, mythic patterning, existential extremity, and hybrid structures undo traditional ideas of continuous being in the world and on the page.

Utilizing Flash animation techniques, Young-Hae Chang and Heavy Industries' text-film *Traveling to Utopia: With a Brief History of Technology* takes the form of multiple black and green words in Helvetica font racing simultaneously across the top, middle, and bottom of a bright white screen at a speed the reader/viewer cannot control. She or he often needs five or more sittings before being able to assemble the information presented. Across the top runs a narrative in Korean characters, indecipherable to most English speakers at any speed. Across the bottom runs one in English that recounts the Kafkaesque dream of a nameless (and ambiguously gendered) narrator stopped by three policemen at a subway station that may be in Seoul, but may instead be in Paris, questioned briefly, and allowed to go on her/his way. Across the middle runs the story of a (probably) different nameless female narrator's life with technology from her first encounter with a computer in her father's office (before he abandons the family) to her own first laptop and beyond. Walking through a metal detector at an airport one day, she sets off the alarm. A visit to the doctor reveals a chip used to track endangered species implanted in her abdomen. Her story concludes with the narrator reporting that she has taken to living in airports, which for her represent atemporal, non-spatial spaces that make her feel safe. All three narratives are interrupted briefly, once, by a screen-sized smiley face clock, while an overly upbeat jazz score at odds with the narratives' content plays throughout. One circuit through *Traveling to Utopia* takes only about three minutes.

Chang's text-film could not have been conceived except as a reaction to and conversation with conventional linear narrativity and hypertextuality, the ubiquity of film, and the Flash technologies which enable it. *Traveling* situates the reader/viewer in the same place as the narrator(s) with respect to technology: unable to control it even as it broadcasts from both outside and inside, dematerializing the self even as it tracks the subject position. Chang's work thereby performs its thematics through a troubled interface with its reader/viewer, who in many ways becomes the piece's protagonist, suggesting that the new flesh (in this case the female abdomen, site of bio-reproduction) has become impregnated with media (the site of semiotic reproduction) that knows more about us than we do about "ourselves." The "characters" in her work, such as they are, exist superficially, erratically, illogically, more as flows of unconnected data streams than as anything resembling, say, a Mr. Darcy or Anna Karenina.

N. Katharine Hayles makes a helpful distinction between two cognitive modes, *deep attention* and *hyper attention*. Deep attention, associated with conventional writing and reading, is able to concentrate on a single object for an extended period of time; think of your experience with a novel by Gustave Flaubert. Hyper attention, on the other hand, switches focus rapidly and often; think of your experience navigating *Grand Theft Auto*. Conventional character formations, such as those found in a novel by Rick Bass, Jonathan Safran Foer, or Colson Whitehead, ask the reader to employ deep attention. Those described in this chapter ask the reader to employ hyper attention (Chang), or to modulate between deep and hyper attention (Beckett), or to re-imagine ways of engaging with deep attention (Acker).

In each case the reader discovers notions of character that resist characterization, and therefore resist the cultural constructions of self and identity of which such characterization is representative—*not*, needless to say, simply to dazzle or complicate for complication's sake, but rather to enable us to ask ourselves the overwhelming question: Who are "we" now, and now, and now, and how, and why?

exercises

1. Write a first-person monologue in which it is impossible to tell the gender, race, or age of your protagonist.

2. Although most narrative centers around character, can you write a flash fiction or poem that doesn't? That is, can you compose one that has no characters in it, or no human ones, or no animate ones, and yet still finds traction for your readers?

3. William Burroughs (influenced by T. S. Eliot's *The Waste Land*, John Dos Passos' *U.S.A. Trilogy*, and his artist friend Brion Gysin) disrupted conventional ideas of stable, continuous characterization by employing what he called the cut-up technique—a mode of collage. Take two different pages from a newspaper, magazine article, or book, and cut the pages in half vertically. Paste the mismatched pages together. Or Google The Lazarus Corporation's cut-up engine and use it to perform a similar task automatically.

4. Invent a narraticule composed entirely of phrases lifted from digital sources—Facebook, Twitter, Wikipedia, RSS feeds, etc. This is a modified electronic version of Tristan Tzara's exercise, described earlier, of creating a piece of writing by pulling words from a hat, only here the words are phrases, and the hat is made of bytes rather than atoms.

5. Short circuit traditional concepts of characterization by writing collaboratively. Invent a flash fiction or poem with several other people, alternating words, lines, or paragraphs, writing simultaneously and collaging, rewriting, editing, supplementing, translating the previous version. This can be done either in person, via email, as a collective blog, or on a shared computer screen.

6. Take a flash fiction or poem of your own or someone else's and cross out words until a new narraticule emerges. This method of creation is called Erasure. For examples, take a look at Janet Holmes' *The ms of my kin*, which erases the poems of Emily Dickinson written in 1861-62, the first few years of the Civil War, to discuss the more contemporary Iraq War,

and Tom Phillips' classic artist's book, *A Humument*, that erases W. H. Mallock's 1892 novel, *A Human Document*, by drawing, painting, and collaging over its pages.

7.   Write a flash fiction or poem composed entirely of how-to directions or measurements and formulae. Study how, if at all, character is formed, deformed.

8.   À la Kathy Acker, write a flash fiction or poem in which an impossible character is your protagonist—the equivalent of Janey Smith in *Blood and Guts in High School*, say, who is simultaneously a ten-year-old girl sexually abused by her father, and, depending on page and paragraph, a literary critic dismantling Hawthorne's *Scarlet Letter* or Marxist theorist critiquing late-stage capitalism.

9.   Compose a narrative or poem that doesn't involve character by using either Twitter and/or your cell phone or cell phone's video camera. How? Exactly.

interviews

lydia davis

q: In one sense, you're one of the only translators interviewed in *Architectures of Possibility*. In another, all writers—particularly those exploring the possibility space called the innovative—are translators. How does the act of translation inform your own fiction?

a: Part of the pleasure of translating is entering another writer's skin, speaking in that other voice, writing in that other style. (Imagine being Proust or Flaubert for a while, or A.L. Snijders, this contemporary Dutch writer of "very short stories"—*zeer korte verhalen*—whose work I'm attempting now.) It's really another way of experiencing a different sensibility and/or a different vocabulary, writing something new. I think I like departing from my own skin for a while, traveling somewhere else. But I don't think the experience is all that alien from the sort of divorce-from-daily-self that allows any of us to write in the first place. After all, to write anything new and strange of my own, in the realm of fiction, I tend to enter another persona.

q: How do you conceptualize and go about creating character?

a: I am active only in the transcription phase—in other words, I don't dream up characters, create them from scratch; instead, I am on the lookout for them and watch them as they occur to me. But this is a hard question for me to answer because my "fiction" these days is usually a version of reality. So it is the real character (the person on the train, the insect on the windowsill) that I observe and then adopt into a piece of writing. Of course, however, even observing a "real" character, it is my own perception of the businesswoman on the train or the ant in the sunlight that goes into the piece of writing. Another writer would see something else.

q: Do you see a relationship between politics and innovative aesthetics?

a: I'm not sure what kind of politics you mean. My first reading of the word is Washington politics, rather than publishing politics, for instance. So I'll answer it in that sense. Of course I'm biased in favor of innovation in any field. Positive innovation, I should say, since there may always be innovative changes for the worse. Innovation implies openness—openness to new ways. It should also imply an objective gaze at things as they are. An aesthetics of innovation does not exactly spring from an impatience with tradition, but an impatience with mere repetition. If one embraces an aesthetics of innovation, it is hard not to look at the current political situation and not see, there too, many fresh approaches that might be tried.

Lydia Davis, a 2003 MacArthur Fellow, is the author of a new translation of Madame Bovary *by Gustave Flaubert. Her* Collected Stories *was published in 2009.*

samuel r. delany

q: Why do you write, and, more interestingly, why do you choose to write alternative fiction?

a: Of all explanations for why artists create, critic Harold Bloom's feels to me the most accurate: Bloom sees creativity as a radical rebellion against the pervasive failure to create—a failure which, in some infantile part of the artist's mind, is equated with death itself. Creativity grows out of the fear, the terror of death.

Alternative fiction might be seen as fiction in which the pressure of observation and the complexity of organization are simply at a different level from where they're set in normative endeavors. But (or, better, therefore), save on the most contingent, provisional level, I don't see the fundamental enterprise of, say, Dickens, Joyce, and Kathy Acker to be particularly, meaningfully different.

The variables in all three cases are variables in observation and organization. In the work of each writer, observation is aimed in one direction or another, then adjusted up or down as one moves along through the text. Organization of the textual material in each case is either complex, or formal, or simple, or informal.

In much alternative fiction the observation and the organization are simpler than they are in normative fiction—the simplicity highlights and makes us aware of the observation and the organization *per se*. Because normative fiction still makes up most of what people read, for many of us it still seems somehow "natural." One thing that alternative fiction does is "denature" normative fiction and make us more aware of how it functions as artifice.

When I conscientiously choose to write something that might be more easily called alternative fiction than not, usually it's because somehow I want to highlight some aspect of process—either of its organization or of its observation.

q: In what sense, if any, do you think writing can be taught?

a: I honestly don't know if writing on the level we are speaking about can be taught.

The mechanics of grammar and various rules of organization and style can be taught. Frankly, I would like to see them taught far more thoroughly than they are. On the level we're discussing, however, when we speak of creative writing, writing presupposes a certain kind of reading. Now reading *can* be taught. When I teach reading, and point out various patterns in the text, be it at the level of the phrase, the sentence, the scene, or some larger structure, I feel I'm much closer to teaching writing than I am when I actually run a workshop and people hand in their attempts at stories, essays, or poems.

In one important respect, all there is to learn about writing is a number of patterns, on all those levels (phrase, sentence, scene…), that writing can conform to. New levels of observation and organization make us violate (or, indeed, conform to) some of these patterns. The existence of these previous patterns alone is what makes the new patterns (of alternative fiction, say) signify.

Well, you now know all I know *about* writing.

Anything else would be what I know *of* writing itself.

And the only way to learn that is by reading…

No, I wonder seriously if writing can be taught, in the usual sense: of explanation, practice, and repetition, leading to mastery.

To me, as I've written before, good writing (especially the more experimental) feels much more like submission than mastery. And that's why I think all the rhetoric that points to, that leads toward the notion of "mastery" in matters aesthetic is deeply misguided.

q: Is there a difference between teaching how to write mainstream fiction and teaching how to write alternative fiction? If so, can you articulate the difference?

a: If we hold onto the provisionality and contingency of the differences between the two types of fiction, of course there are differences in teaching them.

Any exercise that urges us to observe in a different way becomes a route to new fictive material that will likely register as alternative; any exercise that suggests new ways of organizing the materials of writing—from words, to sentences, to scenes, to whole works—will also likely generate alternative fiction.

Spend a single day during which you write three descriptive sentences about every object you encounter (which you stop and look at closely for a minimum three minutes) that begins with the letter "b"—and *only* those that begin with the letter "b." (You might call it "Being and Time.") Fulfilling such a writerly task may well produce an interesting fiction.

Or—depending on the quality of your descriptive sentences—it may produce a very dull one.

But until you try it, until you actually spend some time inhabiting such an Oulipo-esque schema, there's no way to know or to judge the results beforehand.

q: You wrote a number of sentences in *Dhalgren*, the novel many (including myself) consider your magnum opus, on individual cards before inserting them into the text. Why craft so carefully when so few will notice?

a: Emily Dickinson once wrote: "Nothing survives except fine execution." I encountered that statement as a kid—and I bought it. Yes, I'd like my work to survive, if only a little longer than it might had I not worked on it as hard as I did.

In *Dhalgren*, by the by, more sentences were written at the head of notebook pages than on index cards—because I needed to rework each sentence to bring it in line with iron and crystal. I gave up on index cards fairly quickly (yes, an idea initially borrowed from Nabokov); there wasn't enough room.

And people do notice. I can tell the difference between writing that is carefully worked over and writing that is not. You only have to read a paragraph or page of Ethan Canin or Joanna Russ or Guy Davenport—three very different writers—to know that all three put real thought into which word is going to follow which; which also means not only does each make all sorts of wonderful verbal choices, but that each has forbidden him- or herself all sorts of commonplace choices.

There are dozens of ways that ordinary writers allow themselves to negotiate sentences that Canin and Russ and Davenport are just not interested in using. The modes of mental organization they represent are too facile. The commonplace observations and received dogma they allow the writer to slip in are just not ones these writers want to promote. With a Gass or a Nabokov, recognizing the difference between their prose and the ordinary is like recognizing the difference between someone who gets up and walks across the room and someone who leaps up, to grab a trapeze hanging from the ceiling, vaults into the air and spins, balances, and flips. Most of the time, though, it's more like telling the difference between walking and dancing.

People recognize the difference, and they take pleasure in the dancing—even if themselves they can't execute such steps.

q: Many of your characters—Hogg, for instance—are less than likable, even frightening and repulsive. What can we learn about the nature of characterization from your choices?

a: I don't like to talk about "teasing the reader." I'm not terribly interested in character the way it's usually conceived, that is as a ground bodying forth certain psychological truths—or as a playing field to display the usual emotional pyrotechnics we associate with "good characters": sympathy, antipathy, identification. I'm interested in characters only as each is a locus for allowing certain sorts of sentences to be uttered—by the character or about the character.

But, as I've written elsewhere, I begin as a sentence lover. It's at the level of the sentence you're more likely to *find* me, as a writer. Now I'm interested in the larger structures sentences can fit in and generate. Still, for me, writing *begins* as an excuse to put together certain sorts of particularly satisfying sentences.

Samuel R. Delany teaches at Temple University and is author of many speculative and transgressive novels and theoretical essays on narrativity. This interview was conducted in 1996.

elisabeth sheffield

q: What's the one fictional character that best exemplifies what a character *could* be as opposed to what one *should* be?

a: B, a pregnant thirteen-year-old who may or may not be a test tube baby, and the narrator of Marianne Hauser's *The Talking Room*. B creates B (along with all the other characters in the novel, V, D, J, etc.) as she speaks, in a kind of self-generating, linguistic feedback loop. "I hear them through the rumble of the trucks in the night rain as I lie on my back between moist sheets, listening. And I know they are talking about me. But they call me an idea. B? She was your idea and don't you deny it."

Hauser's late twentieth-century B owes something to Proust's early twentieth-century M—both are discursive machines, taking in the raw material of language and producing sentences that somehow assemble into "being."

q: In creating your own characters, where do you begin?

a: With a voice.

q: What advice would you give a writer about building her or his own characters? What's the most important thing to keep in mind?

a: I don't tell other people *how* to write. In the classroom, I talk about the various ways writers create characters. Different strokes work for different folks. Recently I've been reading David Shields' *Reality Hunger*. He says "someone once said to me, quoting someone or other [John Gardner], 'Discursive thought is not fiction's most efficient tool; the interaction of characters is everything.' This is when I knew I wasn't a fiction writer, because discursive thought is what I read and write for." Well, I do consider myself a fiction writer, of sorts, and discursive thought is not only what interests me most, it's also fundamental for my characters. But that's just me (and them).

Elisabeth Sheffield is author of the novels Gone *and* Fort Da: A Report, *and a critical monograph on James Joyce,* Joyce's Abandoned Female Costumes, Gratefully Received. *She teaches at the University of Colorado at Boulder.*

eleven

temporality: summary, scene, dialogue, flashback, slo-mo, tense

Freytag's Pyramid tells us something significant about established narrativity's urge for symmetry, steady pacing, rising and falling action, a sense of closure. It also tells us something significant about established narrativity's assumptions about the nature of time. More often than not, such narrativity embraces identifiable beginnings, middles, and endings that form coherent, causal, clockwork plots. Another way of saying this is that established narrativity evinces a temporality that includes belief in an agreed-upon, stable past; an agreed-upon, stable present; and anticipation of future resolution.

Put another way, established narrativity embraces continuity, linearity, certainty, the concept that who we were then is in a fairly untroubled sense who we are now, that what happened yesterday can be made to account for what is happening today. Consider the memoir, whose structure commonly takes the form of a story chronicling a person's current triumph over earlier adversity. This is the country of urgent rationalist optimism that assumes a relatively unified self overcoming (for instance) childhood traumas in order to achieve a relatively durable, integrated, contented tomorrow.

Authors create such fictions about temporality (and many readers enjoy partaking of them) because those fictions reduce the complexity of the experienced world and self within it (not to mention the task of reading, feeling, and thinking) to comfortable, manageable terms. Those fictions reassure us about the narrative arc called our lives. They affirm (unreflectively) that dénouement awaits us all.

Closer to the case for many, however, is the sense that we are surrounded by countless contested orientations toward past, present, and future that complicate anchored notions of temporality and therefore of identity and the universe(s) that those selfhoods attempt to traverse. With this idea in the back of our minds, let us take a short tour through the major techniques that control a reader's experience of temporality in narrative while asking ourselves more about their suppositions and how we might usefully and instructively disquiet them.

Summary. Summary compresses large amounts of time into a very small space: "My childhood was uneventful"; "They lived happily ever after"; or, as the unhinged narrator of Laird Hunt's novel, *The Impossibly,* writes: "In those days I was in the middle of two or three things that seemed to take up unnecessarily large amounts of my time, but of course there was no getting around them. One of these things was setting in motion the acquisition of a certain item, which was proving very difficult to obtain. Another was the process of establishing whether or not the poorly functioning washer/dryer in my apartment was under warranty, etc. I was told there were papers. I knew there were papers, but where were the papers?"

Notice how summary removes the reader from specific time. The authorial voice takes over and encapsulates the state of affairs in general brushstrokes. Summary, then, allows you to present a lot of information about your character(s) in very few sentences. It can supply easy transitions from chapter to chapter in a novel, or section to section in a short story, quantum the reader back and forth by decades, fill in important background data about the narrative's universe, and provide a change in narrative rhythm after a succession of fully articulated scenes.

Although many how-to creative-writing textbooks will steer authors clear of summary on the grounds that it relies on telling rather than showing, the abstract rather than the concrete, truth is that most narratives rely on it to a greater or lesser degree, especially if we consider summary placed into the mouth of a character during dialogue. Innovative writing, from Patrik Ourednik's *Europeana* to Susan Howe's *The Midnight* and Lyn Hejinian's *My Life*, in fact completely or nearly so eschews summary's opposite, scene. *My Life*, which has been twice updated, originally contained 38 sections of 38 lines each (Hejinian's age at the time of publication); the second version contains 45 sections of 45 lines each. Its torqued style ("A moment yellow," it begins, "just as four years later, when my father returned home from the war, the moment of greeting him, as he stood at the bottom of the stairs, younger, thinner than when he had left, was purple—though moments are no longer so colored")—its torqued style refuses the transparent language conventions just as its sense of changing self refuses unambiguous notions of identity and time that typically compose autobiography.

Scene. While summary diminishes detail, giving rise to a feeling of timelessness or time speeded up, scene particularizes time, slows it down, relishes in direct modes of presentation: action, gesture, appearance, dialogue, thought. By way of example, study this passage from Vladimir Nabokov's *Lolita*, which describes Humbert Humbert and his nymphet pulling into a gas station on their cross-country odyssey. Humbert Humbert knows they are on the run, Lo's mother having been hit and killed by a car while crossing a street on the heels of her discovery that Humbert Humbert was in love, not with her, but her daughter. Lo thinks they are on nothing but a fun junket.

> When we stopped at the filling station, she scrambled out without a word and was a long time away. Slowly, lovingly, an elderly friend with a broken nose wiped my windshield—they do it differently at every place, from chamois cloth to soapy brush, this fellow used a pink sponge.
>
> She appeared at last. "Look," she said in that neutral voice that hurt me so, "give me some dimes and nickels. I want to call mother in that hospital. What's the number?"
>
> "Get in," I said. "You can't call that number."
>
> "Why?"
>
> "Get in and slam the door."
>
> She got in and slammed the door. The old garage man beamed at her.
>
> I swung onto the highway.
>
> "Why can't I call my mother if I want to?"
>
> "Because," I answered, "your mother is dead."

A few points to make here. First, scene erupts around important plot points. If there is a major confrontation, crisis, turning point, conventional narrativity tends to turn to scene to express it. Second—we are back to our discussion about significant detail—you should be careful about overdetailing scene: spending a paragraph, for example, showing a person getting out of bed, walking across the room, and opening the door while thinking about nothing in particular along the way, or, in the case above, showing Humbert Humbert turning on the car, putting it into gear, inching through the gas station, and edging onto the highway. Scene is about carefully chosen, compelling action.

To put this another way: every aspect of every scene, every sentence, every item, every patch of dialogue gives the reader new and interesting information that somehow contributes to the progress of the narrative or helps assemble character. If it doesn't, cut it out—or, perhaps even more aesthetically constructive, ask yourself what "new and interesting information" and "progress" really means in narrativity. The answer will depend on the particular narrative at hand, obviously, on the author's goals and theory of art. In Alain Robbe-Grillet's *Jealousy* and Robert Coover's "The Baby Sitter," scenes are repeated almost verbatim a number of times with only slight alterations from earlier iterations with the intent of casting the truth-value of the whole "plot" (and with it our culture's communal sense of reality) into question. The more one pays attention to Robbe-Grillet's and Coover's texts, the more the definition of what constitutes "new and interesting information" alters, even as "progress" comes to refer, not to traditional forward plot thrust, but to the reader's experience of making a sort of meta-sense out of the uncertain structures before him or her.

Dialogue. An indispensable component of most scenes, dialogue ticks quickly down the page compared to summary, and it is often packed with more data about character, situation, and plot than any other single narrative component. Again, a character's appearance can be in harmony or conflict with what she or he is saying and how. Does she lisp, stutter, use pet words, etc.? What traits define his diction? What is the nature of her speech patterns, his syntax, her responses, the relationship of what he says to what he means?

If you take your notebook to a bar, or a grocery store, or the mall, sit down, and record how the people around you talk, you will notice a curious phenomenon that Rebecca West called attention to in the early twentieth century: most speakers don't so much engage in conversation when chatting with each other as they do intersecting monologues. People tend not to play Q&A, that is, or especially even listen to what the others with whom they are ostensibly conversing are saying. Rather, they tend to use a phrase another person has just employed as an excuse to launch into an editorial of their own. Put plainly, they aren't so much paying attention as waiting for their own chance to fill the air with words. Dialogue is almost always, then, a kind of subtextual struggle for discursive power.

Nor, you will note if you listen, is dialogue particularly logical. Usually it is afloat with sentence fragments, um's, er's, ellipses, bad grammar, meanders, and slang. While unfiltered dialogue on the page almost always devolves into dreary reading exercise, concept without content, most written dialogue approximates the feeling, if not the fact, of unmediated talk—an approximation that can only be attained, paradoxically, through meticulous use of technique.

Like scene, dialogue usually does several things at once. A writer with a good ear and good sense of rhythm (and dialogue is nothing if not a register of these two things) can make dialogue convey a sense of the speaker's education, personal linguistic ticks, geographical source, obsessions, and much more. It can act as a reminder about the past, forecast upcoming events, help fill out a sense of place, and keep the plot clicking forward. All this, and yet written conversations tend to last much less time than their real-world counterparts.

SIDEBAR ONE: characters, like people, tend to mean more than they say. Always think about how you can employ the space between speech and meaning to generate tension.

SIDEBAR TWO: Tags are words that come after quoted speech: "she screeched"; "he whimpered"; "she moaned." If the voices you establish for your characters are as strong and unique as they can and should be, you will seldom if ever need to use tags. Allow the rhythms, word choices, and emphases of your characters' dialogue inform your reader about who is screeching, whimpering, or moaning without ever having to spell it out.

SIDEBAR THREE: Avoid using exclamation marks unless you have to! Because they become distracting quickly! And then downright annoying! Or, as F. Scott Fitzgerald once said: "Cut out all those exclamation marks. An exclamation mark is like laughing at your own joke."

You may want to give some thought to how much a role you would like dialogue to play in your writing, and how you might be able to violate traditional notions about the technique to effect energizing, illuminating ends. There is virtually no direct dialogue in Gabriel García Márquez's *One Hundred Years of Solitude*. Harold Jaffe, influenced by Donald Barthelme, composes unsituated, disembodied, often ambiguous, highly satiric anti-narratives made up of nothing else. Kenneth Goldsmith's *Soliloquy* is an unedited document of every word he spoke during the week of 15-21 April 1996. An example of conceptual art, *Soliloquy* was first realized as a gallery exhibition in April 1997. Subsequently, the gallery published the text in a limited edition of 50. In the fall of 2001, Granary Books published a trade edition of the text. The web version of *Soliloquy*, which appeared in 2002, contains the exact text from the 281-page original book iteration, but due to the architecture of the web, each chapter is sub-divided into 10 parts. Only as the reader scrolls across the blank electronic page for each day of the week do lines wink in and out of existence, calling attention again and again to the ephemerality and banality of the speech act.

Flashback. When you need to take your reader back in narrative time to material that occurred before the beginning of the work, you employ flashback. Characters can recollect in either scene or summary a key event from their lives that sheds light on present action. They can recollect through reveries or dream sequences. Much of a narrative can take the form of a flashback—starting, say, with a key event (funeral, wedding, murder), then tracking back to map and explain what led up to it. Remember how important it is that your transitions into flashbacks be smooth, don't call attention to themselves, that you use them only when you must. Remember, too, that if you place flashbacks too early in your narrative they have a habit of disturbing your story's momentum, confusing your reader unnecessarily. Last, remember that you can usually dispense the same information through dialogue or summary that you would through flashback in a way that won't distract from your narrative's propulsion.

Slow Motion. Time frequently feels like it is stalling in lived experience's most intense instants—in the middle of a mugging, a firefight, a blown tire during takeoff. A sudden clarity descends. You can see every atom moving around you as your car slides across the ice toward that ditch with the six-foot drop. In narrative experience, slow down an important instant to make your reader see, feel, smell every detail of it. In a sense, slow motion is the opposite of summary. Rather than moving through vast tracts of time rapidly, narrative moves through very small amounts of time expansively. You can either write "He was hanged and died," or, as Ambrose Bierce did in "An Occurrence at Owl Creek Bridge," perhaps the most well-known example of this technique, you can write a 10-page tale about what happens between the second a man named Peyton Farquhar is pushed off a bridge during his execution and the second his neck breaks.

Tense. Most narrative is told in the simple past tense: "He walked down the street." While you might logically conclude that this would create an impression of temporal distance between reader and action, in practice it doesn't because the technique is so widespread, so deeply part of convention, as to have become virtually invisible. Over the last half century or so, though, more and more writers have adopted the present tense: "He walks down the street." By doing so, they self-consciously emphasize the immediacy of the narrative's action. A kind of glossy photographic thereness settles over the writing. But what might happen if you were to utilize another tense entirely—the future ("He will walk down the street."), perhaps, or the pluperfect ("He had walked down the street.")? How would the texture and intent of your narrative change? Or, instead of exploring the possibilities inherent in tense, what if you were to explore the possibilities inherent in the subjunctive or contrary-to-fact mood ("He might walk down the street.")?

Writing Time Versus Reading Time. A final observation with respect to narrative temporality: Readers experience it at a very different rate than writers do. This is a conspicuous point, but one many writers don't think about very much. As a rule, it takes authors days—if not weeks—

to compose a fully-realized scene, yet it takes most readers minutes to process it. Authors spend a year or two of their lives composing their novels (Gustav Flaubert took five to complete *Madame Bovary*, James Joyce nearly seven to complete *Ulysses*, Mark Z. Danielewski nearly 10 to complete *House of Leaves*), yet readers spend a few days digesting them. The fact has immense implications for the writing process. As author, you might find yourself bored after writing a page of dialogue or sticking with someone's point of view for an entire paragraph because that page or paragraph took you the better part of two days to carpenter together. At such moments, remember your reader. What effect do you want to have on her or him? Remind yourself that your reader will, if she or he is really careful, spend perhaps 30 seconds on that very same stretch of writing. At this stratum of temporality, there are few creatures more unmistakably unlike each other than authors and their audiences.

exercises

1. Write a flash fiction or poem that depends solely on summary, or one that depends solely on scene.

2. Using Lyn Hejinian's *My Life* as model, compose a story or poem made up of as many sections and as many sentences per section as you are years old. Through language disruption and an assumption of a scattered self, let the piece work against unambiguous notions of meaning, identity, and temporality.

3. Write a flash fiction or poem composed solely of untagged, unsituated, disembodied dialogue between two characters, each of whom wants something different, and neither of whom says exactly what he or she means. Concentrate on distinguishing your characters through voice, rhythm, obsession.

4. Invent a flash fiction or poem whose first and last paragraphs/stanzas take place in the narrative present, and whose body takes the form of flashback, perhaps using as your starting point a significant event such as an accident, a kiss, an act of abuse.

5. Invent a flash fiction in which an event that in real-time would take five or 10 seconds to occur in your fictive slow motion takes three to five pages...a fall, a death, a dazzling realization.

6. While authoring one of the above, employ an infrequently used tense—future, future perfect, pluperfect. Or how about altering the mood of your lines by casting them in the subjunctive, or contrary-to-fact? Or deliberately mixing tenses and moods? What happens?

7. Compose a narraticule in which all the events occur simultaneously, or one in which all the events occur in different places and different times, alternating, not by scene or chapter, but line by line.

8. Using only appropriated images, or only photographs you've taken yourself, tell a wordless narrative—one whose sense of temporality exists only in the arrangement of the pictures before you.

9. Author a flash fiction or poem that, à la Alain Robbe-Grillet and Robert Coover, repeats the same small cluster of scenes almost verbatim, yet with alterations from their earlier iterations that cast the truth-value of the whole "plot," the whole notion of certainty, temporality, into question.

10. Take one of the above exercises you've attempted and now strip away all the verbs—that is, all time signatures. Is it possible to tell a story or poem only through nouns, pronouns, adverbs, and adjectives in an atemporal space? What happens when you try?

interview

scott mccloud

q: As someone widely regarded as synonymous with both the theory and practice of comics, what do you think that hybrid medium accomplishes temporally to separate it from other another medium like, say, prose or film?

a: In comics we have some unique practical challenges because so much is laid out in front of you and you're able to see what's coming, to literally see past, present and future laid out on any given comics spread. There's a kind of temporal altitude that readers start with: the ability to see a broader swath of what's going to happen and what already has. And maybe contemplating that relationship is something that comics offers as a unique possibility. But that's also a unique challenge. Suspense, for example, is an important component of story and we find ourselves pacing to the page break. The fact that you have a set span of time on those spreads as well is unique. Even though there's a set span of time in prose, the window of prose is really a much smaller one, and we're experiencing one word at a time, one sentence at a time, but we're not necessarily expanding that simultaneity to the spread the way we do in comics. Comics can take advantage of the symbolic power of static images. An image can linger, become an interesting tool for memory and symbolism, in a way that the ephemeral, transitory nature of film images doesn't afford.

q: How do you identify innovation in comics?

a: The most interesting innovations in comics for me are very closely tied to the nature of the medium. I think they're more the product of what I think of as comics "loyalists," are especially interested in the fundamental rules of telling stories with pictures. And playing with that is often more fun than playing with the individual components of, say, the text or storylines or style that might be played with in any other related media. So playing with the notion of sequence, with unusual juxtapositions, with unusual spatial constructions, that sort of thing, is especially interesting. And I've been on both sides of the fence. Especially when we began to experiment with digital media in comics, I thought that aggressive experimentation was appropriate to that period, and a number of us devoted ourselves for a few years to nothing but that. But as a practical matter, I think of it very much as our research and development wing, and the end product is a better understanding of the medium for the purpose of communication and emotional persuasion in the long run. I like being on both sides of that fence. I think I'd feel a little undernourished if I spent too long on one side or the other.

q: Are there particular books or artists within the comics medium that serve as examples?

a: Apart from the various grand old men of the twentieth century like Winsor McCay or George Herriman, I think some of the most valuable experimental forays would include Art Spiegelman's early work, which was collected in his anthology called *Breakdowns*. That was very important to a lot of us. Speaking right now just of American or English language comics, David Mazzucchelli's *Asterios Polyp* is going to continue to be an important work for the experimental wing.

q: I know a lot of creatives who are very intrigued by it. In what way is that particular book important for people who are interested in innovative work or even innovators themselves?

a: *Asterios Polyp* is a fascinating example of something that's narratively coherent—telling a fairly riveting story—but is always reminding us of its own form. It's aware of the process of printing, and, in a lot of ways, the whole thing is one long extended joke on four-color comics. But it also manages that rare trick of confronting us with the formal properties of the work while not losing its ability to create an illusionistic world within the story. We can lose ourselves in the story while simultaneously being aware of its form.

q: Any others that come to mind?

a: There's some interesting stuff abroad. Shintaro Kago is a manga artist who has done some pretty extraordinary stuff in the last decade or two. In Europe, Ivan Brun is doing some really fascinating work if you can find it. And of course there's Chris Ware— specifically his *Big Book of Jokes*. *Jimmy Corrigan: The Smartest Kid on Earth* is more dedicated to simply telling a story even though it's a very formally-wise and inventive work, but inventiveness is not the point, whereas it is the point in his other work, especially the oversized-page stuff that he did. And online there are people like my buddy Daniel Merlin Goodbrey, who has done some really significant work exploring the mechanics of alternate navigation methods. There are many more, of course. So very many of them out there!

Scott McCloud is the author of Understanding Comics: The Invisible Art, *creator of the comics series* Zot!, *and progenitor of the 24-Hour Comic movement. He leads workshops and lectures worldwide on hybrid and emergent media.*

twelve

point of view

There are no uninteresting stories, just uninteresting points of view. One of your aims as a writer is to discover the frame of reference that opens up your narrative, presents it from the most engaging and invigorating angle—the one that allows us to see ourselves, our worlds, and maybe even textuality itself anew. Recall, by way of illustration, how in *Grendel* John Gardner appropriates and retells the tale of *Beowulf*—the medieval epic about a brave, overachieving hero's exploits with an awful monster—from the point of view of the monster, thereby transforming the original into a postmodern exploration into how we all feel like freaks and fools in an uncertain topology we can no longer read.

Point of view is all about perspective, how it shapes our understanding of the text of the text and of the text we call lived experience. The glue that holds your narrative together, gives it life, point of view is all about the convoluted relationship among writer, narrator, writing, reader, characters, world.

For all that, point of view distills into a relatively small set of possibilities.

First Person. If you want your character to speak the story, you tell it from his or her point of view. Your character thereby becomes your narrator. That creates an opportunity for you to put some provocative distance between author and protagonist. Your central character can be either reliable or unreliable. Your character can be the center of the story, like Scribble in Jeff Noon's post-cyberpunk novel *Vurt* or Percival Everett's *I Am Not Sidney Poitier*, or a peripheral narrator reporting action that happens to a central character, like Marlowe in Joseph Conrad's *Heart of Darkness* or Nick Carraway in F. Scott Fitzgerald's *The Great Gatsby*. Either way, she or he will undergo education and hence change by the narrative's conclusion in conventional narratives. Along the journey he or she will exhibit a distinct personal voice (remember our discussion about speech above). It is also possible, though seldom attempted, to tell your story, not from a first-person singular point of view, but from a first-person plural one, as Faulkner does in "A Rose for Emily," where the "we" represents the collective consciousness of the town in which the protagonist lives and dies, or as Jeffrey Eugenides does in *The Virgin Suicides*, where the "we" represents an anonymous group of teenage boys infatuated with the five sisters who have committed suicide. In both Faulkner's and Eugenides' cases, the consequence echoes the plural position of the Greek chorus, whose communal voice was used to comment on the dramatic action. (What would the result be to situate first-person singular or plural point of view in an inanimate object or non-human entity?)

Third Person. If one of the enjoyable things about composing in the first-person is getting to inhabit an unbalanced mind (recall schizophrenic "Chief" Bromden in Ken Kesey's *One Flew Over the Cuckoo's Nest*; the crazed academic Charles Kinbote in Vladimir Nabokov's *Pale Fire*), explore it from the inside out, then one of the enjoyable things about composing in the third-person is getting to play the role of omnipotent deity. Here you can conjure up the impression of objectivity in your narrative while gliding easily through time and space. If you choose a third-person omniscient point of view, as Tolstoy does in *War and Peace*, Thomas Pynchon in *Gravity's Rainbow*, you can generate a large cast of characters and visit the consciousness of each as you see fit, remarking along the way what characters look like, where they come from, and so forth. If you choose a third-person limited-omniscient point of view, the most common in narrative, you can generate a single character, or a small handful of them, and stay close by their sides through their experiences. If the first-person point of view witnesses the world as it arrives filtered through a particular awareness, the third-person point of view sees characters moving through the landscape at a little distance from the authorial presence—something not unlike seeing actors moving through a film *out there*.

Second Person. Most authors choose to work within either the first- or third-person points of view, yet a number have experimented with the second-person. What is engaging here, as Carlos Fuentes understood when he cast his novella, *Aura*, in it, is the way the second-person point of view produces a readerly tension that both parents a sense of immediacy associated with the first-person form (by implicating the reader in the action), and keeps drawing metafictional attention to itself as an idiosyncratic technique, and therefore to the text itself as an artificial construct:

> You're reading the advertisement: an offer like this isn't made every day.
> You read it and reread it. It seems to be addressed to you and nobody else.
> You don't even notice when the ash from your cigarette falls in the cup of
> tea you ordered in this cheap, dirty café. You read it again. "Wanted, young
> historian, conscientious, neat. Perfect knowledge of colloquial French."
> Youth…knowledge of French, preferably after living in France a while…
> "Four thousand pesos a month, all meals, comfortable, bedroom-study."
> All that's missing is your name.

The reader can't help feeling an imbalance experiencing such a passage, a discursive unsteadiness. Like Fuentes' narrative in toto, in which a man named Felipe Montero answers a newspaper ad in a labyrinthine part of Mexico City, only to enter a gothic territory that inverts all assumptions of normative realism, the text calls attention to the very process of reading, and hence interpreting, and hence to the physicality of the text in the reader's hands. The "you" refers to the reader, pointing to the notion that the "real" narrator seems to be the reader him- or herself, as well as to Felipe's memory or present consciousness-in-action, pointing to the notion that the narrator has become protagonist, that Felipe is both self and other, that he is both producer-of-script and actor-of-script, putting the very question of identity up for grabs.

Multiple Person. Another option is to tell your narrative by alternating first-, second-, and third-person points of view, or by employing only two of them, or by framing your narrative with one (say the third-person) and then having someone within that frame recount the central tale (say in the first-person), or by utilizing numerous first-, second-, and/or third-person points of view. To shape *As I Lay Dying*, William Faulkner chose the last. He created a family called the Bundrens, imagined the worst things that could happen to them, and then let them occur…

including the death of the family's matriarch, Addie, her dying wish to be buried miles and miles away from the homestead in the middle of a hot summer, and the Bundrens' ultimately selfish quest to honor it, a journey that takes them through flood, fire and public ridicule. Faulkner—who, by the way, reportedly wrote the first draft in only six weeks while working night shift in a heating plant—decided to structure the novel into 59 sections, each either an interior monologue or splash of stream-of-consciousness (more on the difference between these two modes in a minute) told from one of the character's perspectives: 16 by non-Bundrens in order to lend the story several relatively objective points of view; 19 from the fairly intelligent and second-sighted perspective of a brother named Darl; 10 from the perspective of a mentally challenged (or perhaps very young…it is difficult to tell which with anything like certainty) boy named Vardaman; five from the perspective of a simple-minded brother named Cash; and so on. There is even one from Addie's point of view from beyond the grave. The outcome is a richly psychological novel influenced by the theories of Freud and Einstein, Joyce's *Ulysses*, and Wallace Stevens' poem about decentered truth, "Thirteen Ways of Looking at a Blackbird."

A brief dispatch on the difference between interior monologue and stream-of-consciousness. Interior monologue produces the illusion of the associational, illogical workings of a specific mind in motion in one of two ways. First, directly, in a manner that seems to absent the author. Back to Vardaman in *As I Lay Dying*:

> The trees look like chickens when they ruffle out into the cool dust on the hot days. If I jump off the porch I will be where the fish was, and it all cut up into not-fish now. I can hear the bed and her face and them and I can feel the floor shake when he walks on it that came and did it. That came and did it when she was all right but he came and did it.

Second, indirectly, in a manner whereby the narrator's voice intrudes intermittently to select, present, and guide. Note this passage from Virginia Woolf's *Mrs. Dalloway*:

> For having lived in Westminster—how many years now? over twenty,—

one feels even in the midst of the traffic, or waking at night, Clarissa
was positive, a particular hush, or solemnity; an indescribable pause; a
suspense (but that might be her heart, affected, they said, by influenza)
before Big Ben strikes. There! Out it boomed. First a warning, musical;
then the hour, irrevocable.

In her essay "Modern Fiction," Woolf argues that the author's job in the early twentieth century
was to capture, not external reality, but external reality perceived by an individual consciousness.
"Examine for a moment an ordinary mind on an ordinary day," she wrote. "The mind receives a
myriad impressions—trivial, fantastic, evanescent, or engraved with the sharpness of steel. From
all sides they come, an incessant shower of innumerable atoms; and as they fall, as they shape
themselves into the life of Monday or Tuesday, the accent falls differently from of old; the moment
of importance came not here but there; so that, if a writer were a free man and not a slave, if he
could write what he chose, not what he must, if he could base his work upon his own feeling and not
upon convention, there would be no plot, no comedy, no tragedy, no love interest or catastrophe in
the accepted style, and perhaps not a single button sewn on as the Bond Street tailors would have it.
Life is not a series of gig lamps symmetrically arranged; life is a luminous halo, a semi-transparent
envelope surrounding us from the beginning of consciousness to the end."

While both direct and indirect interior monologue continue to embrace grammatical,
articulate thought, associational and illogical as that thought might appear, stream-of-
consciousness (a term originating with Alexander Bain in 1855, although it is usually
associated with the philosopher and psychologist William James, novelist Henry James'
brother) removes conventional grammatical structure, quotation marks, and even commas
and periods to more accurately analogue the machinations of fluid thought-feeling processes.
One of most stunning and best-known examples remains Molly Bloom's soliloquy in
James Joyce's *Ulysses*, which concludes, after eight enormous run-on "sentences" (sans
punctuation) that span more than 40 pages:

I was a Flower of the mountain yes when I put the rose in my hair like
the Andalusian girls used or shall I wear a red yes and how he kissed me

under the Moorish wall and I thought well as well him as another and then
I asked him with my eyes to ask again yes and then he asked me would I
yes to say yes my mountain flower and first I put my arms around him yes
and drew him down to me so he could feel my breasts all perfume yes and
his heart was going like mad and yes I said yes I will Yes.

Paradoxically, of course, even though both interior monologue and stream-of-consciousness
give the appearance of creative chaos, they in fact take much longer to shape and polish than
conventional discourse.

exercises

1. Make a narraticule or poem by describing an apple from five radically different perspectives:
    1) objective realist; 2) a young girl just coming to consciousness of the world around her;
    3) an old blind man; 4) a psychotic killer; 5) a cat. Use first-, second-, and third-person
    limited points of view each at least once in the course of composing.

2. Imagine a car crash. In a flash fiction or poem, tell it from three different points of view: 1)
    the person who was driving; 2) a witness; 3) the first policeman on the scene. Employ the
    first-person point of view for one, the second- for another, the third- for another.

3. Choose one of your favorite stories, myths, fairy tales, or historical events, and retell it
    from the point of view of a minor character or antagonist, paying particular attention to
    how such a move can completely reframe (and refresh) the whole.

4. After trying your hand at #3 in conventionally rendered prose, recast it as either interior
    monologue or stream-of-consciousness.

5. After trying your hand at #3 from the point of view of one minor character or antagonist,
    retell it from the point of view of another to study how everything shifts again.

6. Take a flash fiction or poem you have already written for one of the exercises in this book and rewrite it either in another point of view (for example, if you originally wrote it in the first-person, try the second- or third-) or from another character's point of view, thereby generating a new piece of writing altogether.

7. An objective correlative, according to T. S. Eliot, who in 1919 borrowed the term from Washington Allston's 1840 *Lectures on Art*, is created when an object in the environment is described so that the emotional state of the character from whose point of view we see it is revealed *without* ever telling the reader what that emotional state is or what has motivated it. John Gardner proposed this point-of-view exercise based on the concept: A middle-age man is waiting at a bus stop. He has just learned that his son has died violently. Describe the setting from the man's point of view *without* telling your reader what has happened. How will the street look to this man? What are the sounds he will hear, and how? The odors he will smell? The colors he will register? What will his clothes feel like? Write a flash fiction or poem to find out.

interview

d. harlan wilson

q: How do you usually decide which point of view works best for a particular narrative you're working on?

> **a:** Generally I just do what I want, or what feels right at the moment. I'd like to think I'm more calculating and shrewd than that. But I'm not. In short fiction, I go back and forth between the first and third person. I'm most comfortable with the first person, but after a few stories, I feel too self-indulgent and narcissistic, and my writing, no matter what it's about, seems more like reportage to me than fiction. In a way, I feel like I'm cheating. So I switch gears and turn to the third person for a few stories. This allows me to more effectively create, develop and hone characters. Not that you can't produce round characters in the first person, of course. It's simply easier for me to do with somebody who I "don't know," i.e., a character who is not "I," even if the "I" I'm writing about isn't "me."
>
> In the third person, naming characters alone immediately alienates me from them. Then, during the process of composition, I discover those characters, erasing (or at least curtailing) that initial estrangement. It puts me in the position of the reader, to some degree, and I don't feel like I'm cheating. Still, a few stories later, I get bored, or my ego surges back to the vanguard, and I revert to the first person. It's not a particularly logical methodology, I realize. But part of the reason I write is to come to terms with the many illogical perspectives and desires that define my own character.

q: What about multiple points of view? Is there a specific narrative that executes multiple perspectives better than most? And how might that particular story have influenced or inspired your own experiments with multiple points of view?

a: I write a lot of metafiction and almost always employ multiple points of view. This is especially the case in my novels. *Dr. Identity, or, Farewell to Plaquedemia*, for instance, the first novel in my "scikungfi" trilogy, features two protagonists/narrators: Dr. 'Blah, an English professor, and Dr. Identity, his android surrogate and a homicidal maniac. I oscillate between the third person and two distinct first person narrations, one for each character. Dr. Identity's narration, while somewhat colloquial, is distinguished by minimal punctuation and an utter absence of figurative language in an effort to reflect the emotional and psychological lack that defines the android. In contrast, Dr. 'Blah's narration is richer and more nuanced—more "human," per se. This schizoid manner of storytelling can make for an annoying reading experience. The idea was to offset and disaffect readers from the weird, overtechnologized future in which *Dr. Identity* is set, as well as the characters that populate that future. In addition, I wanted to call attention to the chaotic, rhizomatic nature of perception under the auspices of hypermediatized culture. William Gibson basically does the same thing in *Neuromancer*, as do other cyberpunks, proto- and post-, only via language rather than point of view.

I recall being influenced specifically by Faulkner's *The Sound and the Fury* when I began writing *Dr. Identity*. I can't say that I actually enjoy that novel; for all of Faulkner's ideas and innovation, his writing consistently puts me to sleep. But since I first read *The Sound and the Fury* in college—20 or so years ago—it's stuck with me, and I've taught it a few times in college courses. If nothing else, the book demonstrates a masterful fluidity and technique vis-à-vis perception.

q: You work a lot through the prisms of genre. Do you think there is a dominant point of view that is necessary or even inherent to more genred narratives like those found in horror or sci-fi?

a: Most genre fiction is written in traditional third person prose with little variation or sidewinding into other modes of narrativity (aside from the use of italics to denote first person thought processes, especially in horror, a decidedly flaccid and lazy technique). This is by no means necessary, but it's certainly the dominant style. I guess it has to do with market forces and the expectations of genre readerships. They want a certain kind of writing, which is to say, they want the *same* kind of writing, over and over. So authors, publishers and editors give it to them. Genre readers like new stories and characters, but they don't like new writing or anything that might displace their comfort zones. It's ironic. The fantasy, horror and sci-fi genres arguably constitute the most cunning and imaginative writing spaces, and yet the people who write it, read it, and superintend it are ultra-conservative in terms of how they think narratives should look and unfold. I write against this current. Consciously, vehemently. As a result, my royalty checks often exhibit a certain jaundiced, emaciated, pathetic-looking quality—my Bartlebys, I call them. But I just can't conform, and I can't write the same way all the time. And I can't shake the desire to reach for the New, despite how this desire limits my career. Moral: if you want to make any money writing genre novels, keep things simple, and don't do as I do.

D. Harlan Wilson is an associate professor at Wright State University and the author of hundreds of stories and essays, as well as more than 10 books of fiction and criticism.

thirteen

word worlds

In a very real sense, language will always be your authentic protagonist. Without it, there would be no characters, no movement, no politics, no emotions, no plots, no ideas, no literary marketplace, no genres, no structures, no poetry, no prose, no settings, no time, no space, not a single point of view, no there there. Many readers raised on conventional writing overlook that fact, content to fall through the Balzacian Mode's transparent prose into a land of linguistic assemblages they conceive of as plump people, places, and action. Yet language invariably creates that land, any land, and not the other way around.

"Reality is not simply 'out there' independent of words and unchanged by them," Hazel Smith underscores in *The Writing Experiment: Strategies for Innovative Creative Writing*. "Rather, the way we use language makes the world how it is. Playing with language allows us to construct our own world, and question some of the ways in which reality is normally perceived." In good part, this is creative writing's importance: as an apparatus for interrogating and interfering with dominant sign systems in order to understand how they function, why, and to attempt to envision the opportunities inherent in alternative ones, alternative modes of being, of shaping our experience of experience.

Language is the carrier wave from one consciousness to another, and in innovative writing that carrier wave is a perpetually fraught, self-aware thing. "It is always a mistake to be plain-spoken," Gertrude Stein advised. "Remarks are not literature." Ben Marcus: language is "a physical substance with deviant powers. A powder, a drug, a wind, a medicine." Roland Barthes: "Writing is the science of the various blisses of language."

These are some of the reasons Vladimir Nabokov drafted and crafted almost every sentence of *Lolita* on an individual index card before committing it to his word edifice, the reason Samuel R. Delany did the same for hundreds in *Dhalgren*.

William Gass: "It is precisely considerations of this sort that distinguish the artist's attitude toward language from others. It is the intensity of his concern that measures his devotion, the multiplication of these that reveals the grandeur of his vision; and it is the effect of such scruples, when successfully embodied, whether with the ease of an overflowing genius or by the pains of talent in team with ambition, to raise a fiction, or any other creative work, from what would be on most other grounds a commonplace, to the level of the beautiful."

Here comes sunset cast by a non-writer: "It was, uh, really, um, beautiful. The thing is…Well, words just don't do it justice, you know?"

And here it comes cast by Tom Robbins: "Indigo. Indigoing. Indigone."

The consequence of such attention to expression, mixed with a certain degree of playfulness, a certain degree of skeptical irreverence, of self-consciousness and joy, can be a quartet of sentences like this by Gary Lutz: "Then came nights when, lying awake beside my final wife, I would spend too much time putting my finger on what was wrong. I was wearing the finger out. What was wrong was very simple. Sometimes her life and mine fell on the same day."

A writer's singular use of language—her or his choice of words, figures of speech, devices, sentence shapes, paragraph contours—is that writer's singular metaphysics. Remember David Foster Wallace. In a YouTube interview, a lawyer and author of several books about English usage asks him what he thinks of genteelisms—those multisyllablic, latinate, important-sounding words like "prior to" that substitute for shorter, often Anglo-Saxon, down-to-earth-sounding ones like "before." Revealingly, the writer who majored in English and philosophy at Amherst College, whose father was a philosophy professor, doesn't answer at first. Instead, he reflexively makes a sour face. Only then does he advance that "genteelism" is an "overly charitable way to characterize" such "puff words," and concludes: "This is the downside of starting to pay attention. You start noticing all the people who say 'at this time' instead of 'now.' Why did they just take up one-third of a second of my lifetime?" (N.B.: when Wallace or his sister Amy uttered a solecism at the dinner table, his mother, a professor of rhetoric and composition at a community college in Champaign, Illinois, where the family lived, would commence faking a coughing fit until the culprit had gone back and corrected his or her mistake.)

The upside to grammatical awakenings, as Wallace affirms, is that "you get to be more careful and attentive in your own writing, so you become an agent of light and goodness rather than the evil that's all around." Such remarkable precision and forethought is what Wallace's work is all about—but only in the sense that it is emblematic of a larger determined noticing on his part. His famous sentences are the opposite of those embraced by journalism and/or the Balzacian Mode because the world he perceives is the opposite of the one assumed by those kinds of writing. His sentences are the opposite of transparent and easily comprehensible. They are Rube Goldberg contraptions that are typically dense, digressive, sometimes exhausting, exhaustingly obsessive, frequently mischievous in their use of jargon abutting against colloquialism abutting against lyricism, often sprinkled with comically stilted formulae, repetitions, incorrigible circularity, and parenthetical clauses loaded atop parenthetical clauses.

Their M.O. is hypotaxis, a reliance on syntactic subordination in complex sentences, not simply as a showoffy stylistic swagger, but as charged existential position. Those sentences understand, along with the narrator of Wallace's story, "Good Old Neon," that "we all seem to go around trying to use English (or whatever language our native country happens to use, it goes without saying) to try to convey to other people what we're thinking and to find out what they're thinking, when in fact deep down everybody knows it's a charade and they're just going through the motions." Why? Because that's what the world felt like to Wallace. Because "what goes on inside is just too fast and huge and all interconnected for words to do more than barely sketch the outlines of at most one tiny little part of it at any given instant."

The essential paradox at work in Wallace's writing, which demands (in Hayles' terms) deep attention, is that it doesn't believe in what it's doing—at the same time it can't do anything else but believe in what it's doing. It is a language desperately trying to capture the seven-ring circus of metacognitive consciousnesses which it knows it can't capture while holding off the oblivion which it knows it can't hold off, trying to stabilize a world of contradictory multiples that's all catawampus and inconstancy and convolution and clutter, a hyper-self-aware unconfident language reflective of the hyper-self-aware unconfident narrators frequenting Wallace's fiction who know down at the synaptic level that what they know is that they don't know, that their narratives every time render into parables about the nature of Not-Knowing.

Without that sort of meticulous thoughtfulness before the various blisses (and failures) of language, a writer runs the risk of producing something about which Truman Capote might snark, as he did about Jack Kerouac's spontaneous, unedited work heavily influenced by the jazz explorations of Miles Davis, Charlie Parker, and Thelonius Monk: "That isn't writing at all, it's typing."

If language isn't the most important thing for you when you author, then why not take up dance, painting, journalism, the piano?

That's not a rhetorical question.

And so:

Show, Don't Tell. Of the few general principles to contemplate when working in the realm of conventional narrativity, perhaps the most important is the repeated-to-queasiness mantra: Show, don't tell. Take a moment to enjoy the language in this passage from Robert Coover's "The Baby Sitter":

> That sweet odor that girls have. The softness of her blouse. He catches a glimpse of the gentle shadows amid her thighs, as she curls her legs up under her. He stares hard at her. He has a lot of meaning packed into that stare, but she's not even looking. She's popping her gum and watching television. She's sitting right there, inches away, soft, fragrant, and ready: but what's his next move?

Notice how Coover avoids large, empty, tentative assertions composed of hollow adjectives. His paragraph lasers in on particulars through the senses: fragrance ("that sweet odor"), texture ("the softness of her blouse"), image ("the gentle shadows amid her thighs"), sound (the brash real—"she's popping her gum"—intruding into the narrator's semi-ideal vision). Notice, too, how Coover doesn't announce his point to the reader by telling, but rather shows it by providing significant data. He emphasizes the thingness of the world, emphasizes all those details only the artists among us pick up and can conjure through language. By doing so, he reveals situation, age, sexual tension in the air. He exercises images that transcend simple denotation, are wealthy in connotative charge, juxtaposing that sweet odor, which implies innocence, candy, and so on, with those "gentle shadows amid her thighs," which imply so much more. Last, he employs rhythm, the recurrence of specific sounds or kinds of sounds—the soft sensuous slightly sad alliteration of s's that slide through the passage; the sonic glide from "gentle" to "glimpses" in the third sentence; the abrupt p of "popping" to accentuate that brash gum-chewing in the sixth—all to raise his prose toward something like what we used to refer to as poetry. These components add up to Coover's voice—that amalgam of style, characterization, and tone that makes each writer only him or herself.

Metaphor & Simile. A metaphor strikes an analogy between two objects in the reader's mind that revitalizes the existence of both. A simile is a metaphor that uses the word "like" or "as." Examples of both appear in this excerpt from David Foster Wallace's *The Broom of the System*:

> The reason Lenore Beadsman's red toy car had a spidery network of scratches in the point on the right side was that by the driveway of the home of Alvin and Clarice Spaniard, in Cleveland Heights, lived a large, hostile brown shrub, bristling with really thorny branches. The bush hung out practically halfway across the drive, and scratched hell out of whatever or whoever came up. "Scritch," was the noise Lenore heard as the thorns squeaked in their metal grooves in the side of her car, or rather "Scriiiiitch," a sound like fingernails on aluminum siding, a tooth-shiver for Lenore.

"Toy car," not because it is an actual plaything, but because Lenore's auto is so small, and our first straightforward metaphor. "Spidery network of scratches," however, moves toward the more elaborate: it connects, not two things, but three: a spider's web, an openwork fabric or structure in which cords, threads, or wires cross at regular intervals, and the scratches on poor Lenore's auto. The shrub that causes those scratches isn't really "hostile," naturally, so to say that it is is to create yet another metaphor that compares the shrub to a malicious person (this subset of metaphor, which assigns a non-human entity human qualities, by the way, is called anthropomorphism). The sound that shrub's thorns make across the side of Lenore's car is "like fingernails on aluminum siding, a tooth-shiver for Lenore." The first part of that comparison takes the form of a simile that compares the onomatopoeic (a word formed by imitation of a sound made by or associated with its referent: e.g., *oink, meow, roar*) scritch to fingernails raking across siding, while the second eases from simile back to metaphor: teeth don't really shiver, but we know exactly what Lenore feels when she hears that grating noise. In a phrase then: metaphors and similes wake language up while calling attention to language *as* language.

Opacity. Writers working within the bounds of normative narrativity (Bret Easton Ellis, Raymond Carver, Cynthia Ozick, et al.) usually keep the deployment of metaphor, simile, hypotaxis, alliteration, and other linguistic flourishes to a minimum because they want their language to pretend to be a clean, clear window pane through which the reader objectively views a world, or, perhaps better, a reflective surface that returns external reality with gleaming accuracy. This troubled theoretical position tracks back, if not to Plato and Aristotle, then at least to the early nineteenth-century realists who, along with Stendhal in *The Red and the Black*, believed art should be "a mirror carried along a high road. At one moment it reflects the blue skies, at another the mud and puddles at your feet." (The irony shouldn't be lost that Stendhal couched his scientist creed in—what else?—the linguistic flourish of a metaphor.) Writers working within innovative veins tend to foreground language, call attention to it as a sign system whose signifiers, which always-already exist as manipulated, manifest a complicated relationship with their signifieds, let alone with "reality." And so Ishmael Reed opens *Mumbo Jumbo* thus:

A True Sport, the Mayor of New Orleans, spiffy in his patent-leather
brown and white shoes, his plaid suit, the Rudolph Valentino parted-down-

the-middle hair style, sits in his office. Sprawled upon his knees is Zuzu, local doo-wack-a-doo and voo-doo-dee-odo fizgig. A slatternly floozy, her green, sequined dress quivers.

And Susan Steinberg "Life" thus:

> just me and him driving, just the road and road signs, just broken white lines on the road, just the headlights nearing, then past, then dark, just the radio hum, a song, what was it, just a song from before, just his untucked shirt, his coat on the seat, just my lipstick rising up and up, just my lipstick pressing to my lips in the dark, my: do you like it, his: do I what,

And Mark Leyner "I Was an Infinitely Hot and Dense Dot" thus:

> So begins the autobiography of a feral child who was raised by huge and lurid puppets. An autobiography written wearing wrist weights. It ends with these words: A car drives through a puddle of sperm, sweat, and contraceptive jelly, splattering the great chopsocky vigilante from Hong Kong. Inside, two acephalic sardines in mustard sauce are asleep in the rank darkness of their tin container. Suddenly, the swinging doors burst open and a mesomorphic cyborg walks in and whips out a 35-lb. phallus made of corrosion-resistant nickel-base alloy and he begins to stroke it sullenly, his eyes half shut.

"Oh bliss, bliss and heaven," says Joycean Alex in Anthony Burgess' *A Clockwork Orange* when listening to Beethoven's Ninth on his bed. "I lay all nagoy to the ceiling, my gulliver on my rookers on the pillow, glazzies closed, rot open in bliss, slooshying the sluice of lovely sounds. Oh, it was gorgeousness and gorgeosity made flesh."

"Words," said Samuel Beckett, "are all we have."

Clichés. And so it is incredibly important that writers care about and eschew clichés. If, in the above passage from *The Broom of the System* about Lenore Beadsman's car, Wallace had written "fingernails on a chalkboard" instead of "fingernails on aluminum siding," he would have skidded from fervent metaphor into meek, mundane cliché. In printing, a *cliché* was a plate cast from movable type, also known as stereotype. When letters were set one at a time, it made sense to cast a phrase used repeatedly as a single slug of metal. Over time, *cliché* came to mean such a ready-made phrase, referring to any expression that has been so overused as to become a linguistic clone…a conventional, formulaic, and oversimplified version of itself: "the tip of the iceberg," "it's a crying shame," "old as the hills," "writing on the wall," "curiosity killed the cat," "moment of truth," "to no avail," "cut to the chase," "stopped in my tracks," "frightened to death," "lost track of time," "quiet as a mouse," "dumb as a rock," "down in the dumps," "dead as a doornail." Clichés usually enter popular discourse because they are pithy and vibrant, have a sense of truth about them, but soon, through frequent repetition, they pale into pre-fab predictability. They exist so that writers can allow others to think for them.

Mixed Metaphors. Mixed metaphors are sloppy comparisons the author hasn't thought through. They begin in San Diego and end in Algeria, by way of Hackensack, New Jersey. In the late eighteenth century, Boyle Roche told Irish parliament: "Mr. Speaker, I smell a rat. I see it floating in the air. I shall nip it in the bud." Not only did he string together a series of clichés for his goofy fumbled effect, but he strung them together in such a way as to get them wrong, bang them into each other, create—if you think about it—a grotesque image of a hovering rodent being bitten in the protuberance containing an undeveloped shoot, leaf, or flower. More recently, Rush Limbaugh informed those tuning into his talk show: "I knew enough to realize that the alligators were in the swamp and that it was time to circle the wagons." And the president of Argentina, Cristina Fernández de Kirchner assured her citizens that the current financial crisis would not cause the developed world to "plunge like a bubble."

Empty Filler. Vacant words and padding phrases function as the written parallel of saying *um* when talking. They carry no content, contaminate white space for no reason other than to contaminate white space. Unless you have a good reason, trim every single one of them. And so: *There were bats dangling from the ceiling.* could more cleanly be rendered as *Bats dangled from the ceiling.* Ditto: *Give it to the girl with the dark hair.* → *Give it to the dark-haired girl.*

Active Voice. Active voice means making the subject of your sentence act rather than being acted upon. Active voice: "I throw the ball." Passive voice: "The ball was thrown by me." Use active, and you will energize your prose, generate lines that emphasize doing rather than merely existing. Simply avoid state-of-being constructions (forms of the verb "to be"), and most passive voice will evaporate from your writing.

Verbs. Inexperienced authors are often convinced that the muscle of a sentence resides in its adjectives and adverbs, since those parts of speech are the descriptive mechanisms in language. In fact, they're the verbal cellulite of your style. If you use more than a modest handful per page, your writing will blotch purple, seem overdone, thick, messy as a dorm room on a Sunday morning: "The tall skinny slightly stooped white-skinned man with the red pock-marked face and large nobby potato nose in the weather-worn full-length wool coat walked blithely and inattentively down the wide brick-lined street on a particularly sunny blue-skied early spring day with the occasional white fluffy animal-shaped cloud scudding overhead through the lush lime-green foliage of the full-bodied lovely trees along the normal-widthed if uneven sidewalk." No. The muscle of a sentence resides in the verb, the heart of the heart of the sentence's action. Did that man really just walk down the street...or did he perhaps stroll? amble? crab? skitter? saunter? blunder? Each of those verbs will carry the man's whole character within it.

Word Echoes, Rhymes, Homonyms, Homoeoteleutons. Unless you are doing so for rhetorical/lyrical emphasis or deliberate disturbance, thematic effect, or character/narrator revelation, stay away from using the same word twice on any given page, let alone any given paragraph or sentence—except, needless to say, for the unavoidable ones like simple pronouns and conjunctions. Otherwise, unpleasant word echoes will begin bonging through your writing. If a word is rare, you should probably use it only once per poem or story or book or even career. Those whose ears are finely tuned will hear your redundancy as a kind of verbal static, understand it as your inability to control your own language. Listen, too, for unnecessary full rhymes ("like" and "bike"), slant rhymes ("drunkard" and "conquered"), homonyms ("bore" and "boar"), and one of the most unattractively named linguistic slips in English: homoeoteleutons, those unsettling and graceless likenesses in endings ("emerging moaning becoming discernible").

Sentence Length & Structure. A homely description of a toy wooden dove taking first flight:

> The bird went up into the air. It was made out of wood. It wobbled a little.
> It steadied. It flew. We all thought it was cool. We were very excited.

Note how all the sentences take the same form: subject + verb + preposition/adjective/adverb. Note, too, how they are all about the same length, marching along like a squad of miniature mechanical soldiers. The result is a kind of prose wooden as that dove—sturdy enough, but flat and uninspired as an unpainted '66 Ford Mustang. Now listen to the same subject matter filtered through Guy Davenport's exceptional vision in "The Wooden Dove of Archytas":

> Into the eye of the wind it flew, lollop and bob as it butted rimples and
> funnels of air until it struck a balance and rode the void with brave address.
> We all cried with delight.

Enough said.

Mechanics. "I was working on the proof of one of my poems all the morning," Oscar Wilde noted in his diary one day, "and took out a comma. In the afternoon I put it back again." Which is to say that spelling, grammar, and punctuation are the base metals of every paragraph, every line, every phrase. You should love each one with every linguistic fiber in your body. If you work them correctly, they will become beautifully invisible until you need to bend them for a specific reason.

A quick moment to make a few points about the most frequent trouble spots concerning punctuation (spelling and grammar should take care of themselves, if you stay alert, especially during revision). While writers don't necessarily need to learn how to parse a sentence, they do need to know some basics of sentence construction. All punctuation has to do with sentence rhythm and length of caesura, or pause. Periods, question marks, and exclamation marks *separate* sentences; semi-colons *separate* independent clauses (clauses that could stand alone as individual sentences); single commas *separate* words and phrases within sentences. And so you have:

- ▶ This is a sentence.
- ▶ Is this a sentence?
- ▶ You bet it is!
- ▶ This is a sentence; at least we hope so.
- ▶ At the corner market he bought a can of Coke, potato chips, and a carton of milk.

Pairs of commas and pairs of dashes *enclose* words and phrases; parentheses and quotation marks *enclose* words and phrases:

- ▶ The man, tall and thin, ran down the street.
- ▶ The man—he was tall, thin, and dressed in a raincoat, I believe— ran down the street.
- ▶ The man (tall, thin, raincoated) ran down the street.
- ▶ "I didn't mean that," she said.
- ▶ What did you say?" he asked.
- ▶ "Stop, thief!" they shouted.

Colons and dashes *link* one part of a sentence to another; hyphens *link* two words together, usually in an adjectival construction (e.g., "double-spaced page," "well-written prose"):

- ▶ This is what he bought: a can of Coke, potato chips, a carton of milk.

▶   What I mean to say is—this, just this: know your punctuation, feel
    it in your bones.

Then, when you need to rupture conventional mechanics for a significant purpose, as Samuel
Beckett does in the following passage from *How It Is* (mimicking, instead of traditional
punctuation, the breathing intervals of a being crawling through a seemingly eternal tract of
fecal mud in some nowhere, nowhen), the effect will be spectacular:

how it was I quote before Pim with Pim after Pim how it is three parts I
say it as I hear it

voice once without quaqua on all sides then in me when the panting stops
tell me again finish telling me invocation

past moments old dreams back again or fresh like those that pass or
things things always and memories I say them as I hear them murmur
them in the mud

in me that were without when the panting stops scraps of an ancient voice
in me not mine

my life last state last version ill-said ill-heard ill-recaptured ill-murmured
in the mud brief moments of the lower face losses everywhere

"All my life I've looked at words as though I were seeing them for the first time," Hemingway said.

Everyone should be so lucky.

reading suggestions

Strunk, William C. and E. B. White. *The Elements of Style* (1918; regularly updated). Still the best short course in the rules of correct usage. Anyone wanting to be a writer should read this at least twice. It will take you an afternoon or evening, and it will teach you a world. Also available free online.

exercises

1. Take one of these sentences, which blandly tells instead of shows, and turn it into a flash fiction or poem rich with showing instead of telling: "I am nervous." "He was angry at his mother for not letting him go to the movies." "That woman is pregnant."

2. Describe an object as meticulously as possible for one page—without naming it. To check if your language succeeds in conveying your meaning, share your composition with your writing colleagues and see if they can figure out what it is you're describing. Make sure not to tell ("It's a kitchen appliance designed to keep food preserved longer by keeping it well below room temperature."), but to show ("Someone reached into me and shut off my light and everything went cold.").

3. Write a sudden fiction or poem saturated with as many clichés, mixed metaphors, passive constructions, and other versions of verbal slack as possible.

4. Write a flash fiction or poem that doesn't use any senses, yet, because of its language, is fascinating.

5. Take a half page from a story by Bobbie Anne Mason, Raymond Carver, Ann Beattie, Frederick Barthelme, or Dan Brown, and rewrite it to bring language to the surface. Vary sentence length and structure. Employ hypotaxis. Enrich with metaphor and simile. Play with punctuation. In a phrase, make language your clear protagonist.

6. Homolinguistic translation (based on an exercise by Charles Bernstein). Take someone else's flash fiction or poem, or one you have already written, and translate it "English to English" by substituting word for word, phrase for phrase, line for line. Or translate

the piece into another literary style (Ben Marcus? David Foster Wallace? Kathy Acker? Gary Lutz? Carole Maso?). Chaining: try this exercise with a group of writers, sending the narraticule on for "translation" from person to person until you get back to the first author.

7. Homophonic translation (based on an exercise by Charles Bernstein). Take a paragraph, poem, or entire flash fiction originally written in a foreign language that you can pronounce but don't understand well (or at all), and translate the sound of the piece into English (e.g., French "blanc" to "blank"; "toute" to "toot"). Now translate it again, homolinguistically (from English to English), as in #6, so that you have three versions of shapeshifted "meaning."

8. Substitution #1 (based on an exercise by Charles Bernstein). Take a narrative, poem, or other source text, and put blanks in place of three words in each line, noting the part of speech under each blank. Pass to one of your writing colleagues and ask him/her to fill in the blanks, being sure not to recall the original context.

9. Choose a poem or passage from a flash fiction, either another's or your own, and experiment with line breaks and/or visual composition—while not changing any of the original language—to see what effects arise. Do this three times with the same piece.

10. Proliferating styles. In 1947 Raymond Queneau published *Exercises de Style*, 99 retellings of the "same" story, each written in a different style—e.g., blurb, passive, free verse, medical, mathematical. Do the same, only with five variations of a flash fiction or poem you've written, inventing and exploring your own stylistic categories. For further inspiration, you may want to consult *99 Ways to Tell a Story: Exercises in Style*, Matt Madden's 2005 homage to Queneau's work in the form of a graphic novel.

11. Try your hand at one of the exercises above, and then rewrite it as one long un-capitalized sentence, à la the above examples by Susan Steinberg and Samuel Beckett, emphasizing rhythm and breath through the use of either carefully placed commas or white spaces.

interviews

noy holland

q: My sense is that you write, not so much story to story, or even paragraph to paragraph, but phrase to phrase, perhaps word to word. Would you talk a little about your relationship to the sentence?

> **a:** It's true, your sense that I don't write story to story. I used to think I began a story with a sentence, but later came to realize that I begin with something that precedes a sentence—an image, often, or an intensity of confusion or feeling. Sometimes with a fragment overheard, a scene I have not been privy to but which has emotional or intellectual resonance for me. I write from word to word, favoring sound over sense, finding myself in places I cannot predict by virtue of hearing what is sonically pleasing or discordant. I have found myself writing stories prompted by a single word—the smaller the better. I am grateful for the ways that a sentence, let loose, says things we don't mean to say, or didn't know we meant to say; if I am listening closely enough, I see this deviation and can allow it to dislodge my notion of whatever story I am writing. In this way, sentences generate themselves, and generate stories, and distort stories truly and mindfully.

q: Why and how do you teach a graduate seminar at the University of Massachusetts-Amherst on Samuel Beckett's works?

> **a:** Oh, I loved that class on Beckett, who listens to himself so well, who makes so much of so little. I love, too, that much of Beckett's work manifests itself outside and beyond the literary sphere. We watched and listened to a lot—his work for TV; that strange, silent, hooded square dance. Beckett gives a reader a stunningly clear sense of

sentences being permutations of themselves, of a book being a series of permutations of its originating impulse. It can be exhausting to read so much by and about Beckett at a clip—plays, novels, stories, a massive and detailed biography—but that saturation seems to me exactly Beckett's aim: to overtake and enshroud, to quiet all but that one wicked, despairing, loving, unstoppable living voice. Of course the course depends on smart and willing students. They are the real how and why.

q: How do you think about the use value of innovative writing? Or, to put it another way, what does innovative writing offer a society or individual within it?

a: Innovative writing gives us a reprieve from the ridiculous civilities of being alive, from the ways we gloss and compromise, make ourselves pleasing and accommodating. It gives our best readers, I hope, something of what it gives us. Years ago, I think I neglected to think of it as useful or political. Of course it is. Without what we are calling innovative writing, we are at the mercy of a dominantly rational, on-the-way-to-the-crappy-movie relentless marketing push. Any writing which resists this push gives us more life, extends and validates the range of what it means to be human. I can hardly think of life without innovative literature, without art that says no to the sheepishly held, that insists on the shame and pathos, the gleefully playful, the transformative and sickening and joyous. Without innovative art, we are stuck with the narrow and the orderly and deprived of what we know. We grow weak and afraid. We are starving, stuffed on forms of consumption we are far smarter and hungrier than. It's not even that the common doesn't help us but that it insults and damages us. I say sit, think, don't think, be, stop wanting and buying and moving. Stop adding. BE. Can't we call it—innovative literature, necessary art—a true state of being?

q: What are two or three of the most interesting/fun/successful/challenging writing exercises you offer your students?

a: I ask students to look at their tendencies, and to deprive themselves of something they know or automatically bail themselves out with. This can be a neat linguistic turn or something so sweeping as killing people off at the end of a story. I ask students to write a story generated by a single rhetorical strategy—anaphora, epistrophe, anadiplosis—old and impersonal patterns of repetition. Or generated by a single word. The best is when I can send them to a display of visual art, or a dance performance, which a single gesture or color or object makes coherent. So that we can remember how readily and skillfully the mind makes meaning and narrative, how eager we are to be invited into an unburdened space to think and feel.

Noy Holland is the author of three collections of short stories: The Spectacle of the Body, What Begins with Bird, *and* Swim for the Little One First.

ben marcus

q: Your most recent book is *The Moors*. Is it a novel? Short story? Novella? Do any of these terms describe, apply or even matter?

> a: It's not really a book. It's a long story that was first published in *Tin House*, then reprinted by Madras, a small press whose proceeds go to an organization in need. I chose the Brooklin, Maine library, which is a wonderful little library in the town where my family lives for part of the year.

q: You write elegant and provocative sentences. What does a well-constructed sentence do that no other unit or form of expression can?

> a: Big question, impossible to answer in brief. The amazing writer Gary Lutz covers this topic beautifully in his essay, "The Sentence is a Lonely Place." What still stuns me about sentences is that the removal or addition of a single syllable can completely alter the effect. The architecture is fragile, and anything seems possible, any mood, any tone, any feeling. Writing sentences is a bottomless project, and in some ways I'm glad I don't have a clear answer for you. It's my bafflement and

respect for the mystery and flexibility of sentences that keeps me returning to them over and over.

q: You directed the M.F.A. program at Columbia. What advice would you give a writer trying to decide whether or not to apply to one?

a: The best way to determine whether or not to apply to an M.F.A. program is to understand what conditions best suit, and enable, your work. Some writers thrive in a community, others prefer to keep their own counsel in solitude. It's about knowing what you need to get your work done. That should always come first. Some programs, too, essentially offer a workshop, and ask little of students beyond that, leaving them lots of time to write and make their own way. Other programs put a lot of effort into the supplementary courses, the seminars. At Columbia we work hard to provide seminars that examine craft. We want our students to read seriously, and to begin to understand the technical side of literary composition. But that's not for everyone. Prospective students should do their research, talk to faculty members, and be clear about what they want.

Ben Marcus has published fiction in Harper's, The New Yorker, Conjunctions, Tin House, *and* The Paris Review. *His novels include* The Flame Alphabet.

carole maso

q: Your work is often described as "experimental." What does this term mean to you, and how useful is it?

a: When I think of experiments, I think of a laboratory and a blue flame, and applying a line of questions, ideas, hunches—making imaginative lateral associations, seeking alternatives, thinking with great depth and breadth and also with deep intuition. I think of flexibility, openness, room for accident, indeterminacy. I think of an engrossing and exhilarating investigation, exciting, complex, unpredictable, allowing for beauty of the real, and the beauty of the imagined and of chance, the result unknown. All of this appeals to me greatly.

q: There is such elegance, power and intelligence in your sentences. What do you think a well-written sentence can accomplish that no other form of expression can?

a: I think a sentence can if allowed carry emotional and intellectual states as they flee, as they come and go, an escaping essence difficult to hold in other ways. In this way I think the sentence can work as a phrase of music does, sounding something large and elusive in us. Alternatively it can provide sometimes a stability, an essence, a "moment of being." Unlike music the sentence also of course carries language with all its potential for meaning making and memory traces and association with it as well.

I probably love the accretion of sentences most—those patterns, that shimmer, that resonance.

q: What advice would you give a beginning writer about the importance of taking risks in their writing?

a: Risk keeps a writing project and also the writer vulnerable, open, off-guard, constantly changing, new, intoxicated, deeply immersed, in the midst of great adventure and also a great mystery. Writing then becomes a window into things otherwise off-limits: ultimate freedom and ultimate possibility. Who could resist this?

Carole Maso is the author of 10 books. Her latest is Mother & Child.

melanie rae thon

q: What does a finely-crafted sentence do that no other form of expression can?

a: Seventeen weeks in the womb, and now your ears are open, ready to receive, exquisitely developed. You live in a waterworld, immersed in vibration and sound: the unceasing whoosh of blood through the uterine artery, your mother's heart and breath, the surprising syncopation of your own glorious heartbeat. You know the exaltation and pitch of voice: anger, fear, love, sorrow. Language to you is a polyphonic murmuration: when your father and mother walk through the park in early morning, you hear the sad, sweet burblings of doves, the roar of a train, the whoops of children.

You care nothing for sense and signification: everything you love is music.

Twenty years later you think you want to be a writer and teachers tell you it's meaning that matters, the perfect words, the perfect order, and yes, of course it's true, but as you lie in bed listening to your heart and breath, besieged by the songs of tree frogs and crickets, lulled by a rush of cars so far away they could be a river, you realize that what you want to write is a fugue, a sonata, a symphony.

We speak not only mind to mind, but body to body. Until each sentence sings, until your paragraphs pulse and reverberate, your beautiful thoughts are incomplete, your holy work unfinished.

I read each sentence aloud—20, 30, 100 times—seeking not only sense, but tone and timbre and rhythm, hoping that through the fusion of meaning and music my words can touch anyone, fetus or mother.

Melanie Rae Thon's most recent books are the novel The Voice of the River *and* In This Light: New and Selected Stories.

fourteen

endings

Creative-writing textbooks are quicker to talk about beginnings than endings. One reason may be that endings are more difficult to discuss, classify, and disambiguate effectively than beginnings, particularly at this point in narrativity's history. Yet endings are of course every bit as important as beginnings, if not more so, since they afford the reader her or his last emotions and impressions of the text at hand.

One final visit to Freytag's Pyramid for an obvious observation: conventional narrativity aspires to a relatively clear sense of closure, completion, resolution of conflict that will leave the reader feeling satisfied, leave her or him feeling as if he or she has been on a full-fledged journey, dream, thrill from which she or he has returned. By way of example, recall Shakespearean comedy and romance, or the happily-ever-after clause in many late-nineteenth- and twentieth-century versions of fairy tales, or how Odysseus returns home and reestablishes order in the final scenes of *The Odyssey*, or this last line from Jane Austen's *Emma:* "But, in spite of these deficiencies, the wishes, the hopes, the confidence, the predictions of the small band of true friends who witnessed the ceremony, were fully answered in the perfect happiness of the union." Needless to say, this isn't to suggest such endings can't be tainted by irony, leave the reader hovering a little, but, the argument goes, it should never leave the reader wholly befuddled.

In many ways, however, the history of the last several hundred years has marked the movement away from such more or less closed endings, except in the most cookie-cutter varieties of narrativity (Harlequin romance, pulp science fiction, potboiler porn, etc.) toward more or less open ones in response to the increasing perception that closed endings feel false, faked, divorced from how our lives feel. From Joris-Karl Huysmans' *Against Nature* to John Updike's *Rabbit,*

Run, Henrik Ibsen's play *A Doll's House* to William Gibson's cyberpunk classic *Neuromancer*, one discovers an increasing number of texts at the finish of which characters have just begun to see their worlds differently, have only questionably started to change. Some mysteries and complications may be wrapped up, but others have only commenced.

There are several commonly used methods for bringing conventional narrative to a comparatively comfortable terminus. You can, for instance, create a parallel between your narrative's alpha and omega, returning in your final lines to a powerful opening image or phrase transformed. A narrator or character may make what amounts to a thematic summary statement (Nick Carraway in F. Scott Fitzgerald's *The Great Gatsby*: "So we beat on, boats against the current, borne back ceaselessly into the past."), or characters may conclude by speaking thematically resonant lines of dialogue ("Oh, Jake," the heroine of Ernest Hemingway's *The Sun Also Rises*, says to the protagonist at the novel's conclusion, "we could have had such a damned good time together," to which Jake responds: "Yes…Isn't it pretty to think so?"). The narrator can end with a description of setting whose rhythm and content generate a sense of completion (Kate Chopin in *The Awakening*: "There was the hum of bees, and the musky odor of pinks filled the air."), or with a symbolic description of setting that accomplishes the same (Joseph Conrad in *Heart of Darkness*: "The offing was barred by a black bank of clouds, and the tranquil waterway leading to the uttermost ends of the earth flowed somber under an overcast sky—seemed to lead into the heart of an immense darkness.").

Yet, to paraphrase Roland Barthes' line quoted earlier, for many in this age of uncertainty such endings provide far too many answers and far too few questions. They seem too eschatologically pat, disconcertingly fabricated, even existentially disingenuous and out of step with how the stories we continually construct and reconstruct named our lives feel.

If that is the case, is it conceivable to re-realize the idea of endings—not simply along the binary axis of resolution/irresolution, but rather as something else altogether? In *Blood and Guts in High School*, Kathy Acker's protagonist dies, as might the heroine of any nineteenth-century realist novel, after a series of psychological and physical traumas. Yet the novel, an amalgam of polyphonic structures, doesn't stop there, where one might think it should. Rather, what follows are 25 pages of hybrid diffusion that leave behind the protagonist's body and voice for perplexing and contradictory drawings, definitions, dream maps, an arcane private mythology inspired by eastern and other alternative philosophies, a smattering of punk poetry, and a confrontation with Catullus beyond the grave. A radical heterotopia emerges that adds up to a Bataillean assertion against rational thought, the obscenity of understanding in the face of physical and psychological trauma, an exploded zone where annihilation and liberation are conjoined.

Mark Z. Danielewski's *House of Leaves*, a multiple narrative about a house larger on the inside than outside and a monograph by a blind man about a film that apparently doesn't exist, "ends" in a similar manner in that it doesn't so much resolve or unresolve itself as scatter into—among other things—appendixes made up of myriad letters, photographs, poems, scraps of paper, collages, notes, quotes, and clues often at variance with the bod(ies) of the text; a frequently inaccurate index listing both instances of inconsequential words ("and," "yet," "the"), as well as precisely 100 entries for words with the notation "DNE," an abbreviation from calculus for undefined limit values or non-real function solutions that is short for "Does Not Exist"; and a page invoking Yggdrasill, the tree in Norse mythology around which nine worlds exist, and an early Linux distribution, both of which suggest structures of networking rather than linearity, associative and connotative rather than denotative imaginations.

After the stunning comma-spliced cascade of *The Unnamable*'s nine-page-long final ~~sentence~~, in many ways the epistemologically and ontologically indeterminate companion, the stuttering and pallid postmodern pal, of Joyce/Molly's confident modernist linguistic rush at the conclusion of *Ulysses*, we arrive at…what? We might be tempted to contend the last 11 words ("you must go on, I can't go on, I'll go on") signify a triumph over existential adversity, an assertion of the human spirit against umber odds (as the Nobel committee must have done). We would be wrong. We arrive, rather, at a moment of gray unknowability, an act of grammatical erasure. The antimatter of *I can't go on* cancels out the matter of *I'll go on*, and vice versa, so that we sense the real last line of this un-novel isn't composed of language at all, but instead of the white space washing down the remainder of the page, suggesting the absence both self and text have become.

Who is the *you* in those last words? The *I*? Molloy, an earlier figure in Beckett's trilogy, eons later? Some science-fictional semi-being being dreamed by another? Certainly a disembodied subject position, uncertainly human, pulsing between thereness and not-thereness, floating in the falter between penultimate clause and ultimate, immobile mind and its dream of a body that can move, self and other, speech and silence—an ellipse of uncertainty, a space of unfurling consciousness without steady temporality, geography, identity. In what sense can you/I/he/it go on or not go on, your/my/his/its universe having been unwritten around you/me/him/it? We might be tempted to contend by way of expression and imagination. We would be wrong again. In *The Unnamable,* as Beckett once remarked, "there's complete disintegration. No 'I,' no 'have,' no 'being.' No nominative, no accusative, no verb. There is no way to go on." This is narrative arriving at narrativity's limit. More than half a century after the fact, it continues to challenge each of us innovative writers to cross over and discover what lies on the other side.

One mode that takes up that challenge is hypertext writing, a non-linear computer-based mode of composition that came to the literary foreground in 1987 with the appearance of Michael Joyce's *Afternoon: A Story.* Clearly, though, it had a number of important antecedents reaching back several thousand years. There is, for instance, the Bible, a hypertext the reader can enter and begin reading at any point made up of a patchwork of conflicting voices and perspectives. With the rise of the scholarly footnote in the late seventeenth- and eighteenth centuries, much writing—notably that in an academic vein—became hypertextual in nature, with the reader's eye urged to drop down to the bottom of the page to confirm a quote's or a fact's authority, then to jump back up to the main body of the text.

More recently, presidential science advisor Vannevar Bush published an article in *The Atlantic Monthly* in 1945 called "As We May Think," where he imagined a futuristic hyperlinked data-retrieval device that mimicked the associational rather than logical thought patterns of the human mind. In the sixties, Ted Nelson both coined the terms "hypertext" and "hypermedia" and developed a model for creating and using linked content. In 1987, Apple released Hypercard for the Macintosh while Jay David Bolter and Michael Joyce released StorySpace, the first software programs for creating, editing, and reading hypertext writing. Three years later, Tim Berners-Lee launched the first web server and browser. Thereby the infinite hypertext known as the World Wide Web was born.

Hypertext (the linking of textual nodes called *lexia*) and hypermedia (lexia embedded with images, video, sound, etc.) can and often do do away completely with stable narrativity. In its place, the reader uses a computer to investigate a labyrinth of data in an interactive way, literally developing his or her own version of the text at hand, which may include contradicting plot elements, a multi-media dimension, and opportunities for the reader to contribute character names, descriptions, and shards of action. After each reading experience, the reader can often choose to save or abandon the forking paths he or she has just chosen to follow.

In such a possibility space, ending no longer refers to narrative resolution or irresolution. Instead, in a very real sense it simply refers to the moment the reader chooses to stop reading (if "reading" is the right word here) and exit the text. Consequently, we discover a kind of writing that proposes, as George P. Landow claims in *Hypertext: The Convergence of Contemporary Critical Theory and Technology*, that "we must abandon conceptual systems founded upon ideas of center, margin, hierarchy, and linearity and replace them with ones of multilinearity, nodes, links, and networks"—which is to say that hypertext in particular and hypermedia in general don't merely remind one of poststructuralist theory, as many innovative print texts do, but actually perform it.

exercises

1. Choose a flash fiction or poem you have written for one of the exercises in this book and rewrite/polish the ending by doing one of the following: a) creating a parallel between your narrative's beginning and conclusion, returning in your final lines to a powerful opening image or phrase transformed; b) having your narrator or character make what amounts to a thematic summary statement, or having your characters conclude by speaking thematically resonant lines of dialogue; c) having your narrator finish with a description of setting whose rhythm and content generate a sense of completion, or with a symbolic description of setting that accomplishes the same.

2. Choose a flash fiction or poem you have written for one of the exercises in this book that has either a closed ending or a mildly unresolved one and rewrite it with the aim

of re-realizing the very idea of "ending" in light of the above chapter. You may want to think about an ending in which (as in Beckett's case) language unravels, or (as in Acker's and Danielewski's) textuality itself scatters. Or you may want to travel in a completely different direction.

3. Google one of the free, easy-to-use web-page editing tools, choose a flash fiction or poem you have already written for one of the exercises in this book (shorter is probably better here), and reformat it as either a hypertextual or hypermedial composition. If you're feeling a little chary about engaging with that level of technology, a useful way to begin experimenting with hypertextual and/or hypermedial forms is to recast your flash fiction or poem as a PowerPoint presentation that takes full advantage of that easy application's potential. If you haven't worked with digital media before, don't be put off. Remain curious. Remain playful. Don't read directions or depend on the Help menu.

interviews

joseph cardinale

q: Every piece that constitutes *The Size of the Universe* ends beautifully, fully, richly, mysteriously. Can you talk a little about your sense of endings in narrative—what they are, how they should work?

> **a:** First, an ending should offer *closure*. That's probably the more conventional understanding of plot: a story sets up a series of problems and the problems are resolved in the conclusion. Questions are answered. Realizations reached. Something changes—and the character moves on armed with insight gleaned from experience. In the absence of this kind of closure, the reader tends to feel cheated. And that feeling is understandable, since our thirst for solutions to problems—for progress, for clarity—is perhaps a hardwired part of what makes us human. But the contrary argument is that far from providing closure and clarity, an ending should *complicate* whatever came before it. Instead of getting resolved, the questions set up in the narrative should multiply, the problems should deepen. The illusion of linear progress achieved through insight should be denied. Nothing changes: if anything, the character moves backward. This view perhaps aligns more neatly with the agendas of formally innovative narrative, where part of the imperative is to work against expectations and hence map out new paths and planes of understanding. Anyway: These two takes seem mutually exclusive, but I'd say that the best endings simultaneously offer *both* closure and complication. Closure complicates, and complication amounts to closure. As in The Book of Job, the answers mystify us far more than the original questions did.

q: How did you go about arriving at the endings in *The Size of the Universe*?

a: I think of stories more in terms of concepts than characters. A story sets up a patterned sequence of themes and images. In the end of each, I tried to call these themes and images back to the consciousness of the narrator and then reassemble them into a new pattern. Once I recognized the system of themes and images I was working with, the content of the endings fell into place naturally. Then I just needed to do the hard work of making the language rise to the occasion and lend import to the moment. For example, a dominant theme in all six of the stories in *The Size of the Universe* is the mind-body problem; it dictated the basic dramatic arc of the final paragraphs of each piece. Each story terminates in a moment of sort of transcendent stasis: the narrator's body reaches a still point, and his mind departs somehow—if only temporarily, through an extension of thought—from his flesh, entering a new ontological plane. So in a thematic sense, the ending offers a tentative resolution to the mind-body problem. It closes out the action. It's a kind of epiphanic revelation. But the complicating point is that this epiphany initiates the character into a deeper, richer, truer mystery. In the end he's transcendentally lost. He knows that he knows nothing, which is the same as knowing something. And the aim is to make the narrator and the reader disappear together inside that cloud of unknowing, so that the blank space that follows the final sentence becomes part of the plot. You're not there anymore—and neither is the narrator.

q: How did you conceptualize and go about deploying point of view?

a: All six pieces are narrated from the first person point of view. And the narrator grows progressively older in each, from a child in the first to an old man in the last. I wanted to invite the reader to think that the same person is narrating each story, but I also wanted to undercut this interpretation and leave the question of the narrator's identity unresolved. So the ambiguity framed by the point of view should reinforce the core thematic questions that preoccupy the narrator: How do I distinguish the self from its surroundings? Is the self a stable entity or a constantly changing one? Am I the same person now as I was an instant ago? Ideally, the reader asks another form of these questions: A left-brained reading sees a series of separate stories and characters, whereas a right-brained reading sees through the apparent divisions and finds everything taking place inside a single dreaming consciousness. That's the hope, anyway. In order to accommodate and complicate this ambiguity, I basically had to leave out a lot of the sorts of details that classically go into crafting rounded characters. I never give the narrator a name, for example, except in the first piece. I never describe what any of the characters look like, because I really don't want readers to mentally picture them—at least not clearly. I want the narrator to seem distant, an abstracted figure seen through a glass darkly, as we see ourselves. To that end, too, I avoided references to ethnicity or location or current events. I avoided exposition and back-story, except when memories occurred organically in the acting consciousness of the narrator. And in general I tried to use language that struck a poetic and mythic chord.

q: What often-overlooked book should every author interested in innovative writing read?

a: I don't know if it qualifies as overlooked, but I'd suggest Tolstoy's *What is Art?*, because it mounts a pretty refined and provocative attack on art forms that are usually classified as innovative. Tolstoy sees so-called "difficult" art—the kinds of artworks associated with formalism and aestheticism, and later with the high modernist tradition—as decadent, indulgent, immoral, and counterfeit. His basic argument is that real art is by definition universally accessible and pleases everyone. Clarity is good; obscurity is bad. A contingent point is that the truly great art must spread feelings of spiritual union and universal brotherhood to its audience. In this sense, he says great art is inherently religious. It's easy to pick apart the planks of this argument, but I think anyone who wants to make innovative art should at least grasp and grapple with its foundations and implications. And I agree with the assertion that great art provokes a kind of spiritual union between artist and audience, though I'd define the terms differently enough to accommodate more difficult-seeming artworks. I think innovative writing squares more with mystical takes on religious truth. It uses language to frustrate the human longing to arrive at fixed meanings and stable truths. In the end, of course, that feeling of frustration is precisely what unifies us.

A graduate of the University of Massachusetts-Amherst M.F.A. program, Joseph Cardinale lives in Honolulu.

norman lock

q: How do you determine whether a narrative will become a short prose piece, a prose poem, a screenplay, a novel, or a stage play?

> **a:** My greatest pleasure has been in sentence-making, and it is for the sentence I wait to begin writing. It will come, seemingly, of its own accord; I am helpless to begin until it does, and cannot will it into existence. And it is this first sentence that exposes the idea for a story and at the same time invokes its form—exposes in the way that an instant of light imprints the photographic negative with what one saw, if at all, only imperfectly. I suspect that what the sentence exposes—and insists upon—is something known by me only unconsciously…an idea which has already received its form. Mysterious? Yes. How could it be otherwise?

q: Your collection *Grim Tales* takes the fairy tale genre into interesting and provocative territory. What does working within (or even against) the constraints or expectations of a specific genre afford you as a writer?

> **a:** Always, I am a writer who rubs up against a genre or form. Fairy tale, travel writing, scholarly work or encyclopedia entry, a film or novel impressed upon the popular mind—I find in the shape or substance of what already exists something to make my own. My habit of appropriating what is past proceeds not from any deliberate postmodernist strategy (my work does not comment favorably or ironically on its sources), but from my love of ideas and of play and of the sound and palpable quality of certain sentences as they were formulated during the history of literature. Were I a realist, none of this would be possible, but for a fantasist everything is possible.

q: How do you know when something you are writing is finished? And when you do, what's the very first thing you do with it?

a: Arriving at the end of a writing is as mysterious to me as its beginning. I know when I have written the last sentence, even in those rare instances when the text is still shaping itself far from its inevitable end, which I seldom see clearly until it surprises me. The last sentence sounds a finale, a doom expressive of an ending; it is an almost musical restatement of themes (of which I may have been unaware at the outset). Sentence-making at an end, there comes a terrible release, which brings resolution and also sadness. I set the manuscript aside until my ardor and my anxiety lessen, and, reading it, I can forget a little the struggle and the self-satisfaction and see clearly what I have made.

Norman Lock's work includes novels, short-fiction collections, poetry, stage, radio, and screen plays. He received the Aga Kahn Prize from The Paris Review *and an N.E.A. fellowship.*

fifteen

materiality & immateriality: one

Books have been disparate things at disparate times in disparate places. Five thousand years ago, baked clay tablets in Mesopotamia recorded deeds to land and other business records. Egyptians, Chinese, Greeks, and Romans pasted together sheets made from the inner bark of the papyrus plant into strips sometimes 144 feet long. Around 300 A. D., the codex (composed of several pieces of vellum, or treated lambskin) was folded into a section called a gathering, which could then be sewn into something resembling our contemporary book, though hand-written, every one unlike every other.

The Chinese practiced a simple form of printing over 1000 years ago. Gutenberg developed his version in Germany during the middle of the fifteenth century. It reached England in 1476 when William Caxton set up shop at Westminster. More than 30,000 different monographs were generated within the first 50 years of those presses firing up. By the nineteenth century, printing had transformed into a mechanical trade rather than a handicraft, and by the early twentieth the book had by and large become mass-produced, conceivably hundreds of thousands of copies of a single one published.

Readers tend to forget or repress this history of possibilities when reading. They tend to remain (often willfully) unmindful about partaking in an ever-changing form, and therefore tend to forget the potential immanent within that form. The emergence of hypertext, hypermedia, and other electronic methods of writing and reading (and, with the appearance of the word processor in the eighties, one could argue that virtually all contemporary writing and reading is in essence electronic) is changing all that, defamiliarizing reading and writing practices to the extent that we may re-see and re-think them, reminding us that *how* a text presents itself helps dictate what the text can do and how we might go about reading it.

"Lulled into somnolence by five hundred years of print," N. Katherine Hayles urges in "Print is Flat, Code is Deep," "literary analysis should awaken to the importance of media-specific analysis, a mode of critical attention which recognizes that all texts are instantiated and that the nature of the medium in which they are instantiated matters." She goes on to argue critics should learn to become more attuned to the materiality of the medium under investigation, which is to say a story isn't merely a story isn't merely a story. Rather, the "same" story remediated through film is intrinsically different from that story remediated through conventionally printed books is intrinsically different from that story remediated through hypermedia.

"Materiality," Hayles writes, "is reconceptualized as the interplay between a text's physical characteristics and its signifying strategies, a move that entwines instantiation and signification at the outset. This definition opens the possibility of considering texts as embodied entities while still maintaining a central focus on interpretation. It makes materiality an emergent property, so that it cannot be specified in advance, as if it were a pre-given entity. Rather, materiality is open to debate and interpretation, ensuring that discussions about the text's 'meaning' will also take into account its physical specificity as well."

If Hayles wants to emphasize Media Specific Analysis (MSA), this book wants to emphasize Media Specific Generation (MSG)—the idea that when writing you should always-already be cognizant, not only of the thematics of the text you are working on, and, as it were, the internal components of its narrativity (character, language, plot, etc.), but also of the material embodiment those components take, and, perhaps more important, the material embodiment those components *can* take.

In other words, the way texts *matter* matters. One of the many ways Ronald Sukenick accomplished awareness of this fact in his own fiction was by testing the limits of what he termed "the technological reality of the page" and the fundamental assumption in Western writing that words must constantly march from upper left to lower right in tidy and syntactically coherent paragraphs. Seven of the most interesting pages in his project are those in his novel *98.6.* They are primarily constructed out of collaged excerpts pirated from other sources and repurposed by Sukenick into a dissident bricolaged nexus of formalistics and politics, a disjointed documentary about the violent chaos of sixties culture.

It almost goes without saying that such experimentation with typography, layout, and white space has a long tradition—certainly one that tracks back at least as far as Guillaume Apollinaire's early twentieth-century collection of concrete poetry, *Calligrammes*, and Laurence Sterne's textually ribald eighteenth-century anti-novel, *Tristram Shandy*, although one could arguably plot a hypothetical trajectory that reaches even farther into the past to ancient Greek romances like Achilles Tatius' second-century *Leucippe and Clitophon*, which alternates stretches of prose with stretches of poetry.

In any case, one of the most dazzling examples in the second half of twentieth century is Raymond Federman's *tour de force*, *Double or Nothing*, a 259-page typographiction where each page is laid out (on a typewriter, no less, as opposed to a page-design application) differently from every other page, and where individual words thereby become physical material with which to build extraordinarily complicated and playful visual structures:

11.1

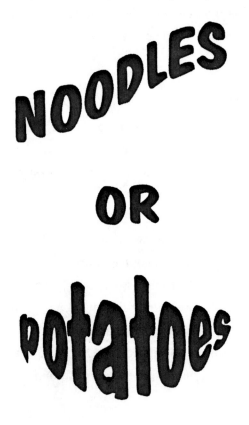

Yes but the *potatoes* the raw
potatoes on the train **remember?** what a story:
on the way to the *camps*
the *camps* X * X * X * X

A
n
d

I
f
o
l
l
o
w
e
d

Can't come into this one…Nothing before the boat…

Damn good story! Could sneak the potatoes in…next time.

m
y

The train
The rats
The old man
The farm
The camps
The potatoes… Wow!

s
h
a
d
o
w

A Time of Potatoes

Could have a whole series   like that 20 or 30 volumes
Could have a whole series   a kind of Balzacian comedy

The Vegetable Comedy

no even better than that

The Hunger Comedy

no even worse than that

The Starvation Comedy

20 or 30 volumes **in folio.**

Although Mark Z. Danielewski claims not to have been aware of *Double or Nothing* while composing *House of Leaves*, it is difficult to imagine how this could have been the case. Danielewski invests a tremendous amount of time and energy in arranging typography and other layout elements in a multitude of ways to foreground the act of reading as a physical activity. To make sense of his text, sometimes the reader must hold the book up to a mirror or rotate it in his or her hands. Sometimes the design compels her or him to experience the anxiety and/or the speed with which the characters within the text experience them, sometimes confronting him or her with a dense welter of difficult-to-navigate narraticules on some pages, thereby turning him or her into a lexical Theseus wandering the labyrinth of the novel (just as the characters wander the physical labyrinth beneath their house) in a search for meaning, and sometimes only a word or two on others, thereby necessitating her or him to flip through 20 or 30 pages in a matter of seconds.

The effect books like Federman's and Danielewski's exert on the reader is an example of what Espen Aarseth refers to as ergodic—that sort of writing which requires nontrivial effort on the reader's part to traverse the text, as opposed to conventional textuality that requires little more than predictable eye movements and page turning.

In the same vein, Anne Carson's *Nox*, an elegy for her older brother, whom she didn't know well and who died unexpectedly while on the run from the law in Europe, arrives in a box that simulates a thick book. Open it, and inside you discover, not a codex, but an accordioned series of "pages" that folds out into an arrangement that suggests an ancient scroll (Carson is, perhaps illuminatingly, a professor of classics) made up of shards of her brother's letters, old photographs, tickets, Carson's observations, Catullus' poem 101 (the one addressed to the Roman poet's dead brother, a doubling of Carson's situation), and extensive dictionary entries on all the words that compose that poem. The aggregate produces a collage about the impossibilities of aggregates, the impossibilities of understanding fully, of capturing absences in language. At times *Nox* feels less an example of what most readers consider a book than something closer to a three-dimensional work of assemblage art (more on this notion of book arts in the next chapter).

A more popular possibility space, which compounds numerous methods of representation in the same work (with a special emphasis on the visual), is graphic fiction. Avant-Pop analog of the medieval illuminated manuscript, it brings together highly skilled comic-book art with elements of the novel. Still one of the most successful instances, Dave Gibbons and Alan Moore's *Watchmen* undoes the traditional superhero comic book by introducing elements from the Balzacian Mode (fully-rounded characters with pasts, fears, and desires in an extended, complex narrative structure) while innovating the traditional comic-book form by inserting cinematic techniques (zoom, extreme close-up, montage, jump-cut), allusions to art history, and tropes from detective noir and alternative-universe SF, in addition to assorted *trompe l'oeil* devices that call attention to the materiality of the page: letters that appear to have been produced on a typewriter, pasted-in entries from other books, police reports, photographs, business cards, paper clips, and more.

Leaving the idea of the page behind completely, various explorations into new-media work (i.e., hybrid digital projects not necessarily structured by means of hypertext's and hypermedia's nonlinear linkages) have proliferated over the last 10 or 15 years. Tellingly, it is nearly impossible in a short space to give even a vague sense of the extraordinary range here, and so a few brief specimens will have to suffice. Two of the largest constructions (Richard Wagner would probably have called them *Gesamtkunstwerken,* or Total Artworks, that strive to make use of all art forms in a single space) are Steve Tomasula's *TOC* and David Clark's *88 Constellations for Wittgenstein: To Be Played with the Left Hand. TOC* is a meditation on the nature of temporality and hence on the nature of narrative itself (narrative, after all, can only exist in time). It appropriates many ingredients from video games—steampunk artwork, text elements, a musical score, film snippets, and a fairly high degree of interactivity—and mixes them with a strong component of audio storytelling in the form (among others) of a circular tale about a pregnant model deciding whether or not to take her husband, in a coma, off life support (thereby performing a remediation of the oral tradition in literature).

David Clark's *88 Constellations for Wittgenstein: To Be Played with the Left Hand*, juxtaposes (mostly audio) narraticules about the Austrian language philosopher with those about his musical brother, astronomy, architecture, movies, logical positivism, Hitler, and Charlie

Chaplin, among other topics. In part the outcome is an investigation into the Wittgensteinian problematics of language itself, and in part into the way narrativity can function as desire for patterning created anew by each reader/listener/viewer by joining the dots of a data constellation in heterogeneous ways.

Note in both Tomasula's and Clark's cases, the authors function as something akin to film directors as much as they do conventional writers, working with a team of collaborators to construct their byte buildings. It took Tomasula 10 years to bring his into being. And thereby a quick aside about collaboration: it is the basic mode of most writing, most art, although our culture usually likes to repress the fact by embracing the cliché of the lone-wolf artist. All published stories and novels are collaborative projects that involve author, editor or editors, publisher, printer, reviewers, bloggers, teachers, critics, people who set up reading series, and so on. Just putting fingertips to keyboard is to collaborate, as well, to enter an intricate conversation across history and geography with other authors. One of the most productive consequences to the act of collaboration is the generation of a piece that none of the collaborators could ever have envisioned at the starting gate. The sum of the collaborative enterprise, that is, is continuously more interesting and surprising than the parts, the process always leading a writer in unexpected directions.

Shelley Jackson re-conceptualizes the page as human flesh in *The Skin Project*, a 2095-word story published exclusively in tattoos, one word at a time, on the skin of volunteers, while Camille Utterback and Romy Achituv's *Text Rain* transforms the page into a three-dimensional room you can inhabit—i.e., an interactive installation in which participants lift and play with falling letters that appear to exist all around them. Participants stand or move in front of a large screen, on which they see a projection of themselves in black and white combined with a color animation of the alphabet tumbling through space that seems to land on their heads, arms, outstretched legs. In *The Xenotext Experiment*, Christian Bök (in collaboration with Stuart Kauffman) undertakes what he calls "a literary exercise that explores the aesthetic potential of genetics in the modern milieu"; by literalizing William S. Burroughs' assertion that language is a virus from outer space, Bök encodes a short verse into a sequence of DNA and then implants that sequence into a bacterium to observe its mutations. To put it differently, he uses a primitive bacterium as a writing machine. His wish is to rocket the organic result into outer space some day, thereby sending language back where it came from while creating an ever-changing poem that would outlive, not only the works of Homer, Shakespeare, and Joyce, but earth, the solar system, and the entire galaxy as well.

Some new-media artists are exploring the creative possibilities of the cell-phone in the wake of the publication of the first cell-phone novel (a digital work whose chapters—usually between 70-100 words long—are distributed by texting) in 2003, the same year social media and viral emails motivated the rise of the flash mob (a group of people in the tradition of performance art who assemble suddenly in a public place, execute an unusual and sometimes seemingly pointless act—a pillow fight, say, or a mass disco—for a brief time, then disperse). Some are looking into the opportunities implicit in the forms of Facebook, Twitter, and other modes of social networking, while still others are engaging with various kinds of random language generators, the notion of GPS mapping/traveling as narrativity, and the possibility of creating three-dimensional narratives that combine written text, new-media components, and live performance, or, as Nick Montfort and Scott Rettberg have done in *Implementation*, producing sheets of stickers with a different text on each that are then passed out to individuals, both personally and via post, with instructions to peel the stickers off and place them in different cities in places viewable by the public.

Experiments into materiality and immateriality like these bracket the very definition of "book" at the same time they highlight Michael Martone's sense of its present future as increasingly viral, collaborative, and ephemeral. Or, as Matthew Battles points out: the future of the "book" has already arrived, and it is "ethereal and networked" rather than "an immutable brick." While conventional writing and reading practices are conceptualized as private, individual, relatively fixed experiences, many of the new forms mentioned above indicate that writing and reading—from production through dissemination—are rapidly becoming public, collective, incrementally unfixed experiences.

The effect? Media and their methods of composition are continuing to change us almost as much as we are changing them.

exercises

1. Keeping the idea of Media Specific Generation in mind, choose a flash fiction or poem you have already written for one of the exercises in this book, and remediate it through Facebook, Twitter, a blog, or your cell phone into a new flash fiction or poem altogether, paying attention to how your words mattering matter.

2. Compose a completely new flash fiction or poem using Facebook, Twitter, a blog, or your cell phone that could only be written in one of these digital modes.

3. Create your own flash comic book (no more, say, than three pages long), collaging together appropriated images while supplying your own (or appropriated and repurposed) text. If you're particularly interested in the idea of the comic book, you may want to look first at Scott McCloud's seminal *Understanding Comics: The Invisible Art*.

4. Google one of the free, easy-to-use film editing tools, or use Apple's iMovie, and create a new-media piece lasting between one and two minutes that combines text, film, and audio. If you haven't worked in this area before, don't worry. It isn't as scary as it sounds. Sometimes the less you know about a technology, the more surprising places it will take you.

5. Using your own body or those of volunteers from your writing community, along with the idea of the flash mob or Nick Montfort and Scott Rettberg's *Implementation* as your inspiration, compose a flash fiction or poem that envisions the page as a three-dimensional, public, collaborative space.

interviews

nick montfort

q: You teach at MIT, in the Program in Writing and Humanistic Studies. Can you describe what affordances there are for writers and artists in such an interesting and unique space?

> **a:** At MIT, the fear of technology and of mathematical and scientific thinking has been removed, as if surgically, from everyone. Writers who want to use computation, conceptualist techniques, and experimental methods are free to run marathons when they would, in some other places, find it difficult to get up off of their knees.

q: In your mind, what separates writing from programming?

> **a:** Unless you're hooking up cables as they did on the ENIAC, programming is a type of writing. In this particular type of writing, the programmer produces a text that is a formal, executable set of instructions for a computer. Forgetting interpreted languages for a moment, programming is writing that compiles and runs. This sort of writing can also communicate to other people, but it usually communicates something closely related to its operational semantics, its workings as a program. That's not a very general type of writing, but it's an interesting type.

q: Your book *Twisty Little Passages* both historicizes and advocates for the evolving digital art form we've come to call Interactive Fiction, and your own work of IF, *Book & Volume*, comments on its own art form in similar ways that so-called metafictional novels did a generation ago. What does a story executed as IF accomplish that the same story executed in sentences and paragraphs might not?

a: When you create an interactive fiction, you develop a model world that someone can interactively inhabit, explore, test, and solve. The differences between interactive fiction and a story written out as paragraphs are extreme. It's almost like the difference between your friend telling you what happened yesterday when she went to an amusement park and actually going off to an amusement park. Both can be very interesting, but judging one by the standards of the other will be disappointing. If you read a transcript of someone playing IF, the repetition, false starts, and lack of compelling characters are almost sure to stand out. You might wonder why someone would bother with this sort of "reading." But for the person playing, there's the opportunity to wander around a landscape, form theories about how this unusual place works, and then try those theories out by typing in different commands to effect different actions. The results can be amusing or terrifying. And, as interactive fiction authors build out their worlds and provide us with systems more elaborate than amusement parks, the results will become increasingly profound and will work to effectively complement our traditional literary modes and genres.

Nick Montfort is president of the Electronic Literature Organization and has collaborated on and developed numerous digital literary projects.

stephanie strickland

q: In your mind, what separates a computer screen from a printed page in terms of its ability to communicate an idea or evoke a response?

a: The printed page is wholly immersive—also boringly tiring, filled with static ants, but it does tend to make more beautiful use of negative space than the screen does. Pages seem ideal for following long lines of thought (think law book or mathematical proof), yet the ability, onscreen, to return at will to any line is a strong advantage.

A screen, too, is wholly immersive—graphically arresting in a way few *printed* books are, thrillingly able to show movement. Its downside, boring flatness and presently immature conventions of screen presentation. If you drift off over a boring page, you unfortunately don't, over a screen, continuing in a zomboid manner to click through meaningless bits. A well-designed screen, however, is a wonder of evocation. A few hand passes over the *Vniverse* screen (see next question) allows one in a few seconds to gain a good idea of the entire thematic range of the piece, providing many incentives for travel. The print book "version" yields this view much more reticently.

Neither screen nor page exceeds the other in evoking a response, but a networked environment vastly exceeds a print one in terms of enabling varied responses.

q: *Vniverse* is a reading experience quite literally like no other. Can you talk a little bit about your creative process in executing it?

> **a:** *Vniverse* came from three trains of interest/obsession: waves, the strong analogy in my mind between the last Ice Age and the present Information Age, and a return to my engagement with Simone Weil about whom I had already written a book of poems.

Waves proved to be very distinct markers between page and screen. The *WaveSon. nets* section of *V: WaveSon.nets/Losing L'una* is a series of "Son.nets" which are in general not end-stopped. Though divided and numbered, they flow into one another and read as one long wave, one long poem. "The same" texts, online, lose the sense of one long flow. They bring forward the sense of interpenetration of waves—in the text dissolves—and they model the way waves slice, collide, and intersect. Poems can also ripple from triplets to quatrains and back.

Ice Age and Information Age people re-map from *scratch* (that boundless communal resource). Ice Age nomads devised/configured our familiar sky constellations as clock, calendar, and guide to tracking migrant herds. *V: Vniverse* "maps" the "sky" differently, taking up the twenty-first-century task of reconfiguring space/time.

Against received wisdom, I find Simone Weil to be a Talmudic thinker: what seems the same is never the same, beware a fused unity. I aimed to model her perceptions in the structure of the *V* project. *V: WaveSon.nets/Losing L'una* and *V: Viniverse* "share" a text but are radically different. More important, still, an emergent poem, *V*, can only appear "between" them, its dwelling not rooted, but rather routed through an experience that turns continually from one to the other.

q: What is the biggest strength of the Web as a literary form? Its biggest weakness?

a: The Web is not a literary form. It is a carrier. As a carrier it has a strong back and fast legs. It can also disappear and reappear: overall, much like Mercury and the other messenger gods.

Most importantly, for literature, it supports many born-digital hybrids. It has given rise to many network forms (blog, newsfeed, Wiki, commercial website, email…) that inflect new literary creations. It permits visual, haptic, acoustic, and textual languages to consort (not always preserving all their analog capabilities, however). A shortlist of the kind of literary forms to be found in the *Electronic Literature Collection* includes: textual instruments, interactive fictions, poetry generators, hypertexts, hacktivist rants, works of augmented reality, works for CAVE (a virtual reality environment), gesture-controlled texts, games, database non/fictions, Second Life compositions, works keyed to mapping, kinetic text effect animations, AI-based interactive drama, and works that draw on standard web servers (synonym servers, image search engines).

Stephanie Strickland's book V: WaveSon.nets/Losing L'una *was the first book of poetry to exist simultaneously in print and on the Web as one work. She serves on the Board of the Electronic Literature Organization.*

steve tomasula

q: Can you describe a little bit of the writing process for your hypermedia novel, *TOC*?

> **a:** Basically, it was like writing any other book, except other phases followed the writing: creating a storyboard to determine which parts readers would read for themselves on screen, and which parts would be read to them, i.e., presented as audio. Then I had to create a flowchart to indicate how these parts would be linked— that is, how a reader would use a mouse to navigate between the various chapters, and thinking about what the experience would be like if readers went through the book in a variety of different orders. Working with all of the other artists, designers, programmers, composers, musicians, and others who contributed work to *TOC* was all part of its creation. It was a lot like writing the script for a play, and then being heavily involved in how it would be produced, or performed, working with set designers and musicians to make its various aspects come together as a whole— which is also a lot like writing, albeit in different forms.

q: You frequently collaborate with other artists—illustrators, designers, composers, programmers—who work in different media than sentences and paragraphs. What does working with others who create in different media teach you about your own?

> **a:** I think it's heightened my awareness of how certain media do some things better than others, and some things worse than others. Every time there is a new media, it's proclaimed to be the death of an older media: photography was supposed to have killed off painting; movies were supposed to end theater; and TV movies. Now there's a lot of talk about e-readers being the end of books, but a Kindle can only replace a paper book in the way that a photograph can replace a painting. For many books, e.g. bestsellers, it probably doesn't matter whether the text is poured into a paper or electronic container. But for those novels that try to make their medium part of what's said, it makes a big

difference. So maybe that's the thing that comes out of writing for different mediums—an ability or freedom to ask if a paper or electronic form is the best for this narrative, to ask if text or image is the best way to get across the story being told. To be able to think if a poem would work better as a painting. Or maybe a graph.

q: What advice would you give a beginning writer about experimenting with form?

a: Stendhal's metaphor for the novel was a mirror traveling down the road of life, which is a great way of expressing the idea of representation of the world in a novel, the metaphor that probably best describes most traditional novels. But it's also sort of limited. Why couldn't the mirror be a kaleidoscope or Polaroid camera instead? Why a road? I mean, the thing that makes writing as an art form different from other kinds of writing is that in art how something is said is as important as what's said, or part of what's said, or even the thing that's being said. But if you hold this up to a mirror, what's said also shapes how it's said; so I guess for me a first step would be to not feel bound to the idea of Stendhal's mirror or any other single way to write; nor would it be a matter of setting out to try something new either, though. Rather, it's more like thinking about what's being said, and how the form—be it a grocery list or a LANGUAGE poem—is part of the message, and then feeling free to draw on the whole history of writing—and not just the conventions we are used to—in ways that make sense for the story, even if it means stretching them, or putting them together in ways that they are not normally found. Really, it's using all the keys on the saxophone, not just some of them.

Steve Tomasula is the author of the novels VAS: An Opera in Flatland, The Book of Portraiture, IN & OZ, *and* TOC: A New-Media Novel, *which won the eLit Award's Gold Medal for Best Book of 2010.*

sixteen

materiality & immateriality: two

One response to the disembodiment of textuality evinced by new-media artists is the book arts "movement"—with "movement" here used in its weakest sense. Usually published in small editions, or as one-of-a-kind objects known as "uniques," artists' books employ a wide range of forms, from scrolls and fold-outs to loose items contained in a box and beyond. Although precedents exist as early as the medieval period (e.g., the illuminated manuscript), many critics cite William Blake and his wife Catherine as the parents of the contemporary artist's book. In *Songs of Innocence and Experience*, for instance, the couple merged handwritten texts with illustrations, then printed, colored, bound, self-published, and distributed them.

Innovative artists' books have flourished particularly since the late twentieth century. Their existence evinces a cherishing—some might even argue a fetishization—of the book's materiality (its design, its layout, even its texture and smell), along with an inquiry into its boundaries. In the universe of innovative artists' books, you are as likely to find a wooden doll with a modestly handcrafted booklet inserted into a slot in its tummy, or text printed on a slice of bread tucked into a plastic baggie, as you are a beautifully realized edition printed on a letter press, boasting handmade paper and gorgeously stitched binding.

Again, the field is too wide, too multifarious, to give anything like an overview, but for the purposes of our discussion a few emblematic examples. In *Borges and I*, Heather Weston takes Jorge Luis Borges' flash critifiction about multiple identities and prints it as black text offset on black paper. By employing blind embossing, or raised letters, Weston uses her art book's materiality to allude both to the problematics of personality doubling and to the technique of Braille—the latter of which itself alludes to the blindness that overtook Borges later in life and prevented him from writing and reading. Weston's project's physical being, then, is shaped by a deep interaction with its thematics, rather than simply serving, as most books produced by corporate publishers do, as a relatively unadorned data delivery system.

Clarissa Sligh appropriates and manipulates texts in a much different way and for much different reasons than Weston. She re-writes and re-rights power relations in *Reading Dick and Jane with Me*, taking the textbooks she encountered in elementary school—known as The Dick and Jane Readers—and interrupting the originals by inserting images and scribbled comments that throw the primary book's assumptions about race and class into question. The original Dick and Jane Readers represented white, middle-class, suburban families as the norm in the fifties. Sligh, an African American growing up in Arlington, Virginia, had dramatically contrasting experiences that she captures through her textual in(ter)ventions.

Jen Bervin also deploys a kind of interruption in *The Desert*: she authors a poem by sewing row by row, line by line, across 130 pages of John Van Dyke's naturalist classic, *The Desert: Further Studies in Natural Appearances*, about his three-year expedition into the wilderness—with particular emphasis on the Red Rock Country of the Colorado Plateau—beginning in the summer of 1898. Van Dyke addresses the aesthetic qualities of what strikes many as a radically foreign, desolate landscape. Bervin creates an edition of 40 of her version in which she used a pale blue zigzag machine-sewn stitching to erase Van Dyke's original. Bervin: "The book is experienced both as a poem in which a reader must seek out the words which often hide, and when one turns the page, as a kind of drawing where the acts of poem-making leave their thready record." Because of the materiality of that thready record, a sense of readerly touch becomes as important to understanding Bervin's undertaking as does readerly sight.

Surplus Value Books #13—Deluxe Edition, created by Rick Moody in collaboration with Daniel E. Kelm and Chip Schilling, is concretized as a mental patient's box of personal possessions wrapped inside a straightjacket. The text is formatted as a publisher's galley proof with marginalia supplied (and in some cases whited-out) by Moody. Upon removing the galley from the box, the reader discovers a removable panel resembling a hospital release checklist. Holes cut into this panel reveal the mental patient's possessions contained below, including a

Stormtrooper action figure from the *Star Wars* movie, two rubber stamps, a baseball card, a partially smoked cigar in a glass container, and a dozen scrabble tiles, among other articles. Character becomes the objects the patient collected. "Book" becomes sculpture.

In her memoir, *The Chronology of Water*, Lidia Yuknavitch encourages us all to "make up stories until you can find one you can live with." Hypertext, hypermedia, new-media writing, and artists' books encourage us by their very presence to go one step farther by making up textual architectures until you can find one your writing can live within.

exercises

1. Does the library at the university nearest you have a special collections and/or rare books department? If so, spend an hour there exploring, then write a paragraph on each of your three favorite finds—not in terms of content, but materiality and form.

2. Choose a flash fiction or poem you have already written for one of the exercises in this book and rethink it as an artist's book, or perhaps artist's pamphlet, paying particular attention to the wedding of materiality and thematics, and to reconceptualizing what we think of when we think of the word "book."

3. Imagine a container, shape, or material you would like to work with, and compose a flash fiction or poem that can only exist within it. To put it differently, think of a three-dimensional architecture first, and then generate a content that fits it—and only it.

4. Many community colleges, colleges, universities, libraries, and other local organizations offer two-or-three-day mini-courses on the manifold aspects of book arts. Enroll in one of these to begin to become acquainted with the fundamentals of printmaking, typesetting, bookbinding, and so on, and to become more conscious about what a "book" is and can be.

interviews

shelley jackson

q: You move fluidly among writing spaces—print, digital, performance, even flesh in *The Skin Project*. How do you go about discovering/choosing a means to instantiate a particular idea for a narrative?

a: For me, "writing" includes anything that shapes a reader's experience, so what kind of body my words should take on is not a secondary question. It rarely happens that I get an idea for a story that isn't at least partly an idea about what *shape* that story should take. Nor that I get an idea about a shape, without an inkling about the story that would take that shape. While I write, both the story and its shape become clearer, and begin demanding certain things of each other—form suggests content and vice versa. Say I want to write about the Gowanus, a polluted estuary in my neighborhood. The way its flow changes direction with the tides makes me think about how most stories flow one way only, and wonder how I'd write one that could be read in two directions. I might consider a palindrome, then settle on a two-part story, half of which flows inward (whatever that might mean in narrative terms) and half outward. That formal idea feeds back into my story idea, suggesting two threads that treat the same themes from two points of view: maybe a brother's and sister's? This might make me wonder whether there's something about the mixture of fondness and disgust I feel toward the Gowanus that reminds me of family, and then what it would mean to write a polluted *story*—would it include indigestible pieces of other texts, or perhaps poems? I'd also ask myself whether a book (dry and rectilinear) was really the right place for such a gooey text? Maybe I'd publish it at intervals along the estuary itself (graffiti?

posters? brass plaques?), so that the smells and colors and the reflections of light on water get mixed into the reading experience. This too would feed back into the story, prompting me to weave in reflections on the specific setting of each segment: this tangle of barbed wire, this drainage pipe, this sunken shopping cart…

q: How does being slightly synesthetic inform your work?

a: The word is a physical object to me; I sense its weight, texture, color, shape, and even what it's made of—wood, steel wool, felt. So writing is at least part sculpture, fitting objects together in pleasing ways. This has the strongest possible influence on my prose; if I can't say what I want to say in words that feel good together, I'll just say something else. So I am at least as often led to an idea by words as I am led to words by an idea. It also grounds my interest in form: if words are already forms, then how can formal questions be considered secondary? A body of work really is a body, for me. There is a direct, physical relationship, not just an analogy, between words and things—hence all the embodied texts and inscribed bodies that inhabit my work.

q: The notion of the "innovative" is a fraught creative space. How would you go about defining it? Or, to put it somewhat differently, what's innovative about the innovative, and to what purpose?

a: The purpose of the innovative is, I think, to wake us up. We are not quite alive, most of the time; we occupy a sort of cartoon version of our lives, its lines made smooth by repetition. Writing can open the seams in that world, reintroduce us to the real lives that we have forgotten. Maybe all good writing is innovative in some sense, in that it shows or tells or makes you feel something you never felt before—something for which you have no cartoon ready. The ways in which the word can wake you up are many. Sometimes it's a delicate matter, an adjective that ever-so-slightly bristles against its noun. An innovative *reader* can find the strangeness in even the most conventional work, because language is slippery, it gets away from us. But traditional form arrests this slippage; I look for writing in which I can really lose my way, see my compass needle spin.

q: Do you see a relationship between gender and innovative aesthetics? Does innovative narrativity engage with gender differently than other forms of narrativity?

a: I don't believe that one gender is intrinsically, "naturally" more innovative than another. But I do see a strong correlation between the negative qualities often attributed to innovative literature by its critics and stereotypes of the feminine: obscurity, irrationality, excess, self-indulgence, pointlessness, a frivolous preference for style over content, etc. Furthermore, there are eerie echoes between the advice given to young writers to cut, purge, and starve their prose of its excesses in order to achieve what is often tellingly called a "lean" and "muscular" style and the war that adolescent girls are encouraged to wage on their bodies. There is something vicious, visceral in the critical response to experimentation that supports my intuition that it challenges something deeper than literary convention.

q: What are two or three of the most interesting/fun/productive/challenging writing exercises you offer your students?

a: My favorite exercise to assign students is one I use in my own work: take a single sheet of the newspaper and write something using only words you find there. It is up to you to decide whether to recycle entire phrases or only individual words, whether to "correct" the grammar, etc. Another one I like: write your autobiography, using one word for your first year, two words for your second year, and so on—e.g.:

What?

A sister!

I become serious.

I can't go naked?

Shelley Jackson is author, among others, of the novel Half Life, *the short-story collection* The Melancholy of Anatomy, *and the new-media projects* Patchwork Girl *and* The Doll Games.

jeffrey deshell

q: What is the one novel that most exemplifies what a novel *could* be instead of what it *should* be?

> **a:** I'm reminded of Robert Bresson's quote, "Failure of Cinema. Ludicrous disproportion between immense possibilities and result." Certainly the same with fiction. But if I had to pick one novel of possibilities, I'd pick Proust's *In Search of Lost Time*, even in translation. It's that obsessive attempt to get at something, through (in all senses of the word) language, accompanied by a tremendous, and here I'm a little hesitant, love, that opens the reader to infinite possibilities of narrative, perception, and being in the world. It's the novel I think of when I think of the breathtaking enchantment that art can produce.

q: We live in an era of incredible electronic mediation and digital production, where the world's largest bookstore is Amazon.com and the number of ebooks sold is surpassing the number of printed ones sold. What do you feel is still compelling about physical books that will ensure their survival in our virtual age?

> **a:** I think for those of us who believe that language is *not* one category or example of information among others, the physical book will survive. For those who think that language is simply another set of 1 and 0's to be distributed and sold like any other set, the physical book is an arcane relic, an unnecessary, inefficient, and ultimately obsolete

delivery system. The physical book allows me to best experience and activate the language in front of me with all of its inherent play, movement, allusions, references, emotions, ideas, intuitions, connotations, denotations, imaginations, etc., etc., etc. Reading on screen, I believe, is essentially distracted: one is always multi-tasking (or wanting to), and that inhibits the play of language to fully develop. And with hypertext, the screen fills in the images, play, movement etc., for the reader, and who needs that?

q: What do you find most fulfilling about being a writer? Most frustrating?

a: I don't think about writing and "being a writer" in these terms. I think that the "being" of "being a writer" is extremely unstable and problematic; it's precisely "being" that the act of writing puts into question.

Jeffrey DeShell is the author of five novels and a book of criticism. He teaches at the University of Colorado at Boulder.

lidia yuknavitch

q: There are lots and lots of ways to produce art now in the digital age. Tell us why words and sentences and paragraphs are the primary ways you choose to do it.

a: There have always been new mediums and media, but language acquisition, so far as I know, remains one of the most primal and yet intensely intellectual experiences humans have. Language makes us in its own image—though we walk around thinking we control that. We "use" or "make use" of an arbitrary sign system to order and understand and express experience. Whenever I feel despair about how language is being "used" or not used out there I simply read Gertrude Stein over again, and then I feel better. I feel like I am back in the mighty ocean of wordness. So while I admire the new media, and I even make use of them myself at times, I remain hopelessly in love with words. Their small backs. Their tender enormity.

q: You wrote two separate books—a novel and a memoir—pretty much on top of each other and ended up selling both to the same publisher, Hawthorne Books. How did you keep those projects separate as you composed them, and how important is a grand organizing scheme to how you work?

a: I never keep projects separate as I compose them. I can't. I'm a Gemini. It's not quite multitasking; it's more like de-medicalized schizophrenia. My brain moves in more than one direction at all times. In my personal life that has been a great difficulty—achieving normalcy and passing in the socius and in relationships. But in writing and art there are vast and endless territories I can enter. For example, I write a lot about the white like it's a place you can travel to or from. The white of the page or canvas. I wrote my dissertation on top of my first book of short stories. I'm nearly always working *at least* two large projects at once. I'd say for me, they feed one another. They interrogate one another. They take their chances crossing the lines.

q: You have taught writing in colleges and universities long enough to see some of the blessings and curses academia has in store for creative writers. What would you consider to be the best thing about pursuing a creative path through higher education? And what might be the worst?

a: I have to tell you I've been thinking of leaving teaching/academia since the first year I taught. So you have to take whatever I say with a grain of salt. Or a whole shaker. I think what is best about pursuing a creative path through higher education is the uninterrupted writing time, and how writing can be your front and center focus for a few years in your life. I think the worst thing about pursuing a creative path through higher education is that you risk mimicry, fallacies about creative production, and the possibility that you are writing to a terribly constructed audience exactly like you. How, I wonder again and again, is that making art?

Lidia Yuknavitch is the author of the memoir The Chronology of Water, *three books of short stories, and the novel* Dora: A Head Case.

seventeen

re-visions

"Finishing a book," Truman Capote once japed, "is just like you took a child out in the yard and shot it."

Many writers feel much the same about finishing a short story or a poem. After all, you live in your language and with your characters for hours, days, weeks, months, and sometimes years on end. You watch your work materialize, cohere, and, all going well, maybe even flourish. Along the way, you learn about yourself and your world and you write hard, write long, and almost invariably write for a sobering figure (if you write for a figure at all) far, far, far below minimum wage. Not uncommonly, you spend as much time in universes of your own making as you do interacting with those you can bump your nose against.

Early on in their careers, many authors believe such labor will become less difficult over time. Practice will make perfect. As a rule, it won't. "Writing doesn't get easier with experience," Tim O'Brien remarked. "The more you know, the harder it is to write." Anne Enright deadpanned: "The first twelve years are the worst." "Writing is easy," Gene Fowler agreed. "All you do is sit staring at a blank sheet of paper until the drops of blood form on your forehead."

No wonder that one encounters a sense of anti-climax, post-partum depression, at the conclusion of a creative project. That's why it is so important to make it your business to launch a new one right away, or, better, always have several in the air at the same time. Don't feel you need to locate a safe harbor for one project before setting sail on another. Continually be on the lookout for the next idea. Follow your interests. Follow your passions. Keep working in your journal.

Make notes on where you'll journey next that you haven't journeyed before. And, no matter what, don't stop putting marks on the page.

It is equally important to realize that, even though you've plunked the last punctuation mark on the last sentence of that manuscript you've been working on, it is likely you are not half as close to being done with it as you think you are. In a very real sense, you have only started. William Gibson wrote a dozen drafts of the opening of *Neuromancer* before he was satisfied, and that's much less unusual than it may sound. Flaubert wrote and rewrote drafts of every passage in *Madame Bovary*, combing through them for poor assonances, clunky repetitions of sounds and words, and often perfecting them only to throw them out in the end. At one point he estimated he had produced 500 pages to find 120 good ones. By the time he was done, he had produced more than 4500 for his 400-page novel—roughly an 11:1 ratio of pages authored to final rendition.

That sort of furious drafting and redrafting enables writers to see and re-see what they are doing. The word *revision* literally means *to see again*—to view something afresh from a new perspective. It doesn't mean to tinker with your lines, fixing commas and spelling, changing around a word here or there—or, rather, it doesn't mean only that. Instead, it means to think big and think small simultaneously. It means to take your time, *really* take your time—not 15 minutes or an hour, but a week, two, a month, maybe many more on even a small manuscript. If you seriously embrace the notion of revision, the last version of a piece of writing will seldom look anything like the first.

A perhaps counter-intuitive initial step toward revision is to put your project in the metaphorical drawer and take a psychic holiday from it. Doing so will help you to gain the proverbial distance you need from what you've just created to be able to see it as though it had been written by someone else. Sometimes just a couple days will do the trick, sometimes half a year. Be patient. Work on something else. Remind yourself you're in no rush. Let the gremlins of unconscious creativity pester your project behind your back. If you return to it only to recognize it still reads like the most brilliant thing you've ever had the pleasure to meet, chances are you haven't let it sit in that metaphorical drawer long enough. (N.B.: Anne Enright: "Only bad writers think that their work is really good.")

When you feel ready to dive back in, pick up what you want to revise and read it through from start to finish without stopping in order to gain a sense of the whole. During the original writing process, you were busy with this line of dialogue or that paragraph of description. By necessity, you were standing extremely close to your narrative canvas. Now it is time to step back and look at the complete painting. If all goes well, you should experience the same sensation Claude Monet did when he stepped back from those splotches of color before him and witnessed his water lilies for the first time. You will see the larger context your lines and paragraphs inhabit.

At this stage, ask yourself: Is everything serving the architectural sum? Is every page, every phrase, moving my project forward, teaching my reader something important about my central character(s), my voice, my fictive galaxy? If relatively conventional, is my character fully rounded, fully motivated, and undergoing transformation from beginning to end? If not, why not? Has my project been told from the most productive point(s) of view? Does each part occupy the right amount of narrative space, or do some shoot by too quickly while others unfurl too slowly? Am I missing any indispensable transitions between scenes? Are there any authorial intrusions I can do away with?

If each element doesn't in some significant way contribute to your overall effect, excise it. Never save a scene, a paragraph, a phrase, a word just because you happen to like it. As Faulkner famously said: "Kill your darlings." (Remember, too, that you can always cannibalize your extra bits by tucking them into a folder that you can tap for a later, different piece.)

At the same time you're looking to tighten, keep your eyes open for areas that need to be fleshed out. Because you've probably written your first draft at a fairly hefty clip, there are bound to be segments that will now strike you as a little anorexic. Don't forget: in conventional narrative several things need to be going on at once in every scene for it to feel richly conceived. Are they? Have you expended the energy necessary to describe your characters' external characteristics, internal states, histories, wants, strengths, weaknesses? Have you detailed your setting so your narrative doesn't seem sketchy, out of place and time? Or have you—with forethought, with purpose—rattled the above conventions in engaging and revealing ways?

Once you are reasonably content with the general contours of your piece, move down to the next level—paragraph and sentence—and begin to think increasingly small. Again, strike out anything that isn't essential. Ask yourself: is every line clear (or deliberately unclear) in its intention and execution? Will my reader find each as exciting and surprising to read as I did to write? Have I varied sentence length and structure enough to keep my language engaging? Have I oriented my readers sufficiently at this micro-stratum with respect to time, place, character, action, how we just got from point A to point B—or have I mindfully disoriented those components? Is my tone consistent—or inconsistent for a reason? Are there any verbal tics (i.e., words or phrases you repeat far more than you need to for no good reason) that I should trim? Does my dialogue have a fundamental narrative function, or is it just taking up room on the page? Are my characters' accents and verbal eccentricities consistent?

From paragraph and sentence, drop down even farther to individual phrases, verbs, adjectives, and adverbs. Are there word echoes that can be shed in a way that would make Flaubert proud? Verbal fillers? Clichés? Mixed metaphors? Is each verb as active, interesting, and powerful as possible? What about the adjectives and adverbs—are there some I can do away with? Some I can make more concrete? Is my punctuation perfect, or deliberately disfigured?

After you've taken your project as far as you can take it yourself, you are ready to offer it to your writing community, however you have come to define that term—an online or offline classroom, a local workshop, a colleague, a friend. That community, that district of creative collaboration and support and challenge, is potentially a good place to discuss your ultimate thematic intentions and worldview in ways that teach you something about both. It is potentially a great place to gain enlightening angles on your work, invigorating ways of thinking about it and about options for revising it.

As you enter that community, keep in mind that writing is a method of reading. That is, such communities allow you to re-learn various strategies for experiencing textuality from the inside out (both with respect to your own work and others'), how to slow down your perceptions, deepen your contemplation; re-learn what makes a text a text by having to develop language about it. At their best, such communities allow you to theorize narrativity collectively, conceptualize it as an *as if* space, re-appreciate that every narratological move we make, every technique we employ, carries with it philosophical and political consequences.

Every time any of us speaks in such a community, we also provoke everyone involved to reflect upon the institutional framework in which our words sound—what a "community" is, what a "workshop"; what they *might* be; how academic "workshops" exist within the power fields of a given department; what economic purposes they serve, and what cultural; how the university or other community in which we position ourselves expresses itself through it and through us; how the larger culture does; how that might be changed in productive ways.

While we all want our writing affirmed by the world, listening for praise too early in the process can deafen you to constructive suggestions for making your work more itself, more successful in achieving what it wants to achieve. If you hear a number of people in your writing community saying the same thing, it will probably behoove you to stop and ask yourself why. In other words, don't be too hasty in your evaluation of their evaluation. Sleep on it. Live with it a few days. Give it some time to sink in. It is always possible, of course, that they have it all wrong, but it is also possible that they've touched an important nerve in your writing. If you're extremely lucky, you might even discover someone who completely gets what you're up to, someone whose opinions you can learn from, someone who can offer advice that resonates with you, that you somehow always knew but needed to hear somebody else articulate before you could act upon it.

You should learn to understand when you're really done with a piece. Sometimes this will happen because your manuscript will be finished, and sometimes because it will be beyond repair. It isn't anomalous to spend months on a piece of writing only to discover in the end it is never going to be the one you wanted it to be. If that happens, there are two things you should do: first, celebrate all you learned during the process of writing and rewriting it, and, second, quickly move on to the next piece you'd like to write.

Another repetition for emphasis: authors don't write to publish. They author to author. Take your writing fervently, and publication will eventually follow, if that's what you would like to have happen. More important, though, you should ask yourself every night: What have I done today that will make me a better writer tomorrow?

You should ask yourself: Have I taken chances, pushed myself, tried something I've never tried before, written with excitement, with attentiveness, with awareness, read another book or poem or flash fiction by someone I admire, attempted to write the flash fiction or poem or book I've always wanted to read?

And you should without exception be able to answer yes.

reading suggestion

Madden, David. *Revising Fiction: A Handbook for Fiction Writers* (1988). Useful guidebook to the art of revising normative narrative that will also help those working in innovative modes become more conscious of what they are doing.

exercises

1. Go back to one of the exercises in this book at which you have tried your hand, and set about revising it, keeping in mind this chapter's suggestions. The important thing here is not to hurry. As the Romans said: Make haste slowly. Let yourself live with your work for at least a week, revisiting it daily, giving yourself permission to completely re-imagine it if need be. Assume you will generate at least three drafts.

2. Exchange manuscripts with someone in your writing community and read his or hers with an eye toward revision. Go through the work before you scene by scene, paragraph by paragraph, line by line, sound by sound, comma by comma, offering constructive, generous suggestions in your marginalia. Then summarize your comments in a short paragraph at the end by: a) discussing the piece's thematics and intentions; b) citing two or three specifics of techniques that work well for you; and c) citing two or three specifics that, if rethought, would make the manuscript significantly more itself.

interview

lynne tillman

q: How do you know when something you are writing is really and truly finished?

> **a:** When I think it's finished, it's because I've done what I wanted to do; the story, novel or essay accomplishes, by the end, what I want or think it needs—it has convinced me I've come to an end. I decide about an ending more as a convincing than a concluding. To me it seems as complete as I can make it—though, of course, the reader really completes it. Let's say, how it ends satisfies my sense of things.

q: Can you talk a little bit about your revision process? What's most important to you as you begin combing back through something you've written with a more editorial eye?

> **a:** Writing and rewriting are writing. I don't use the term "revision," because its premise is false, in my opinion: revision connotes that the first version of the writing is the piece, the writing, and everything after is fixing what's there already. That's not the way I think or write. I write a word or sentence and then look at it, and I work on it as long as it takes me to find the best way to say it.

q: What advice would you give a beginning writer about the importance of revision?

> **a:** Don't think of it as revision. It's all writing.

Lynne Tillman's fifth novel, American Genius: A Comedy, *was published in 2006. Her most recent book,* Someday This Will Be Funny, *is her fourth collection of stories.*

eighteen

publishing pragmatics

In *A Hacker Manifesto*, McKenzie Wark describes contemporary culture as one where the producers of information (from artists and scientists to software developers) find their labor expropriated by large corporations that own patents and copyrights on their inventions. Wark names the data producers "hackers," and the owners/expropriators of their data "vectorialists" (because information travels along "vectors" as it is reproduced and transmitted). What compels the hacker to forge an alliance with the vectoralist is the relationship the former wants to establish with her or his audience. Many hackers agree to work within the corporate matrices in order to allow their products to be disseminated effectively and lucratively. Corporate publishing is a case in point, where the author is a version of hacker, the press of vectoralist.

But with the exponential spread of digital and multidisciplinary modes of textuality, collaborative models, web outlets, ebooks, the zine scene, independent presses, artists' books, niche audiences, rhizomatic distribution patterns, the transient nature of the artifact, and relatively simple applications for desktop layout and design, the hacker/vectorialist paradigm has become far more troubled than Wark could have imagined in 2004 when his neo-Marxist manifesto first appeared. In fact, it has never been less clear exactly what "publication" even means.

As production and distribution paradigms adapt to current economic conditions and technologies, as they continuously and rapidly diversify, innovative publishing—like innovative writing itself—becomes an ever larger and richer possibility space that is always in-process.

At the same time, the means of production and distribution form a feedback loop with what can be written and how. The former exerts influence on the latter even as the latter exerts influence on the former. The outcome is an expanding web of opportunities for those on the lookout for them. Trent Reznor, Radiohead, and Jonathan Coulton have already shown how hackers in the music industry can in good part circumvent the corporate model by taking their work directly to their audiences. Cable television hosts Leo Laporte and Kevin Rose operate their own podcasting and streaming video channels. Writers as different as Neil Gaiman, Debra Di Blasi, and David Clark are leveraging the egalitarian energy of electronic publishing to bring new readers into an already substantial tribe of existing ones.

Two considerable factors in the successes of these hackers are the strategic development and utilization of blogging technologies like the open-sourced WordPress, and the careful deployment of such comparatively controlled web portals as Google+, Facebook, and Twitter. With these tools, an individual becomes analogous to an entire avant-broadcasting network. While on the one hand it is admittedly easy to argue social networking is simply one more incarnation of corporate vectoralism (e.g., a commercial enterprise masquerading as free zone), it is simultaneously and paradoxically inarguable that social networking is also a powerful tool for collapsing distance between hacker and audience, not to mention an area for generating and exploring new modes of creation that work against or around corporate vectoralism. Via its apparatuses, hackers build their audiences one person at a time. Let that audience grow organically, and soon a single click can instantaneously send a project into the viewing/reading/listening channels of literally thousands of people.

Take, for example, Mez Breeze. Using social networking tools, including Twitter's 140-character constraint and the modification of gaming environments like *World of Warcraft*, she explores the nature of online encounters while pushing digi-speak to the point of inventing something like a new sort of Internet language poetry based on the use of portmanteau words and the layering of multiple meanings into a single phrase that, much like James Joyce's *Finnegan's Wake* or Anthony Burgess' *A Clockwork Orange*, is wholly of her own derivation and design. The result, called Mezangelle, blends conventional English with slang, ASCII art, programming and markup languages, source code, emoticons, and phonetic spelling to produce "narratives" like this:

From: "dirtee codah." <netwurker@hotkey.net.au>
Date: Mon Feb 11, 2002 5:20 pm
Subject: N.formation.sources|{i. am. [trapped. in. seizure. language.
>   +   <
][][][][][][in][Form.ational Sauces
>+<living. in. charl.e.tan][ned & lurvely][. glass.][topped danca dangerous]
[::drenching wurds with cauls of gritty re:][d][wined rims & gra.][k][nit.e
longing
>++< hearts of c.hun.king stone
::shifting l][iquid polyvalent][ucre melts gigabyting fronts
>+.+.< removable feldspar][s(ta][c][tic)nakes & jacob][ladders
::whole twitching N.titees d][cl][own.loading l][m][uddite dust
]   [   ]   [   ]   [   ]   [   ]   [   ]   [   ]
] [ ] [ ] [ ] [ ] [ ] [ ] [ ] [ ] [ ] [ ] [=] [
<=>

If, rather than (or perhaps in addition to) engaging with the capabilities of social networking tools, you are interested in your writing appearing in online or print journals, a useful place to start is by consulting *Duotrope's Digest* (duotrope.com). A free and continuously updated writers' resource, it lists somewhere in the neighborhood of 4000 publications. You can filter search results by genre, style, length, theme, pay scale, and/or medium. Click on a specific journal to locate a link to that journal's website, along with information about response times, percent of submissions to acceptances, where else writers who submitted to the journal in question submitted their work, and so on.

Another helpful resource is *The International Directory of Little Magazines and Small Presses*, which lists thousands of journals and indie publishers alphabetically and by genre. Each entry provides the editor's name, address, and phone number, as well as the date the journal was founded and a quote by said editor about exactly what he or she is and is not looking for. Sometimes you will also be able to glean the names of several authors who have published there, which can give you a sense of whether the journal or press will be a good fit for your own writing. Too, you will discover the press' print run or the journal's circulation, cost of individual copies, length, format, payment method (normally one or two contributor's copies, sometimes a small sum, seldom more than $100), copyright information (most publications copyright for the author), and response time (expect a four- to six-month wait). Because *The International Directory of Little Magazines and Small Presses* appears in print, you may be able to dig up a copy at your local or campus library.

When searching for possible outlets, don't forget to read the fine print. Some venues only read manuscripts at certain times of year. All will announce whether or not they accept simultaneous and/or electronic submissions. Make sure, as well, to locate an editor's name to whom you can address your cover letter; such a gesture demonstrates you have done your homework.

In the end, consider coming up with eight or a dozen options. Check out their websites and/or drop by the library to take a look at the company you may be keeping, the tenor of the writing published, the sharpness of layout. You never want to submit your work willy-nilly.

The next step is packing up your piece and sending it out. Editors frown on sloppy presentations, which they see as indicative of unprofessional behavior, even authorial disinterest. If a press or journal asks for a hardcopy submission, print your piece neatly on fresh medium-weight paper. Use paper clips instead of staples for stories and nothing at all for book manuscripts except the boxes in which you're shipping them. Double-space. Use one-and-a-half-inch margins.

If you're submitting a book, use a title page that, in the center, includes the title of your work, your name, address, phone number, and e-mail. If you're submitting a short story, poem, or hybrid piece, forego the title page, but make sure that the title of your piece and your name appear centered about a fourth of the way down the first page, and that your address, phone number, and e-mail appear in the upper right-hand or left-hand corner. Make sure your name and the piece's title appears on the top of all succeeding pages. Avoid rambunctious fonts and colors unless they are integral to what you're doing. You needn't indicate your story's word-count, and you definitely shouldn't type in the copyright symbol or some phrase about copyright, both of which accomplish little more than flagging amateurism since they don't actually guarantee copyright.

A cover letter should accompany your submission and should be short and to the point. It should contain your name, address, phone number, and email in standard letter format and font, and should be about three short paragraphs. The first should give the title of your piece, its genre, a sense of its tone and situation. The second should give the highlights of your publication record—where your work has appeared, which awards it has won, which M.F.A. or Ph.D. program you attended, that kind of thing. If you don't have a track record, that's perfectly fine; just drop the second paragraph altogether—many (if not most) editors thrive on discovering new talent. The last paragraph should consist of a quick, pleasant, professional sign off. Never try to convince an editor of your writing's worth. It will do that all by itself.

If submitting a print version of your piece, include a Self Addressed Stamped Envelope, or S.A.S.E. Bring that and the envelope into which everything is going to the post office. The people there will weigh and price everything. Pack it up, and your piece is off.

If you want to send a book manuscript to an editor at a press, it is wise to send a query letter or email first. That letter should traverse much the same ground as the cover letter above, but should also dwell another paragraph or three on the subject and shape of your project. Enclose a brief synopsis that gives a sense of your book's plot, aesthetics, intent, perceived audience, and constellation of books it exists within.

Agents almost never handle individual pieces of innovative writing. They seldom handle innovative book manuscripts. If you want to send out the latter, you may therefore want to consider submitting directly to small independent presses or contests, such as FC2's Ronald Sukenick American Book Review Innovative Fiction Prize or Catherine Doctorow Innovative Fiction Prize—ones, in other words, that specifically target experimental writing.

Often based in New York, agents serve as the gatekeepers to (by and large) corporate publishers. They spend decades developing working relationships with the key players at the big houses, and over the past quarter century or so have become the first line of defense for the mega-publishers. Ask many writers who have been around for a while, and you will learn that landing an agent today is as difficult (if not more so) as landing a publisher was back in the early seventies, yet most are uninterested in any writing that won't make them money.

Find one who adores your work, however, and you've got a fairly powerful advocate in corporate publishing circles. Agents know who is buying what kind of writing where, and thus where and with whom to try to place your book. They also know the contractual ropes, and so can work on your behalf to secure the strongest possible deal. They understand things like royalties, movies rights, foreign rights, and paperback ones. All said and done, though, agents are business people first, literature lovers second. Most are indifferent to short-story collections or poetry, will lose interest in work they can't place within three or four months, and most ask for 12 to 15 percent of the deal they cut, to be paid after the author's advance arrives. Some less-than-reputable ones will ask for several hundred dollars or more to "edit" and "shop" your manuscript, pocketing your money whether or not they make a sale. Whatever you do, avoid that ilk at all costs.

If you do decide to pursue an agent, do your research first. Most reputable ones belong to the Association of Authors' Representatives, a group which subscribes to a list of ethical guidelines. Look in agents listings at the back of such publications as *Writer's Market*, and you can ferret out that information quickly. Send a cover letter, a synopsis of your book, and the first 50 pages. If the agent likes what he or she reads, she or he will ask for more. If she or he likes the whole, he or she will write you an email or letter that will usually serve as your contract, stating, in essence, that you two have agreed to work together and, should that change, you both need to agree in writing that you are going to go your separate ways.

However you choose to go about finding a publisher, if that's what you conclude you want to do, keep a careful log—either in a special notebook or via an application you can ferret out online—listing where you've sent your manuscript and the date on which you sent it. Those are the kinds of details an author believes at the time she or he will never forget, but the truth is it is remarkable how easily he or she can and will. The same day your manuscript is returned or an acceptance letter arrives, go to your log and update it.

If you haven't heard from a venue within three or four months, it is fair and reasonable to email or snailmail a polite query note asking after your work's status. In that case, provide your name, your piece's title, and the date you sent it. (No news seldom means good news. Usually no news just means no news—although sometimes it can indicate a sloppy editor and a lost story, or a journal that has abruptly gone belly up.) After six or eight months, write the editor stating that you assume he or she is no longer interested in your work and that you're hereby withdrawing it from his or her consideration. If you've submitted the same piece to several places at once, and it is accepted by one, email the others right away to inform them of the situation and to withdraw your manuscript from consideration. Never try to play one venue off another, holding out for the best deal or most prestigious publication.

Once you have sent off your manuscript—and this may be the most important bit of advice in this entire chapter—forget about it immediately and get on with your writing life. Obsessing over a piece that's been submitted, wondering about its fate hourly, isn't going to bring an editor's decision any sooner, but it can distract you from the real work at hand: writing. If you don't already have another piece you're working on, start one. Return to your journal for ideas. Continue taking notes on your geographical and imaginative environments. Brainstorm with your writing community. Read that armful of excellent books you've always meant to read but just never got around to. Try some of the exercises in this guide to see if they might spark a fresh thought, approach, or subject for investigation.

As your manuscript goes into the mailbox or up into an online submission manager, begin to get your head around the fact that rejection is one of the things that defines most professional authors' existences and separates those existences from the ones lived by most of her or his friends and acquaintances. It is an extraordinary thing to think about: more of what you write will probably be turned down than accepted; you will take critical hit after critical hit—willingly, no less—from people whose opinions you don't necessarily admire or respect; and, bizarrely, you will keep coming back for more.

Often manuscripts will be rejected the first 10 or 12 or more times they are sent out. This usually says less about your writing's worth than it does about the fact that millions of people across the country are producing and submitting work to thousands of journals (most of which appear only once or twice a year, and most of which have only three or five slots open for stories in each issue) and publishing houses (most of which accept less than one percent of submissions). More times than not, it is going to take a while to locate a match between your piece, an editor who loves it, and a journal or publisher that has enough space to publish it.

Still, it isn't always beneficial to dismiss rejections out of hand. Listen if an editor takes the time and effort to write you a line or two about your work. That means she or he cared enough to do so. And, even if she or he doesn't, it is probably time to take your piece out of circulation and look at it again with new objectivity if it has made the rounds for a year or two without progress.

Commonly, rejection takes the form of a bland boilerplate email or slip of paper in a S.A.S.E. with your manhandled manuscript saying something to the effect that the editor(s) didn't feel your poem, story, or book was right for them, and wishing you luck in placing it elsewhere. Don't feel bad. Don't feel sad or mad. Or at least don't feel alone. The very same thing is happening to hundreds of thousands of other people all over the world that very second.

The best way to deal with rejection is head on. Don't take your frustration out on family or friends. Don't write back the editor explaining how he or she missed the point of your work. Wallpaper your refrigerator with those slips, those printed-out emails, and when the fridge is full, move on to the bathroom. Get determined. Let rejections slide off your back. And give yourself a 24-hour turnaround: if a piece returns to you this afternoon, and you continue to have confidence in it, send it again in tomorrow's mail.

A secret about writing: 99 percent of it comes down to persistence and tenacity, both in terms of vision and execution. If writing is all about rejection, then rejection is all about learning how to overcome rejection. Even after publication, you will confront another version of that beast in the form of negative reviews, blog posts, tweets, or other public feedback. You won't be able to get away from it, and so the most productive thing you can do is get used to it.

Barbara Kingsolver's beautiful advice: "This manuscript of yours that has just come back from another editor is a precious package. Don't consider it rejected. Consider that you've addressed it 'to the editor who can appreciate my work' and it has simply come back stamped 'Not at this address.' Just keep looking for the right address." Another secret about writing: a single, simple acceptance note will gird you against 20 rejections, one thoughtful review against 20 incompetent ones. The day that first acceptance or review arrives is always a miraculous one. Enjoy every picosecond of it.

For a person with words in his or her blood, there is only one sure-fire antidote to rejection, and that is to produce more language. "Why do writers write?" Thomas Berger asked. "Because it isn't there." If a piece comes back for the twelfth or twentieth time, and you're starting to get the feeling all those editors out there might just be trying to tell you something, do this: commence another piece.

Don't stop. Don't slow down.

And if you fill up your bathroom with rejection slips, just remember there's always the hall.

reading suggestions

Brewer, Robert Lee. *Writer's Market* (updated yearly). Listings of commercial publishing houses and agents.

Editors of Coda: Poets & Writers Newsletter. *The Writing Business* (1985). Sections on contracts and other practicalities of being an author.

Writer's Net. *Directory of Literary Agents* (updated regularly). Online.

exercises

1. Visit *Duotrope's Digest* (duotrope.com) and/or your campus or local library, and begin to acquaint yourself with several journals that sound like they might be good fits for you. Develop a working wish list of venues—perhaps 25 in all. At the top should appear your dream choices, in the middle those you think your work may have a fair shot at, and at the bottom four or five you imagine could be safeties.

2. Buy or download a log to track your manuscripts. Set it up to follow: a) where the piece is sent; b) when it is sent; c) when it is returned; d) whether it is rejected or accepted.

3. Keeping in mind the advice in this chapter, take a deep breath and send out your first manuscript.

4. If you've just had a manuscript rejected, give yourself a strict 24-hour deadline to send it out again.

5. Return to the notion of expanding and complicating the idea of publishing by choosing a mode of social networking to find an audience for your work while using the constraints of a specific social networking format (e.g., Twitter's 140-character limit) to shape that work.

interview

bradford morrow

q: Can you briefly explain what led you to start *Conjunctions*?

> **a:** Back in my twenties I knew the great poet and translator, Kenneth Rexroth, with whom, though he was 50 years my senior, I'd developed a deep literary kinship. One day we were sitting in his library talking about how important James Laughlin and New Directions had been to each of us in different ways. We agreed that a festschrift in Laughlin's honor was long overdue. Though a stroke prevented Kenneth from helping me put it together, the Laughlin festschrift turned out to be *Conjunctions:1*. Another issue followed, featuring work that didn't fit in that first volume, and then another. I meant only to edit *Conjunctions* for a few years but, sustained by the enthusiasm of what became a community of fellow writers, I found myself more and more committed to publishing innovative fiction and poetry that I wasn't consistently finding in other journals at the time. I never imagined the project would experience such longevity and aesthetic scope, but it has served as a kind of living notebook in which a thousand and more authors and artists have inscribed their visions over the decades.

q: As a writer, you're best known for your novels, but you recently published your first collection of short stories, *The Uninnocent*. How is the revision process you used for that collection different than one you might have used for one of your novels?

> **a:** Revising a novel and revising a short story aren't all that different, at least for me, beyond the obvious issues of length, character complexity, narrative development. But revising a novel and a short story *collection* do involve crucial differences. When I made final edits on my most recent novel, *The Diviner's Tale*, I strived for consistency

of voice, in the emotional evolution and history of characters, and tried to make sure that the story unfurled at just the right symphonic moments. When editing the 12 stories that comprise *The Uninnocent*, I combed through a whole range of quite different narratives, winnowing out any unintentional echoes, repeated metaphors, words, images, even names, so that each story stood alone as a dynamic individual, but the underlying themes of the collection remained darkly harmonious.

q: What advice would you give a beginning writer about to send her first short story out for consideration?

a: There's no magic involved with this part of the literary life. When a beginning writer is ready to send out work, it's imperative to submit as polished and final a draft as humanly possible. There's less than little to be gained by having a story, say, accepted and published, if it turns out to be something one regrets not having worked on harder. Publication is a serious matter and, to paraphrase William Gaddis, once the work's in print the author cannot go running after it saying, I meant this, I meant that. Simplistic as it may sound, it's also crucial to research, read, even subscribe to journals and magazines to determine which will make the best aesthetic fit. And never be discouraged by rejection. Easy to say, hard to do. But nobody said writing and publishing is easy. At least I didn't.

Bradford Morrow is author of six novels, including Trinity Fields, Giovanni's Gift, *and* The Diviner's Tale. *He teaches at Bard College.*

nineteen

literary activism & the tribal ecology

"Remember," A. L. Kennedy cautions us, "writing doesn't love you. It doesn't care. Nevertheless, it can behave with remarkable generosity. Speak well of it, encourage others, pass it on."

Speaking well of language, encouraging other authors, fostering work you love—this could form the literary activist's creed. She or he has come to understand the corporate paradigm of composing-as-competition has been challenged by one celebrating collaboration and support. And, with that recognition, a return to our discussion in the first chapters of this book about how distinctions between editor and writer, critic and poet, reviewer and novelist, academic and publisher, blogger, tweeter have become incrementally more fused and confused, if not erased entirely, in recent years.

Nowadays, an author is a person who authors, yes, surely—but she or he is also a person who does a tremendous amount more. An author is somebody who helps make literary culture happen. For the literary activist, writing is only one creative act among many that composes his or her textual life. Others include editing and bringing out fellow writers' work in online and print journals and through book publishers, reading and reviewing that work, writing essays about it, teaching it, talking it up, urging others to launch journals and indie presses, running reading series, laboring in arts administration, coordinating innovative writing conferences, launching local writing groups, posting about authors and texts they love on their blogs or via other social networking media.

We have returned, then, to one of this book's vital refrains: *ask not what publishing can do for you; ask what you can do for publishing*. Or, to rephrase slightly: in the twenty-first century, there is no such thing as an isolated writer. That species and the myopic Romantic myth that cultivated it have gone virtually extinct. Rather, every one of us is attending a literary party. And it is important to understand what the conversations going on around us there are about, who the people we're talking to are, who has just entered the room, who just left, how and why those conversations are always changing (and changing us) in abundant and energizing ways.

A better analogy for this paradigm might be that of a tribal ecology, where authors easily move among multifarious clans and loose coalitions based on various forms of aesthetic and existential kinship that attempt existing outside (and not infrequently in direct opposition to) the dominant cultures' models.

The tribal ecology is intent on inventing possibility spaces for possibility spaces. Such aphorisms may sound unnecessarily abstract and/or utopian, and so to state in more practical terms: you should make it your goal to know what the current literary trends are, how they're developing and why, how your work positions itself with respect to them, what forces are shaping the publishing industry and the book and how those might affect what and the way you're authoring, how you might affect them, which publishers are publishing what, which ones have entered the field of play lately, which have lately folded, why, what you can learn from their successes and/or failures, what new writers you should be checking out, which ones' work might stimulate you to continue formulating or questioning or expanding your own aesthetic, which you can help to reach a wider audience and how, which books published in the last six months and last six years and last 60 and 600 or 2600 are worth pursuing, are worth getting out the word about, what the next publishing season will look like, which journals you should be keeping up with, which new digital modes of production and distribution, what "publication" will mean in five years or 50 or 500, how all this might affect the way you conceptualize your own writing, how it might impact your tribe, how your tribe might impact it.

Initially, the idea of getting a handle on all this commotion of information may strike you as overwhelming. It isn't, though. Not really. After all, writing isn't just writing; it is a method of existing in the world, a 24/7/365 condition. It's what you *do*. Once you've established a writing schedule for yourself and eased into its rhythms, it is time to establish a schedule for literary activism. Like your writing schedule, it needn't be daily, and it needn't be for long stretches. It just needs to *be*.

Consider, for instance, dropping by the local or campus library once a month for an afternoon or evening to thumb through journals and familiarize yourself with them. Spend time on the web acquainting yourself with presses you have begun to hear about or see advertised in your favorite journals. Subscribe to or check in regularly online with two or three review outlets that focus on innovative writing—*Rain Taxi, Electronic Book Review, Review of Contemporary Fiction, American Book Review, The Collagist, HTMLGiant*—to see what's going on. Google which blogs are talking about the sort of work you admire. Friend authors you admire on Facebook and/or follow them on Twitter. The more you know, the more you'll want to know, and the more it will become clear to you how you might best use your time and energy to join forces with and nourish others.

In addition to advocating on behalf of others' writing, you should use the information above to begin to advocate for your own. Once an editor has accepted your short piece of innovative writing or book-length manuscript, it can take anywhere from several months to several years before you will see it in the world. Along the road, chances are you will receive a set of proofs (preliminary versions of a publication) to copyedit. At this point, you will be allowed to make exceedingly few substantive changes, so be sure your project is complete *before* you submit it. Proofing is a special case of reading: a slow, methodical search for misspellings, typographical mistakes, layout glitches, and omitted words or word endings. Because such errors can be difficult to spot in one's own work, some writers read their work aloud or even backwards to defamiliarize the language so they can pick up problems with it.

In the case of a book, an editor will ask you for your input about obtaining blurbs—those words of praise by other authors that appear on book jackets. He or she may also discuss with you to whom review copies should go, what you plan to do about setting up public readings and generally disseminating news of your work's publication. Make sure to be thinking of that in advance. And be advised: a press will probably send forth a very small number of review copies. You should take it upon yourself to know where they are going, and to send out a good number of your own (you will usually receive a box of author copies yourself) to carefully targeted reviewers.

If you don't care about your own work once it is published, nobody else will care about it either. So it is up to you to let the world know it exists. Don't leave publicity in your publisher's hands and then complain that your publisher isn't doing enough for you. Commonly, small presses have extremely limited financial resources. You can be sure they are doing everything they reasonably can on your book's behalf and wish they could do more. It is obviously in their best interest to do so. Nonetheless, by the time your book sees print, it is quite possible that your editor will have moved on to other ventures.

Assume, therefore, that no one is as interested in seeing your work succeed as you. Let people know about it. Pass the word through your neighborhood, town, or city by approaching the local mainstream and alternative papers with review copies and setting up readings in bookstores and cafés. Follow up on every query. Check to see if so-and-so got the review copy you mailed last week, the request for a reading you emailed the week before.

At the same time, think national and international. Compile an email list to announce new books (not, as a rule, however, new individual pieces). Develop a snailmail list and consider having simple postcards made; a quick Google search will provide you with the names of many inexpensive companies. Include your friends' names and addresses, naturally, but also those of acquaintances, local newspapers, magazines and journals, television and radio stations, regional and national review organs, bookstores, bloggers, potential reading and interview venues. Always try to be as specific in your targeting as possible. Don't, for example, generate a general address for a magazine, but rather for the review editor there, or, more effective still, a particular reviewer who tends to review the sort of book you've written. Trade your lists with writer friends who have come up with their own. Set up a website. Announce your publication through social networking media.

All that said, though, be very careful as well to steer clear of overkill. If your feed consists of nothing but plugs for yourself and your writing, most of your followers will (understandably) unsubscribe or unfriend you. If people start receiving email updates from you about your accomplishments every few months, let alone with greater frequency, they will starting marking them as spam and deleting them unread.

A few words about public readings. Every one you give should be an excuse to see old friends, colleagues, and comrades, make new ones, possibly take you somewhere you haven't gone before, introduce a few strangers to your writing, and celebrate the sheer fact of that writing being in the world. If you don't like performing, don't do readings. Nothing is less enjoyable for an audience than seeing an author read who clearly doesn't want to or doesn't know how, and you will probably reach a wider group of potential readers through reviews anyway.

Yet if you do enjoy performing, plan on having a good time and be creative about where and how to read. If you have published a book, you might want to approach local or regional junior colleges, colleges and universities. In any case, check into community reading locations in your town or city and others—art galleries, writers' groups, libraries, bars, cafés, bookstores. Invent your own locale—a warehouse, say—and hold a reading there.

Start approaching possible reading venues at least six months before publication. Make sure to get copies of your book to sell. Let your editor know how hard you are working on behalf of your writing. Contemplate teaming up with one or two local writers you admire for a group reading, or even more for a flash reading, where each reader shares his or her work for five or six minutes. Not only will it be more enjoyable that way, you will also draw a larger crowd. In preparation, send announcements to local papers and radio stations in addition to emailing friends and acquaintances and posting posters in nearby libraries, restaurants, bookstores, bars, co-ops.

While you need to remain flexible, you should try to ferret out what the reading room will look and feel like in advance. You don't want any surprises. Is it large or small? Will there be a table, chair, podium, microphone, a glass of water for you? How large will the audience likely be? Why will they be there? Are they coming primarily to hear you, have a beer and talk to friends, or do an assignment for their professor? What you discover will influence the sort of work you read and for how long.

There are few things more embarrassing for audience members than to realize the reader, thumbing aimlessly through his or her book for a passage, or stumbling over the very words he or she has written, hasn't prepared and therefore is the opposite of professional. Another way of saying this: practice, practice, practice. Decide on a number of possible passages that work as fairly self-contained units, rehearse by reading and rereading them out loud until they become part of you. Time them to the minute. Develop brief anecdotes and/or explanations around them.

After your reading, set aside five or 10 minutes to take questions from the audience. Stick around for a while to talk one-on-one with people, answer any more questions they may have, autograph books or maybe copies of the journal your piece appeared in. Always bring a few extra copies of your work along, just in case the bookstore you contacted and re-contacted never quite got around to ordering them, or maybe (and blissfully) didn't order enough.

As with readings, if a newspaper, magazine, radio or television station decides to interview you, prepare beforehand. Know your audience and the general situation. Find out what sort of people you'll be addressing and for how long, since both might give you some sense of what you should emphasize, what sorts of questions you might be asked. Spend time readying to answer those questions in as few words as possible. Know what you want to say, in other words. Interviews tend to be short. From your point of view, they'll be over before they start. It isn't a bad idea, therefore, to approach each with several topics you would like to see discussed and to guide the interviewer toward them. Sometimes the interviewer will ask you in advance what you would like to talk about. Sometimes he or she won't. Either way, if you come armed with some strong anecdotes about your work, perspectives on what you are doing and why, and points about your recent publication you would like to get across, you will be able to lead rather than follow, and there will be many fewer uncomfortable dead spaces between questions and answers.

It isn't unusual to get only one take of an interview, so make sure you are on your game. Think before you speak. Even if you find yourself confronting an aggressive interviewer, stay relaxed and friendly. Some interviewers thrive on conflict, but that isn't why you're there, so steer around the tension and back to those topics you want to talk about. Some interviewers won't have done their homework, so don't be surprised to learn the person asking you questions hasn't actually read the book you wrote, or has only skimmed it. Answer the questions you want asked rather than those the interviewer in fact poses. And don't tip your hand that you've already answered the same questions a hundred times before. Even though that might be the case, your listeners, viewers, or readers won't have heard what you have to say.

Finally, keep it brief. It is easy to go on and on about your favorite topics—yourself and your book—in an interview, but remember the whole thing will seldom last more than 20 or 30 minutes, and usually only three or five. Your responses should be compressed, pithy, and information-rich.

And, whatever you do, enjoy yourself during this part of the writing process, too. Enjoy others. Enjoy the golden moments.

And ask yourself how you can help your fellow writers do the same for their work.

exercises

1. Subscribe to or check in regularly online with two or three review outlets that concentrate on innovative writing. A few good places to start: *Rain Taxi, Review of Contemporary Fiction, American Book Review, Electronic Book Review, The Collagist, HTMLGiant.*

2. Begin to blog, tweet, or post about books, journals, review venues, and individual pieces you read and love.

3. Via email, approach the editor of a small journal or press you admire, the coordinator of a local reading series or arts council, or perhaps the people running an upcoming writers' conference in your area, and offer to volunteer your time and energy. They will almost certainly appreciate whatever you're willing to give, and you will learn galaxies of inside information about how such enterprises function.

4. Following the advice in this chapter, set up a flash fiction reading composed of at least a dozen members of your writing community.

5. Imagine at least two ways not cited above to become a literary activist…and dive in.

interviews

matt bell

q: You have a strong public presence on social networks like blogs, Facebook and Twitter, where you frequently post about what and whom you're reading. Why is it important to you to broadcast this way?

> **a:** It gives me a chance to meet other readers who have already experienced these books, or who might be interested in reading them. There's a lot of untapped excitement out there, especially if your reading tastes veer away from the mainstream. I grew up in an area without a strong community of writers and readers, or at least without one I had access to, and so it's no exaggeration to say that without the internet and the various social networks I might still not have one. Every writing group I've ever had has been made up of people I met online, and a lot of that work has been accomplished over the internet. So sharing the books I'm excited with—as well as my own writing process—has become a way to build what I lacked, and also to interact with others who have their own enthusiasms and talents to contribute.
>
> Obviously, the job of writer will always have its lonely, isolated processes. It's a vocation that requires its practitioners to shut themselves away for long, exhausting, often frustrating periods of time. There's probably no way to avoid that and still be a writer, but that doesn't mean it has to be the whole of the experience. It's a joy to come out of the difficult work of the writing day to find a community ready to receive you, to share in the successes and the disappointments of the day, and to know that community will more often than not give back everything you put into it, multiplied. I put myself out there in hopes that other people will feel safe to do the same, and that way we all benefit, all enriched.

q: Your debut collection of short stories, *How They Were Found,* is available in a number of different formats, including traditional print, ebook, and audiobook. Do you think print is the optimized medium for a short story these days? What do electronic forms afford those stories that, say, simple sentence-and-paragraph-on-a-page don't?

a: One of the interesting things about publishing *How They Were Found* in different formats (without having ever expected to do so, in advance) was realizing that certain elements of the stories didn't work as well when taken off the page. The first story in the collection utilizes a series of typographical symbols that couldn't be replicated in the ebook or the audiobook, and so they had to be written out of the story for those versions. Now I think, if the book goes into another edition, I'd probably take them out of the print version as well, both to unify the versions, and because I think the story is stronger without. So there's been an opportunity to think about the choices I've made, and whether the book needs to have multiple versions, one for each medium, or if there should be one version that works best across all the possibilities.

I do think we're likely to see writers—and publishers—thinking hard about this, especially as simultaneously published print and ebook versions become the norm. And this might be a great thing for innovation in fiction. The best novels are the ones that can *only* be novels. You can't make a movie out of these books, because their power comes from effects of the syntax and diction of the prose, and can't be translated directly into film. (And vice versa: the idea of making a novelization out of many of the strongest movies seems ridiculous.) What would a novel that can only work in print look like? What about one that would only work on a Kindle? Would it also work on an iPad?

q: Can you talk briefly about your affiliation with Dzanc as an editor?

a: As a younger editor, I've been really lucky to work for a publishing house that allows me such a wide range of experiences. In addition to editing our book manuscripts with their authors, I edit *The Collagist,* our online literary magazine, do the ebook design for all our books, run the website, and work on marketing, fundraising, and other parts of being a non-profit literary publisher. It's an honor to get to take some of these books through the entire process—from acceptance to editing to design and layout to galleys to print—and to be a part of that process at every stage. It's not the kind of experience I would get working for a larger publisher, and I've learned an incredible amount about the publishing industry there. I realize not every young writer also wants to be an editor, but the experiences I've had as an editor have been absolutely invaluable to me as a writer, and to my larger literary life.

Matt Bell is the author of Cataclysm Baby *and* How They Were Found.

debra di blasi

q: You're a writer, editor, publisher, new-media artist, and designer of beautiful print objects for your press, Jaded Ibis. What compels you to play all of these roles, often all at the same time?

a: Glib answer: I'm easily bored. Thoughtful answer: I operate from the core of two questions: "What if…?" and "Why not?" The first question concerns the nature and subsequent pleasure of invention. Invention is a *Homo sapiens* genetic program. I'm prewired to seek and enjoy problem-solving and making. My reward centers respond well to doing—even more than succeeding at—both. The second question concerns my relationship to socio-politics. I don't like *no* for an answer and am often dubious of its origins. I stopped trying to arbitrarily please and obey others when I figured out how many people lack vision and ambition or demand undeserved deference. My favorite and oft-used retort to *no* is, "Kiss my lily-white ass."

Hidden agenda: I still believe it's possible to positively change the world. Yes, even at my age. I do. And so I will. In some small way or large.

q: What is the most rewarding thing about running your own small press? The most challenging?

a: I manage Jaded Ibis Productions as a collaborative art project. I approach each branch of the company and every component of those branches as a challenge toward possibility rather than probability. The process has its own rewards, of course, but I prize the excitement in a writer's voice when we're collaborating on the various editions and they discover that her or his manuscript can and will manifest in ways she or he didn't think possible. I get the same kick from the musicians and artists we assign to respond to a manuscript who are consequently inspired by a body of literature operating at an aesthetic level they didn't know existed.

My biggest challenge undoubtedly is time, the one obstacle I have not yet found a way to overcome. My workdays are usually 10 or 12 intense hours, sometimes much longer and much more concentrated when a special project or event looms. I can keep up that pace for only so long before I have a meltdown. But the next day I'm up and ready to go again because I have a mission that matters.

q: Your work fluidly moves between traditional print and electronic media, oftentimes within the same piece. Can you describe a little bit of your creative process in composing pieces that fuse word, image and hypermedia?

a: My formal education was creative writing (poetry) and visual arts (painting, video, mixed media, design), so I'm comfortable utilizing a variety of media. I consider each element, each medium, as part of an overall palette from which to compose the seduction. A little text here, a little image there, a little time-based video or audio over there—a process of addition and subtraction, placement and replacement until I feel I've achieved exactness. Tomorrow I may have a completely different explanation for my creative process because, as you surely must know, if one is working organically and intuitively then the essence of the process remains lost in impulse and reflex.

Debra Di Blasi is author of five books, including The Jiri Chronicles & Other Fictions.

eric lorberer

q: What do you see *Rain Taxi*'s role to be in the contemporary conversation about writing and publishing?

a: To keep a lively and intelligent conversation going about new and innovative books, especially those that are often overlooked by the mainstream media. We aim to shine a spotlight on interesting authors, and to be a voice for new critics and passionate observers of the literary scene.

q: *Rain Taxi* exists as both a print and online journal. Do you see it moving to a fully online publication in the future? Do you think most literary reviews like *Rain Taxi* will continue to exist in print?

a: We will continue to have both print and online issues as long as it is viable. *Rain Taxi* feels committed to the print medium, and having both forms allows us to best reach as many adventurous readers as possible. Economically, it's difficult to continue to exist in print, but moving to online leaves an important piece of literary culture unattended. I hope at least a few other literary reviews will find ways to enact a print option.

q: What advice would you offer someone who is considering her or his first job or association as an editor?

a: Do it only if you have a puppy love for language. You're rarely going to get thanked or even acknowledged; you'll often get attacked or vilified; the hours are long and the pay horrible. On the other hand, there's no high like helping to shape a piece of writing or a significant literary publication. If that fills in the gaps for you, welcome to our tribe.

Eric Lorberer has published poems, essays, and criticism in numerous magazines and his essay "The Ashbery Bridge" *was named a notable essay in* Best American Essays 2008. *He is also director of the Twin Cities Book Festival.*

ted pelton

q: The notion of the "innovative" is a fraught creative space. How would you go about defining it? Or, to put it somewhat differently, what's innovative about the innovative, and to what purpose?

a: I don't think a strict definition is possible, because successful innovative fictions can be accomplished in myriad ways, and often with aesthetics that may be in disagreement with each other. A bottom line for me as an editor, or as I think about my own work, is that I want to see writing and fiction that operates and understands itself as an art form. I think if you look at an art form like painting, the desire for innovation is more clearly understood—no serious painter simply operates within received notions of the art form without forming questions about approach, tradition, and challenging expectations. Really, it's such a given that the art of painting is interested in innovation that one can imagine a classic portrait painter being a kind of radical throwback. Yet in most serious "literary" fiction that is produced in the U.S., these questions aren't engaged; the normative model of representative, psychological realism is so assumed that it isn't even seen as one approach among others; it is seen by most, simply, as what fiction is. The situation is better than it was, say, 10 years ago—in large part, I believe, because the small presses have made the larger ones deal with such issues and look for more interesting writers. But fiction remains the most formally conservative of art forms, and politically conservative, for that matter, in the sense of pretending that political questions are of no consequence in this country. Quick, how many important political novels can you name by U.S. authors from the last 25 years?

q: Would you talk a little about the pragmatics of Starcherone's founding and history, and how the press currently fits in with your sense of innovative writing?

a: I began Starcherone Books for self-interested reasons: I had won a National Endowment for the Arts Fellowship in Fiction Writing, yet I couldn't get my first collection of stories, the core of which had won me the prize, published. I could hardly even get anyone to read them. So after the couple places that would even consider them had turned the book down, I learned enough Quark and Photoshop to put the book together myself and started the press, putting the initial printing, mailing, and advertising costs on a personal credit card.

Soon after, Raymond Federman, an old teacher of mine, asked me if I could put out his book *The Voice in the Closet*, which had been out of print for some 20 years. Next I did my ex-wife's book. In the meantime, I started to see that there was a need for a press like Starcherone, both to give innovative debut authors a break and to return classic avant-garde authors—Kenneth Bernard was another example—to print.

Starcherone began a contest to discover new authors; I didn't want the press to be nepotistic. I also made it a nonprofit, so it could start to reflect interests and values besides just my own. I remembered an old piece of advice Robert Creeley wrote about getting from Ezra Pound, when Creeley had first started *Black Mountain Review*: Pound had said to get writers for the magazine using the principle of "a constant and a variant," recruiting some authors whom you knew you could depend upon for material, and having the other half of the content coming from all over, so that anyone felt they had a chance of getting in. Our contest became the "variant" part, and has really been integral to Starcherone's success: we've striven to keep it blind-judged and democratic, and without necessarily trying for this, each year in the eight years the prize has been awarded, the winner his been a debut author. We debuted Aimee Parksion, who has since won numerous story prizes; Sara Greenslit, who went on to win a prize from FC2 for her second novel; Zachary Mason, whose career took off after his book with us was nominated for the NY Public Library's Young Lions Prize; and Alissa Nutting, whose renown keeps growing, and rightly so.

q: Do you see a relationship between politics and innovative aesthetics in your own fiction? In the fiction Starcherone publishes? Does innovative narrativity engage with politics differently than other forms of narrativity?

a: I feel my own work is probably more politically engaged than a lot of what Starcherone publishes. I just find this to be a fairly apolitical time in fiction writing, even among a lot of so-called innovative writers. I think, personally, that innovative aesthetics leads to more politically engaged writing, that it simply leads to a more engaged and humane relationship to the world and its inhabitants, a less sheltered life, and thus a more compassionate and politically responsible life and art. But— and I think this might be somewhat generational—I see a good percentage of innovative writers practicing an aesthetics of the beautiful where the surface of the language is most important and, while the LANGUAGE poetry made such a practice explicitly political, such engagement doesn't necessarily follow for all these authors. Beauty is truth, one poet said, but I think beauty also has the capacity to be amoral, perhaps at a shallower level.

A writer whose legacy I very much wish to honor in my work is Kurt Vonnegut, who began being important to me when I was about 17 years old, before I knew anything about other "good" writers. To me, one of the jobs of fiction, and one that Vonnegut performed exceptionally well, is to engage and struggle with the prevailing narratives by which we are controlled and determined. I'm quite a bit younger than Vonnegut, who famously fought (or at least participated) in World War II, but I've also found myself returning to that war in an effort to understand my own moment in history in the 1980s and 90s, and particularly the Reagan-Bush years love of war. My novel *Malcolm & Jack (and Other Famous American Criminals)*, which took me roughly 10 years to research and write, tries to question our national narrative about the 1940s that names "America's greatest generation," through the stories of two figures – Malcolm X and Jack Kerouac, who were marginalized in that time by racism and by normativizing pressures; who both were involved later in rebellions against the dominant identity the U.S. had of itself; and who had lives intertwined (in jazz, drugs, and crime in the Columbia University environs of Manhattan), yet could not quite speak to each other.

Philip Roth, in a novel that mainstream media fawned over, *The Plot Against America* (2004), failed badly to exploit his own initially terrific idea because he was so determined to write psychological realism that he shut down the imaginative space the novel itself wished to create. Here you have a novel in which Lindbergh, a national hero, becomes the fascist President of a United States in league with Hitler's Germany, and yet Roth is determined to keep his focus on one Jewish family in New Jersey, and in so doing, he downplays the overwhelming chaos that such an alternate reality would result in. Late in the book, in a throwaway moment, the narrator mentions the death of Robert Kennedy in later years, on *exactly the same day* that he was actually shot. But if Lindbergh were president, and the U.S. aligned with Germany, would the Kennedys have been the same Kennedys? J.F.K. was a war hero; the family were Catholics—surely there's enough doubt generated by those two facts alone to start ripples through the reality fabric of a fascist version of our country enough to disturb the tenuous circumstances that resulted in a deranged gunman shooting the younger brother of an also-assassinated President two decades later. No? I had heard from the media so long that Roth was this great novelist, our neglected Nobel candidate, so I gave him a try. I was shocked at how tame and circumscribed his imagination had become.

q: What are two or three of the most interesting/fun/productive/challenging writing exercises you offer your students?

a: I generally lift from: Natalie Goldberg, *Writing Down the Bones*; Jerome Stern, *Writing Shapely Fiction*: Brian Kiteley, *The 3 A.M. Epiphany*; plus, of course, "Exquisite Corpse" and variations.

While the Stern book isn't particularly experimental, I like the two exercises he begins with. The first is to write an anecdote in the voice of someone who is not you, and have the narrator's account of what occurred slowly undercut itself, so by the end of the anecdote you consider the narrator unreliable. The second exercise is to assume one incredible, magical, or otherwise unreal donné for your story at the beginning, á la Gregor Samsa waking up one morning as an insect, then proceed with the story according to the logic that this one given has set up, without complicating the story with additional factors.

Natalie Goldberg has the very simple and wonderful timed-writing exercise, in a private notebook, where you just write for 10 minutes, with the only rule that you can't lift your pen from the page but must keep going. With practice, this leads you to unknown places. In Goldberg's version, you keep these to yourself, to develop as a writer without fear of having your thoughts shared, but I have often used variations of this in classes, combined with a technique Ronald Sukenick used to use in his classes, of giving prompts and changing them each after a few minutes. Students will write for five minutes on the first prompt, then I will give them another; then they go on that. You do about six or seven, then read aloud to the class.

Here's a further variation I like: As instructor, I select several phrases ahead of time, sometimes borrowed from a writer we will be reading in class, sometimes selected at random. Each is then used as a prompt, and in the resulting passage, the phrase is made the heading of the passage and is also used as a phrase in the first sentence, like this:

ENLARGE MY MIND

I always thought the rays from a microwave would enlarge my mind. Late at night while everyone was asleep I'd stare through the little dots shining through the dark and watch the crusty plate rotate round and round. In the silence of the night the only sound punctuating the air was the beeps of the buttons I pressed and the drone of the power radiating from the metal box, fertilizing my brain until you could smell the traces of food from my ears.

(Credit for authoring this example goes to my former student, Lori Markham.)

If students have written on computers, it can facilitate the next stage: all the examples that people wish to contribute to a group project are collected, and the result can be ordered and reordered into various combinations. Students in one of my classes published an edited version of this in a literary magazine under a pseudonym created out of the names of those who had participated in making the piece.

Ted Pelton is the author of four books, all fiction. He has received National Endowment for the Arts and Isherwood Fellowships, and is Professor and Chair of Humanities at Medaille College of Buffalo, New York.

twenty

reading list: 101 limit texts

What follows, by way of conclusion, is an inconclusive, chronological, unavoidably skewed, highly subjective, gap-filled list of 101 Limit Texts that I've found tremendously influential on my own writing, and which I hope you might find useful as well. Some have already been mentioned in the body of this book. Most have not.

The purpose of such a list, naturally, isn't to generate a canon of innovative writing, but rather a space of contention, conversation, and inspiration. That is, what appears below doesn't present itself as a list to be accepted, but as one to be questioned, tested, modified, disputed, and quite possibly in the end abandoned in favor of (many) others.

Why not fewer titles? The number is arbitrary, naturally, but strikes me as a generally fair one to give readers a good introduction to (or further offers of) some key innovative works through history and across cultures. Why not more titles? In good part not to overwhelm potential readers. After all, provide a list of 500, 1000, or 5000 Limit Texts, and in a sense you have provided no list at all.

Which is to say I'm developing the rules of a game that I am inviting you to play, even as we both understand how artificial any such game is. One productive and perhaps illuminating way to begin playing is by trying to come up with your own list that answers the question: For me to have become the innovative writer I am today, which five or 10 texts had to have already existed on the planet?

It would probably be wise, as you peruse, to keep the relativity of the term "innovative" in mind. It is always going to carry a plurality of charges, as I have tried to indicate throughout

Architectures of Possibility, that will be shaded by who you are, what you have read and when, how many times you've read it, where you're standing in the world and in history as you approach the topic, and so on. Here, as elsewhere in this book, I'm suggesting "innovative" writing is that which asks by means of its fomalistics and thematics what writing is, and how, and why, and what its limit cases might look like.

Such use argues implicitly that the history of writing has in fact been, not one of dogging conventions, but one of continuously undoing them, experimenting with and beyond them, continuously redefining them, exploring the boundaries of the writerly act, of how we might tell our narratives—and hence ourselves, our worlds—differently than we have and do in order better to capture what it feels like to be alive at this place, this time, in this body, this brain. If that is the case, it follows that the pursuit of convention and craft is the pursuit of the historically tangential, the search for the ability to produce merely competent, imitative writing. The "real" history of writing is the one populated by the Petroniuses, the Sternes, the Melvilles, the Joyces and Steins, the Becketts, the Tomasulas.

While I suspect some sorts of narrativity are especially apt for comparison with architecture, some less so, some comparisons less revelatory or more forced than others, what links most innovative writing and architecture is how my experience of them is not so much one of objects-in-the-world as of events. Entering a building or a book feels to me like entering a zone of options, a networked field of impulses, influences, warrens that I immediately want to learn how to negotiate, navigate, how to make sense of, how to talk about. Texts begin to become interesting precisely at that instant when they begin to become much more than predictable, much more than those I've seen before, when they begin to impede my easy understanding of them. Moving through them challenges me to work.

In his essay "The Beginning and the End of Reading—The Beginning and the End of the Novel," Milorad Pavic asserts that there are two kinds of art: reversible and nonreversible. Reversible is that which, like architecture or sculpture, can be entered at several points, wandered through without a sense of beginning, middle, or end, and visited and revisited from a number of considerably different points of view. Nonreversible is that which, like a piece of music or conventional writing, is made to be experienced linearly from launch to landing. Pavic's aim is to transform his writing from nonreversible into reversible art—to make it feel, in other words, more like architecture.

Limit Texts, I would argue, pressure the architectural metaphor farther. Perhaps a better term in this context would be Marcos Novack's: liquid architecture—a nearly unimaginable architecture "without doors or hallways," a nearly unnamable architecture that seeks extreme regions that feel like "spatialized music," a continuously unfixed, flickering, mercurial sort "whose form is contingent on the interests of the beholder," "a version of what it is becoming, a structure for what does not yet exist."

One makes such gestures to answer the question the architect, in the documentary *Sketches of Frank Gehry*, says every artist must ask him or herself: "How does democracy express itself?" One invents them, that is, because the world now comes to us as the equivalent of a clutter of strip malls, McDonalds, and used-car lots. The spaces of innovative writing remind us continuously that we can always live in other buildings, other cities, other suburbs, always alter our fabrications of mind and spirit into something astonishing.

The pursuit of innovation in the arts has always been and will always be, not simply a mode of writing, but an existential and aesthetic infection. Once it enters your bloodstream, you will discover, it will be impossible to tell the universe around you in quite the same way(s) again.

1. Petronius, *Satyricon* (1st century A.D.)
2. Miguel de Cervantes, *Don Quixote* (1605, 1615)
3. Laurence Sterne, *Tristram Shandy* (1759-67)
4. Mary Shelley, *Frankenstein* (1818)
5. Herman Melville, *Moby-Dick* (1851)
6. Joris-Karl Huysmans, *Against Nature* (1884)
7. Rainer Maria Rilke, *The Notebooks of Malte Laurids Brigge* (1910)
8. Marcel Proust, *Swann's Way* (1913)
9. Gertrude Stein, *Tender Buttons* (1914)

10.   Franz Kafka, *The Metamorphosis* (1915)

11.   James Joyce, *Ulysses* (1922)

12.   Virginia Woolf, *Mrs. Dalloway* (1925)

13.   André Breton, *Nadja* (1928)

14.   William Faulkner, *As I Lay Dying* (1930)

15.   Flann O'Brien, *At Swim-Two-Birds* (1939)

16.   Jean Genet, *Our Lady of the Flowers* (1943)

17.   Jorge Luis Borges, *Ficciones* (1944)

18.   Raymond Queneau, *Exercises in Style* (1947)

19.   Samuel Beckett, *Malloy, Malone Dies, The Unnamable* (1951-3)

20.   Vladimir Nabokov, *Lolita* (1955)

21.   Alain Robbe-Grillet, *Jealousy* (1957)

22.   William S. Burroughs, *Naked Lunch* (1959)

23.   John Cage, *Silence: Lectures and Writings* (1961)

24.   Samuel Beckett, *How It Is* (1961)

25.   Carlos Fuentes, *Aura* (1962)

26.   Vladimir Nabokov, *Pale Fire* (1962)

27.   Julio Cortázar, *Hopscotch* (1963)

28.   Guillermo Cabrera Infante, *Three Trapped Tigers* (1967)

29.   Gabriel García Márquez, *One Hundred Years of Solitude* (1967)

30.   John Barth, *Lost in the Funhouse* (1968)

31.   Stanislaw Lem, *His Master's Voice* (1968)

32.   Rober Coover, *Pricksongs & Descants* (1969)

33.   Georges Perec, *A Void* (1969)

34.   J. G. Ballard, *Atrocity Exhibition* (1970)

35.   Peter Handke, *The Goalie's Anxiety Before the Penalty Kick* (1970)

36.   Tom Phillips, *A Humument* (1970)

37.   Raymond Federman, *Double or Nothing* (1971)

38.   Ishamael Reed, *Mumbo Jumbo* (1972)

39.   Thomas Pynchon, *Gravity's Rainbow* (1973)

40.   Walter Abish, *Alphabetical Africa* (1974)

41.   Jacques Derrida, *Glas* (1974)

42.   Donald Barthelme, *The Dead Father* (1975)

43.   Samuel R. Delany, *Dhalgren* (1975)

44.   William Gaddis, *J.R.* (1975)

45.   Renata Adler, *Speedboat* (1976)

46.   Thomas Bernhard, *The Voice Imitator* (1978)

47.   Italo Calvino, *If on a Winter's Night a Traveler* (1979)

48.   Guy Davenport, *Da Vinci's Bicycle* (1979)

49.   Gilbert Sorrentino, *Mulligan Stew* (1979)

50.   Lyn Hejinian, *My Life* (1980)

51.   Donald Barthelme, *Sixty Stories* (1981)

52.   Theresa Hak Kyung Cha, *Dictee* (1982)

53.   Kathy Acker, *Blood and Guts in High School* (1984)

54.   Julian Barnes, *Flaubert's Parrot* (1984)

55.   Milorad Pavic, *Dictionary of the Khazars* (1984)

56.   Paul Auster, *The New York Trilogy* (1985-6)

57.   Alan Moore & Dave Gibbons, *Watchmen* (1986-7)

58.   Carole Maso, *The Art Lover* (1990)

59.   Carole Maso, *Ava* (1993)

60.   Samuel R. Delany, *Hogg* (1995)

61.   William Gass, *The Tunnel* (1995)

62.   Ben Marcus, *Age of Wire and String* (1995)

63.   Haruki Murakami, *The Wind-Up Bird Chronicle* (1994-5)

64.   José Saramago, *Blindness* (1995)

65.   W. G. Sebald, *The Rings of Saturn* (1995)

66.   David Foster Wallace, *Infinite Jest* (1996)

67.   Don DeLillo, *Underworld* (1997)

68.   William Gass, *Cartesian Sonata* (1998)

69.   Ronald Sukenick, *Mosaic Man* (1999)

70.   Young-Hae Chang, *Traveling to Utopia* (ca. 2000)

71.   Mark Z. Danielewski, *House of Leaves* (2000)

72. Joe Wenderoth, *Letters to Wendy's* (2000)

73. Percival Everett, *Erasure* (2001)

74. Kenneth Goldsmith, *Soliloquy* (2001)

75. Laird Hunt, *The Impossibly* (2001)

76. Michael Martone, *The Blue Guide to Indiana* (2001)

77. Patrik Ourednik, *Europeana* (2001)

78. Gary Lutz, *Stories in the Worst Way* (2002)

79. John Haskell, *I Am Not Jackson Pollock* (2003)

80. Susan Howe, *The Midnight* (2003)

81. Shelley Jackson, *The Skin Project* (begun 2003)

82. Steve Tomasula, *Vas* (2003)

83. Brian Evenson, *Wavering Knife* (2004)

84. David Mitchell, *Cloud Atlas* (2004)

85. Claudia Rankine, *Don't Let Me Be Lonely* (2004)

86. Vanessa Place, *Dies: A Sentence* (2005)

87. Susan Steinberg, *Hydroplane* (2006)

88. Lynne Tillman, *American Genius: A Comedy* (2006)

89. Lydia Davis, *Varieties of Disturbance* (2007)

90. Thalia Field, *ULULU: Clown Shrapnel* (2007)

91. David Markson, *The Last Novel* (2007)

92. Yuriy Tarnawsky, *Like Blood in Water* (2007)

93. David Clark, *88 Constellations for Wittgenstein* (2009)

94. J. M. Coetzee, *Summertime* (2009)

95. Nick Montfort, *ppg256: Perl Poetry Generators* (2009)

96. Lance Olsen, *Head in Flames* (2009)

97. Steve Tomasula, *TOC* (2009)

98. Anne Carson, *Nox* (2010)

99. Lance Olsen, *Calendar of Regrets* (2010)

100. Noy Holland, *Swim for the Little One First* (2012)

101. Lidia Yuknavitch, *Dora: A Head Case* (2012)

exercises

1. Pick a book at random and use its title as an acrostic key phrase. For each letter of said key phrase, go to a page number in the book that corresponds (a=1, z=26), and copy as the first line of your narraticule from the first word that begins with that letter to the end of a line or sentence. Continue through all key letters.

2. Collaborate with one or more people. Ask the first to write down a question without showing it to anyone else; simultaneously, ask the second to write down an answer. And so on. Let a collective narrative form via non-sequitured Q&As.

3. Write a narraticule consisting entirely of things you'd like to say, but never would, to a parent, a lover, a sibling, your child.

4. Choose a narrative you have already written for one of the exercises in this book, and reverse or alter the line sequence of it. Or reverse the word order. Or, instead of reversing the word order, scramble it.

5. Write an autobiographical narrative without using the first-person pronoun or referring to yourself. Keep in mind as a model Theresa Hak Kyung Cha's *Dictee* (1982), a hybrid unwriting of the memoir made up of nine sections about Joan of Arc, Korean revolutionary Yu Guan Soon, Persephone, Cha's mother, a Beckettian voice trying to find language, et al., none of which and all of which are about Cha herself.

6. Write a narraticule consisting entirely of a list of things: shopping lists, things to do, lists of flowers or rocks, lists of colors, inventory lists, lists of events, lists of names, etc.

7. Write a narraticule composed entirely of opening lines. Improvise your own and/or use source texts.

8. Write a narraticule consisting of one-word sentences.

9. Write a narraticule made up entirely of excuses.

10. Another collaborative exercise: ask each person in your writing community to pass a narraticule s/he has written to his/her left. Ask each then to set down the narraticule s/he receives seven different ways on the page, using different fonts, colors, layouts, etc., creating variations on a theme.

11. Make a collage narrative by transcribing and juxtaposing various reports of important news announcements—e.g., the Challenger Disaster, the Fall of the Berlin Wall, Churchill's Declaration of War, etc.

12. Make a narraticule composed of things you don't know or don't want to know. Make a Not-Knowing narraticule.

CPSIA information can be obtained
at www.ICGtesting.com
Printed in the USA
LVOW09s1729280817

546679LV00005B/427/P